Translation Project Management

This textbook provides a comprehensive overview of the processes, principles, and constraints of project management in the translation industry. It offers readers clear insights into modern-day project management practices specific to translation services and an understanding of critical inter-related aspects of the process, drawing on key works in business studies on management, aspects of economics relevant to project management, and international standards on project management processes.

Developed on the back of a successful module titled Intercultural Project Management, *Translation Project Management* provides a coherent account of the entire translation project management lifecycle from start to finish and pays considerable attention to the factors influencing decision-making at various stages and how external forces shape the way in which a translation project plays out. Through an array of real-world case studies, it offers readers opportunities to explore, analyse, and engage with six fundamental project constraints: cost, time, scope, quality, benefits, and risk. Each chapter offers discussion points, possible assignments, and guided further reading.

This is an essential textbook both for all project management courses within translation studies programmes and for professional translators and translation service providers.

Callum Walker joined the University of Leeds as a Lecturer in Translation Technology in September 2020, where he teaches computer-assisted translation technology, project management, translation theory, and specialised translation. He has previously taught at Durham University (2012–2020), University College London (2018–2019), and Goldsmiths College University of London (2020), as well as being an Honorary Research Fellow in Translation Studies at University College London (2020–2022). He has published a monograph (*An Eye-Tracking Study of Equivalent Effect in Translation: The Reader Experience of Literary Style*, 2021) and co-edited a collection on eye-tracking research in translation (*Eye Tracking and Multidisciplinary Studies on Translation*, co-edited with Professor Federico M. Federici, 2018), in addition to a number of journal articles and book chapters on the topic.

Routledge Introductions to Translation and Interpreting
Series Editor:
Sergey Tyulenev holds a PhD in Linguistics and a PhD in Translation Studies. He is the Director of the MA in Translation and Russian Studies at the School of Modern Languages and Cultures, Durham University, UK. He teaches courses in translation theory, translation history, and sociology of translation.

Advisory Board
Luise von Flotow, University of Ottawa, Canada
Ricardo Muñoz Martín, University of Bologna, Italy
Kobus Marais, University of the Free State, South Africa
Nike K. Pokorn, University of Ljubljana, Slovenia
James St André, Chinese University of Hong Kong, China
Michaela Wolf, University of Graz, Austria

Routledge Introductions to Translation and Interpreting is a series of textbooks designed to meet the need for teaching materials for translator/interpreter training. Accessible and aimed at beginning students but also useful for instructors designing and teaching courses, the series covers a broad range of topics, many of which are already core courses, while others cover new directions of translator/interpreter teaching.

The series reflects the standards of the translator/interpreter training and professional practice set out by national and international competence frameworks and codes of translation/language service provision and are aimed at a global readership.

The books encourage students to reflect on how a discussed aspect of translation or interpreting is practiced in their home country and in the countries where they work or plan to work. All topics combine both practical and theoretical aspects so as to ensure a bridging of the gap between the academic and professional world, and all titles include a range of pedagogical support: activities, case studies, etc.

Most recent titles in the series:

Translation Ethics
Joseph Lambert

For more information on any of these and other titles, or to order, please go to https://www.routledge.com/Routledge-Introductions-to-Translation-and-Interpreting/book-series/RITI

Additional resources for translation and interpreting studies are available on the Routledge Translation Studies Portal: http://cw.routledge.com/textbooks/translationstudies

Translation Project Management

Callum Walker

LONDON AND NEW YORK

Designed cover image: Getty Images | DKosig

First published 2023
by Routledge
4 Park Square, Milton Park, Abingdon, Oxon OX14 4RN

and by Routledge
605 Third Avenue, New York, NY 10158

Routledge is an imprint of the Taylor & Francis Group, an informa business

© 2023 Callum Walker

The right of Callum Walker to be identified as author of this work has been asserted in accordance with sections 77 and 78 of the Copyright, Designs and Patents Act 1988.

All rights reserved. No part of this book may be reprinted or reproduced or utilised in any form or by any electronic, mechanical, or other means, now known or hereafter invented, including photocopying and recording, or in any information storage or retrieval system, without permission in writing from the publishers.

Trademark notice: Product or corporate names may be trademarks or registered trademarks and are used only for identification and explanation without intent to infringe.

British Library Cataloguing-in-Publication Data
A catalogue record for this book is available from the British Library

Library of Congress Cataloging-in-Publication Data
Names: Walker, Callum, author.
Title: Translation project management / Callum Walker.
Description: Abingdon, Oxon ; New York, NY : Routledge, 2023. |
Series: Routledge introductions to translation and interpreting |
Includes bibliographical references and index.
Identifiers: LCCN 2022027838 | ISBN 9780367677831 (hardback) |
ISBN 9780367677732 (paperback) | ISBN 9781003132813 (ebook)
Subjects: LCSH: Translating services. | Project management. |
Translating and interpreting–Economic aspects. | LCGFT: Textbooks.
Classification: LCC P306.94 .W35 2023 | DDC 418/.02–dc23/eng/20220917
LC record available at https://lccn.loc.gov/2022027838

ISBN: 978-0-367-67783-1 (hbk)
ISBN: 978-0-367-67773-2 (pbk)
ISBN: 978-1-003-13281-3 (ebk)

DOI: 10.4324/9781003132813

Typeset in Sabon
by Newgen Publishing UK

Access the Support Material: http://routledgetranslationstudiesportal.com

Contents

List of Figures vii
List of Tables viii
List of Boxes ix
About the Author x
Series Editor's Foreword xi
Acknowledgements xiii
About this Textbook xv

1 Translation Project Management 1

PART I
From Cradle to Grave: The Translation Project Lifecycle 19

2 Pre-production 21
3 Production 49
4 Post-production 82

PART II
Triangles, Diamonds, and Stars: Evaluating Translation Project Constraints 111

5 Timescales 113
6 Costs 129
7 Scope 144
8 Quality 171

9 Benefits	194
10 Risk	213
11 Post-mortem	237
Index	259

Figures

1.1	Translation project models	6
1.2	Outsourcing model	7
1.3	The evolution of project constraint models	14
2.1	Analysis report in memoQ	29
3.1	ISO 17100:2015 waterfall production workflow	51
3.2	Example of proofreading comment in final PDF	75
3.3	Annotated translation production workflow	79
4.1	Aggregation of marginal gains over one year	85
4.2	Example of different post-delivery invoicing approaches	93
4.3	Example of staggered payments tied to project milestones	95
4.4	Specimen invoice	98
4.5	Example of 'cleaning' a TM	102
5.1	Time zones example	124
6.1	Supply and demand curves	133
6.2	Price elasticity	139
7.1	Visualisation of the Kano model	167
8.1	LQA error functionality of memoQ	180
8.2	Example Pareto chart based on LISA error categories	184
8.3	Short-term cost of quality	189
8.4	Long-term cost of quality	189
8.5	Cost of quality	190
9.1	Stakeholder benefits	209
10.1	Project risk and cost of changes over time	215
10.2	Risk management procedure	217
10.3	Example risk breakdown structure (RBS)	219
10.4	Example probability/risk matrix	224
10.5	Example quantified probability/risk matrices	225
10.6	Example Pareto analysis in risk management	227
11.1	Summary of contemporary translation industry challenges, pressures, and changes	239
11.2	Principal–professional relationships in client–LSP–vendor interactions	243

Tables

2.1	Vendor costs calculation	37
2.2	Client costs calculation	38
3.1	Linguistic conventions and project specification examples	58
7.1	Client-side MoSCoW analysis	160
7.2	LSP-side MoSCoW analysis	164
7.3	Summary of Kano model categories	165
8.1	Features, principles, and examples of LQA and QA	176
8.2	LQA score card example	177
8.3	Long-term analysis of LQA score cards	178
8.4	LISA error typology model	179
8.5	Example Pareto distribution table	184

Boxes

2.1	Project enquiries	23
2.2	Project analysis example	29
2.3	Project schedule example	31
2.4	Resource assessment example	34
2.5	Quotation example	37
3.1	Example of a translation brief	56
3.2	Checking example	59
3.3	Pre-editing example	62
3.4	Light post-editing example	64
3.5	Full post-editing example	66
3.6	Revision example	70
3.7	Review example	73
3.8	Proofreading example	75
4.1	The aggregation of marginal gains	85
5.1	Types of logical relationships and dependencies	117
5.2	The Goldilocks principle	120
6.1	Supply and demand	132
6.2	The effects of exchange rate fluctuations	137
6.3	Price elasticity	138
7.1	Buyers' guides	147
7.2	Samples of different translation services	152
8.1	LQA score card	177
8.2	LISA error typology and implementation	179
8.3	The Pareto principle and Pareto analyses	183
9.1	Business case	197
9.2	Translators Without Borders	203
10.1	Describing attitudes to risk	217
10.2	Risk breakdown structure (RBS)	219
10.3	Probability/impact matrices	224

About the Author

Dr Callum Walker joined the University of Leeds as a Lecturer in Translation Technology in September 2020, where he teaches computer-assisted translation technology, project management, translation theory, and specialised translation. He has previously taught at Durham University (2012–2020), University College London (2018–2019), and Goldsmiths College University of London (2020), as well as being an Honorary Research Fellow in Translation Studies at University College London (2020–2022). His research interests cover two contrasting fields. More recently, his research has focused on translation industry studies, with a specific focus on project management, the economics of translation, and the interaction between technology and translation workflows, culminating in a recent journal article in *Translation Spaces*, plus two conference papers. He also maintains a research interest in the comparative reception of source and target texts using experimental methods and has published a monograph (*An Eye-Tracking Study of Equivalent Effect in Translation: The Reader Experience of Literary Style*, 2021, Palgrave) and co-edited a collection on eye-tracking research in translation (*Eye Tracking and Multidisciplinary Studies on Translation*, co-edited with Professor Federico M. Federici, 2018, John Benjamins), in addition to a number of journal articles and book chapters on the topic.

Concurrently with his academic roles, he has worked as a freelance translator specialising in legal, business, and financial translations from French and Russian into English (beginning in 2009) and runs his own small translation business. He is also a Chartered Linguist, Member of the Chartered Institute of Linguists, and Member of the Institute of Translation and Interpreting, and he actively contributes to professional translator networks to bridge the gap between academia and the translation industry.

Series Editor's Foreword

Translator and interpreter training programmes have become an integral feature of the present-day professional educational landscape all over the world. There are at least two good reasons for this. On the one hand, it has been realised that, to work as a translator or interpreter, one needs more than to speak a couple of languages; special training in translation and interpreting is a must. On the other hand, translator/interpreter training programmes are seen as a practical way to start a career in the language service provision industry or to earn a degree as a translation/interpreting studies scholar. These programmes may be part of a university curriculum or standalone courses in various formats of continuing studies or qualification upgrading.

Yet there is still a dearth of teaching materials geared towards novices in translation or interpreting. In every class, students are either given sheaves of handouts, which, by the end of the course, build up into a pile of paper, or referred to a small library of publications for a chapter here and a chapter there. As a result, the student struggles to imagine the subject area as a coherent whole, and there is no helpful textbook for references while on the course or after.

The lack of coursebooks makes life no easier for translator/interpreter trainers. Even if they find a suitable book or monograph, a great deal of adaptation must be done. The instructor would have to adjust the book to the length of the course and individual teaching sessions, and add exercises and assignments, questions and topics for presentations to facilitate students' engagement with the materials and help them go beyond the 'read-only' mode of working with the recommended book(s).

The purport of the series *Routledge Introductions to Translation and Interpreting* is to put into the hands of the translator/interpreter trainee and trainer ready-made textbooks. Each textbook is written by an expert or a team of experts in the subject area under discussion; moreover, each author has vast experience of teaching the subject of their textbook. The series reflects what have already become staple courses and modules in translator/interpreter training, but it also introduces new areas of teaching and research. The series is meant as a kind of library of textbooks – all the books together present various aspects of a translation and interpreting training programme viewed as a whole. They can be taken as a basis for developing new programmes and courses or reinforcing existing ones.

The present textbook is on translation project management. To be able to manage a translation project is a necessary skill that any translator should have. The translator may need to manage a project either at the request of the organisation s/he works in or because s/he is involved in a project that cannot be accomplished single-handedly.

The book will be useful for interpreters, too. More often than not an interpreter may also find him/herself in a situation where they need to handle an ambitious interpreting project. Interpreters often work with one or two partners. Sometimes a small team of colleagues may be involved or perhaps a project is a series of events that requires the coordination of human resources and efficient time management.

The present book *Translation Project Management* is written by Dr Callum Walker in such a way that it can be used for an entire course or as a part of a larger course. This textbook is also suitable for self-teaching.

Sergey Tyulenev
2022

Acknowledgements

So many people contribute to the drafting of a textbook like this in so many different ways and, as I write this, I'm immediately conscious of the fact that there will inevitably be people whom I have unintentionally overlooked in these remarks. So I would first like to start by thanking anybody and everybody with whom I have spoken about this textbook, project management, or the translation industry more generally at some unspecified time in the past. All of these discussions have both shaped and challenged my perspectives and contributed to the end product that you are now reading.

In an attempt to be more specific, I'd first like to thank the series editor, Dr Sergey Tyulenev (Durham University), for offering me the opportunity to write one of the first books in this brand-new series. You've provided a huge amount of guidance throughout this project, from the initial proposal stage right up to your reviews of the final drafts, and I'm eternally grateful for all your support.

I would also like to thank Dr Joseph Lambert (Cardiff University) for the many and varied discussions that we've had over the last couple of years about practices in the translation industry and the academic field of translation studies. I'm very grateful for your comments and suggestions (and attention to detail) on my draft chapters and I've enjoyed our chats about various aspects of this textbook and the 'bigger picture' that underpins much of the content in this book.

Special mention should also go to Raisa McNab, CEO of the Association of Translation Companies (United Kingdom), for her detailed and incredibly helpful comments on Chapters 2 to 4 of this book. I wish that I'd had more time to allow Raisa to review the remainder of the book too, but I sincerely hope that it is greeted with her seal of approval when she comes to read the book as a whole.

Professor Maeve Olohan (University of Manchester) and Dr Christopher Mellinger (University of North Carolina at Charlotte) both provided some incredibly useful recommendations and feedback on the initial proposal and a sample chapter in the early stages of this project, and I hope that my finished product appropriately reflects their insightful suggestions and expectations.

xiv *Acknowledgements*

I also owe a debt of gratitude to the 2020/21 and 2021/22 cohorts of the MA Applied Translation Studies at the University of Leeds, both of which served as 'guinea pigs' for various chapters in the early and later stages of drafting. Their feedback has been very helpful in making sure that this textbook really satisfies the needs of the primary target audience.

And finally, thank you to my wife, Megan, for your love and support throughout this long project (and especially in the final stages of preparing the manuscript for submission). It's taken a great deal of work on my part and you have always been on hand to support me both pragmatically and emotionally when I've needed it. And to my children – Kieran, Oliver, and Bethan – thank you for just being you and being your usual adaptable, patient, and thoughtful selves… most of the time!

Despite all the help that I've had in putting this book together, all responsibility ultimately rests with me. Any errors or inaccuracies are most definitely my own.

About this Textbook

Translation Project Management is intended to offer an accessible introduction to a topic that is crucial to the success of the translation industry. For such a critical topic, this field has received comparatively little treatment in academic literature more widely, let alone introductory-level books such as this one. This textbook aims to provide a comprehensive overview of the processes, principles, and constraints of project management in the translation industry. It offers readers clear insights into modern-day project management practices specific to translation services and an understanding of critical inter-related aspects of the process such as cost, time, and quality, drawing on key texts on management studies, aspects of economics relevant to project management, and relevant international standards.

Developed on the back of experience teaching translation project management at a number of UK universities, the textbook is intended to support both students on translation studies and related programmes and instructors looking to develop new dedicated project management modules or to bring project management content into existing modules with a view to enhancing students' career prospects. While the content is aimed predominantly at a postgraduate taught level, the intended student readership of *Translation Project Management* is broad, encompassing undergraduate, postgraduate, and even doctoral students in translation studies and related disciplines. Practitioners of project management – i.e. 'real-world' translation project managers – may also benefit from seeing their practice formalised in this book and learn about some of the novel perspectives that some of the later chapters, in particular, can offer to their practice. Newly recruited project managers may not have received formal training in project management and might therefore like to supplement their on-the-job learning with additional reading from this textbook.

When the textbook was first conceived, the European Masters in Translation (EMT) Competence Framework was an important driver behind the intended content and skills that can be developed through appropriate training in translation project management. One of the core competences of this framework is 'Service Provision', which specifically references 'language services in a professional context – from client awareness and negotiation through to project management and quality assurance' (European Commission, 2017b, p. 11). But project management goes beyond service provision alone. Indeed, the Competence Framework specifically stipulates that students should receive personal and interpersonal training in time and workload management, deadlines, project instructions and specifications, and teamwork from a personal perspective (European Commission, 2017b, p. 10), as well as content on industry demands and job profiles, prospecting and marketing, project requirements, negotiation, the organisation, budgeting, and management of translation projects, standards for language services, quality management, and networking (European Commission, 2017b, p. 11). Indeed, the 2017 Mid-Term Review mentions the addition of compulsory project management modules at many EMT member universities, further adding that 'best practices' would involve 'adding formal and explicit project management training' to programmes (European Commission, 2017a, p. 5). It was these goals and the underlying EMT Competence Framework that fed into the taught modules from which this textbook is derived.

Translation Project Management is not intended to be prescriptive. While it is, of course, based on the international standard for translation services ISO 17100:2015, project management, like translation more generally, is a varied practice and there are many different ways to approach a problem or find an appropriate solution. The aim, therefore, is to provide insights into different approaches by drawing on principles and ideas from a wide range of fields. Many aspects of project management – and even more basic aspects such as professional skills in invoicing, handling feedback, etc. – will be entirely unknown to readers. Hence, there are some elements of this textbook that are necessarily rudimentary in nature. But for the more confident reader, there are also thought-provoking ideas and perspectives intended to stimulate debate, further exploration, and, ultimately, creativity or 'thinking outside the box'.

Instructors

Translation Project Management is aimed at instructors with students that are entirely new to the world of project management. The textbook has been structured with a one-semester dedicated module in mind, following the common UK practice of eleven standard teaching weeks, including one 'reading week', manifested in this textbook through ten primary 'content' chapters (i.e. Chapters 2 to 11) plus the Introduction in Chapter 1. However, many institutions are not blessed with the space, resources, or opportunities to deliver a dedicated optional (let alone compulsory) module on translation project management. For those in this situation, my recommendation would be to focus on the pragmatic technical content in Chapters 2 to 4 as a priority (on pre-production, production, and post-production), with the chapters on time (Chapter 5), cost (Chapter 6), and scope (Chapter 7) and/or quality (Chapter 8) as secondary priorities. All of the chapters have been written with independent study in mind and can easily be set as further reading to follow on from taught content on the earlier, more process-oriented chapters.

The chapters also feature a scattering of discussion points at various junctures. These are signalled by bullet points in the form of a question mark (?). These questions can be readily used by instructors when delivering taught content in classes and offer a point of discussion with which students can engage in class, either with the instructor directly or in smaller groups (perhaps then feeding back to the group as a whole). They can also form the basis for short assignments or in-class practical tasks (some of which could even feed into dedicated classes on CAT tools, for example).

At the end of each chapter are several recommended texts for further reading. These can be fruitfully set for students to explore in their own time to reinforce or expand upon content taught in class. The further reading resources are also accompanied by suggested assignment topics. These assignments could take the form of formal (assessed) written essays, individual or group presentations, or in-class practical or discussion-based exercises. More suggested assignment topics are available on the TS Portal. Instructors can also use the various case studies on the TS Portal to design alternative assessments or practical tasks such as devising project quotations or feasible project schedules, which can be delivered and assessed in various ways.

Students

Students are the primary target audience of *Translation Project Management*, and the content and style of the book has been designed in such a way that students will be able to study independently. Since the vast majority of content on translation project management in translation studies has appeared only in edited volumes or journal articles, the aim was to provide a coherent 'narrative' with a clear sense of direction, focusing on what is deemed to be relevant to those undertaking a module in translation project management, or even a taught component on this topic, as well as the wider future demands of the profession (including freelance translators, who will inevitably use many of the skills, principles, and ideas set out in this book too).

It should be noted that practices in project management will differ, and students should not view this textbook as *the* definitive resource on how translation project management *should* take place. It is intended as a guide and a source of inspiration. Readers should also be aware that practices will not only differ from one language service provider (LSP) to another, but also from one country or region to another, and from one sub-sector of the language services industry to another. As such, my hope for this textbook is that it serves its diverse readership – studying translation studies in Europe, China, the USA, Canada, Africa, the Middle East, or anywhere else – as a springboard to consider how practices might change or how certain tasks or interpersonal interactions might be handled differently.

Each chapter begins with a set of learning outcomes that are intended to point not only to the content of the chapter but also to a series of tangible goals in terms of the knowledge or skills acquired or perspectives broadened. Many of these objectives are quite practical in nature, but others encourage reflection on theoretical dimensions of project management, especially where practice intersects with the necessarily socio-economic dimensions of the industry. The chapters close with proposed further reading to enhance your knowledge further and to seek out additional sources for assignments. There are also some proposed assignment topics that can be used either in their own right or as inspiration for self-designed assignments. Many universities offer students opportunities to design their own essay questions or presentation topics, and these suggestions are designed with this in mind. For those looking to pursue more extensive study in project management, they could also serve as a starting point for a dissertation (at undergraduate or postgraduate level) or even a PhD proposal.

Finally, a glossary of key terms is available on the TS Portal alongside other key resources such as the aforementioned case studies. Students are strongly encouraged to make use of these resources in their work in order to maximise their understanding of key terminology and bring in examples from the realistic case studies provided.

Final Notes

As noted above, this book is complemented by additional learning materials on the Routledge Translation Studies Portal ('TS Portal'): http://routledgetranslationstudiesportal.com. In particular, the case studies to support of some of the additional tasks, discussion points, and assignment suggestions can be found on this portal. To find the relevant resources for this textbook, readers should click on 'Resources' and 'View by Book' before clicking on the link for *Translation Project Management*.

On a practical level, to avoid complexities surrounding currency conversion, the currencies used in the worked examples are British pound sterling (£ / GBP), euros (€ / EUR), and US dollars ($ / USD), given the relative stability of these currencies and the broad familiarity with their respective symbols. It should also be made clear that all of the case studies on the TS Portal are based on or adapted from real-world projects, compiled from my own experience as well as the experiences of numerous project managers who have taken the time to share such examples with me. Finally, the vast majority of the company names in this textbook are invented, with the exception of instances where readers are explicitly asked to think about well-known translation companies or companies operating in other domains outside translation.

References

European Commission. (2017a). *EMT Mid-term Review 2017: Report on the State of Play of the EMT Network 2014-2019*. Retrieved 17 May 2022 from https://ec.europa.eu/info/sites/default/files/mtr-ares_3730430-en_0.pdf

European Commission. (2017b). *European Master's in Translation: Competence Framework 2017*. Retrieved 23 July 2021 from https://ec.europa.eu/info/sites/default/files/emt_competence_fwk_2017_en_web.pdf

1 Translation Project Management

> **Learning outcomes:**
> - Appreciate the importance of translation project management in the wider context of the rapidly growing translation industry
> - Situate translation project management as a practice and scholarly discipline within the broader discipline of translation studies
> - Understand the specialist terminology used in the field of translation project management
> - Learn about the development of project constraint models
> - Reflect on the role of translation project management and project managers, and the influence of project constraints on translation projects

There is a well-known adage, referred to as Murphy's law, which holds that 'anything that can go wrong will go wrong'. Effective project management is about trying to thwart this supposedly inevitable phenomenon. In many respects, therefore, project management is about risk management: proper planning and organisation will in most places remove (or at least mitigate) the chance of things going wrong. This textbook covers the processes involved in translation project management across the project lifecycle, focusing on the practicalities of managing projects and understanding key project constraints such as timescales, costs, and quality. However, one important caveat should be stated from the outset: just as there is no single 'correct' way to translate a particular text, so there is no single 'correct' way to manage projects. The aim is to provide a structural framework, based on recognised standards and practices within the translation industry and across a wide range of industries more generally, and to raise key issues and factors that influence the success with which a project is managed and carried out. As Keiran and Elena Dunne succinctly put it in the subtitle of their edited volume, translation project management is about 'the art of the possible' (Dunne & Dunne, 2011b).

2 Translation Project Management

The language services and technology industry was estimated to be worth between $49.6 billion and $53.5 billion in 2019 and is projected to reach $70 billion by 2023 (CSA Research, 2019; Nimdzi, 2019). Language services now include a vast panoply of different forms, including written translation (translation in its basic sense, transcreation, software localisation, etc.), audiovisual translation (subtitling, dubbing, voiceover, respeaking, etc.), interpreting (consecutive interpreting, conference interpreting, telephone interpreting, sign-language interpreting, etc.), machine translation (including pre- and post-editing), terminology management, multilingual content management, language education, and many more besides. Translation itself (broadly defined) takes place in fields ranging from law through medicine to tourism and everything else in between, and it is practised in a wide array of workplace settings (in-house translators, institutional translators and interpreters at the European Union, United Nations, etc., freelance translators and interpreters). Because of the immense diversity of what the language services industry comprises, this textbook will of course only focus on a small slice of the sector, shining a spotlight specifically on translation project management and the slightly narrower sense of the translation industry itself. The result of this is that the term 'translation' will be used throughout the textbook as a (admittedly imperfect) hypernym to cover the vast diversity of translation-related services that are on offer in the industry.

It would be wrong to assume that the knowledge presented in this textbook is useful only to those either currently working or wanting to work as a project manager; indeed, project management is not a task carried out solely by project managers working for language service providers (LSPs). Project management is a skill and process practiced by *everybody* in the translation industry to some degree or other. For example, freelance translators and interpreters have to manage their schedules effectively – often with multiple on-going projects – to ensure that projects are delivered on time and in line with the required specifications; some freelancers also integrate an element of outsourcing into their business model, working with colleagues in language pairs or domains beyond their own area of expertise who carry out work on their behalf in precisely the same working arrangement as larger LSPs work with freelancers.

Situating Project Management in Translation Studies

Drawing on Dunne and Dunne's opening chapter to their edited volume *Translation and Localization Project Management* (2011b), translation project management is a field that spans the vast diversity of translation studies as a discipline, from the 'pure' side of Holmes's 'map' of the field (Dunne & Dunne, 2011a, p. 1; see Toury, 1995/2012, p. 10) across to the 'applied' side. Of course, the applied branch of the field is where translation project management sits most naturally, but there are elements of the pure realm, such as the descriptive translation studies paradigm and functionalist theories of translation, to offer two examples, that are in dialogue with the very practical nature of translation project management.

That notwithstanding, translation project management is a field that has been subject to relatively little attention in translation studies. This observation may be surprising to many readers, given the prominent role that project management plays in the way in which the translation industry operates. Perhaps the best known publication on this topic is the aforementioned edited volume by Dunne and Dunne (2011b), which compiles a diverse array of chapters on the strategic dimensions of localisation project management, application of the Project Integration Management methodology to translation projects, scope management, time and scheduling, quality management, effective communication, risk management, the role of the project manager, and relationship management, among others. All of these chapters offer insightful contributions drawing on literature from business and project management to discuss some of the unique complexities of the translation industry. The book is undoubtedly a leading contribution to this field, but by its very nature – as an edited volume – it does not offer a comprehensive, systematic coverage of project management as a whole, but rather fascinating snapshots of specific components of the project lifecycle or the wider context in which translation project management takes place.

One book that goes some way towards addressing this gap is Nancy Matis's ebook *How to Manage Your Translation Projects* (2014). The book is a noble contribution to the field, as it provides a highly pragmatic guide to setting up and running a translation project, with a great deal of technical detail on specific tasks such as quotations, pricing, and scheduling. Where it is lacking, however, is in some of the depth beyond these technical outlines in terms of why these approaches tend to be common practice or indeed how some of these common practices could be improved by integrating common standards and frameworks, and perspectives from project management as a discipline.

Another notable contribution to the field is Hanna Risku's *Translationsmanagement: Interkulturelle Fachkommunikation im Informationszeitalter* [Translation Management: Intercultural Technical Communication in the Information Age] (2016), which is now in its third edition and is based on a primary research carried out at an Austrian LSP. Sadly, this book is not yet available to an anglophone readership, and many would derive considerable benefit from the first-hand insights that it offers to readers.

A recent edited collection that brings new perspectives to this area is Angelone et al.'s *The Bloomsbury Companion to Language Industry Studies* (2020b). While not specifically focused on translation project management *per se*, all of the chapters touch in different ways on how the industry operates, which in turn feeds indirectly into the ways in which industry processes are managed. As the editors rightly point out in their introduction:

> The language industry consists of many moving parts. The constellation of these parts vary from one task to the next, which makes sound project management all the more important. Indeed, the type and scope of projects we see in the language industry on a daily basis are manifold, with varying degrees of logistical complexity. ... Needless to say, the working conditions and environments of language industry professionals (and non-professionals) are far from uniform.
> [Angelone et al., 2020a, p. 1]

Of particular note to translation project management in this volume are the chapters on researching workplaces, translators' roles and responsibilities, the corresponding chapter on interpreters, tailoring translation services for clients and users, pre-editing and post-editing, and others, which intersect with topics such as non-professional translation, terminology management, and translation technology. The volume makes an important contribution to the field, and scholars in this area have warmly welcomed the publication as well as calling for even more work in this still nascent area of research.

Of course, translation project management intersects with so many aspects of what we research in translation studies, from translation technology to the sociology of translation and translation networks, ethical issues in translation practice, and the economics of the translation industry. A plethora of academic articles, book chapters, and even full monographs and textbooks exist in many of these areas, which all have some bearing on translation project management, but given that project management is addressed in only a limited manner, or indirectly, if at all, it is impossible to offer a comprehensive review or outline of all such articles without necessarily missing out some contributions.

Frameworks

PMBOK and PRINCE2

This textbook draws on two popular project management frameworks: the *Project Management Body of Knowledge* (PMBOK), produced by the Project Management Institute, and *PRINCE2* (*PRojects IN Controlled Environments*), which was developed by the UK Government for information systems projects. These two frameworks – or methodologies – should not be considered mutually exclusive; they are in fact complementary to one another (as recognised by the drafting organisations themselves). However, the ways in which both frameworks are drafted differ. The PMBOK is generally considered to be *descriptive* – it explains how project management techniques *tend to be* implemented in practice – while PRINCE2 is *prescriptive* – it sets out how project management techniques *should be* implemented in practice (see Matos & Lopes, 2013). As such, the PMBOK focuses more on the processes involved in project management, while PRINCE2 is product driven, focusing on product delivery and quality. It is not the intention of this textbook to advocate one methodology over the other, but rather to draw insights from two widely accepted approaches to project management to achieve a more comprehensive perspective on the different factors that influence project management processes.

ISO 17100:2015

The selected insights from the PMBOK and PRINCE2 will be used to build on the main framework running throughout this book: ISO 17100:2015 'Translation Services – Requirements for Translation Services' (International Organization for Standardization, 2015). This international standard lays down specific requirements for translation services in relation to the quality and provision of translation services, including requirements on linguist qualifications, resource management, and any other processes involved in delivering a quality translation service:

> This International Standard provides requirements for the core processes, resources, and other aspects necessary for the delivery of a quality translation service that meets applicable specifications [including] those of the client, of the translation service provider itself, and of any relevant industry codes, best-practice guides, or legislation.
> [International Organization for Standardization, 2015, p. 1]

To clarify, it is not a requirement that all language service providers (LSPs) adhere to this standard, but, in order to sell a particular service as 'ISO 17100:2015-compliant', it is a strict requirement that all of the standard's provisions are respected. In this sense, compliance with the standard can be marketed as a guarantee of the quality of the service provided. It is important to note, however, that an LSP that holds this particular standard is not required to fulfil the provisions of the standards on all projects, but only on projects or components that have been explicitly agreed as such with the client.

ISO 17100:2015 breaks down the translation process into three distinct parts: **pre-production, production,** and **post-production**. This delineation of three clearcut project stages has been adopted in this textbook as it provides a simple but effective model of the translation project from start to finish. Alternative models of the translation project have been proposed but are far more complex. Rico Pérez (2002), for instance, proposed an alternative model comprising commissioning, planning, groundwork, translation, and wind-up stages, and Matis (2014) split the project lifecycle into eight stages: client contact, reception/distribution of a new project, identification

6 Translation Project Management

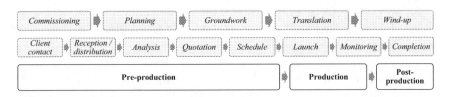

Figure 1.1 Translation project models
Source (from top to bottom): Rico Pérez (2002), Matis (2014), International Organization for Standardization (2015)

and base analysis of a project, quotation, schedule, project launch, project monitoring, and project completion. While the specificities of project management are open to different interpretations and categorisations, both of these models are needlessly complicated. When these two models are juxtaposed alongside that of ISO 17100:2015 (see Figure 1.1), it becomes clear that both Matis's and Rico Pérez's models break down the phase prior to the primary linguistic tasks into much smaller units (some of which are not clearly defined), resulting in a very 'front-heavy' design, perhaps at the cost of some of the processes that take place during and after the main linguistic tasks themselves. The advantage of the ISO 17100:2015 model is its sheer simplicity: pre-production concerns everything that takes place before the main act of translation; production concerns all of the main tasks associated with the creation of the deliverable product; and post-production comprises any tasks taking place following delivery of the product to the client.

This textbook adopts the workflow model set out in ISO 17100:2015, not only on account of its simplicity, but also because the very aim of the ISO is to standardise processes and terminology across the industry. It therefore makes the most sense to acclimatise ourselves to this structural overview in light of this drive for standardisation.

Scope and Terminology

As noted above, translation projects are carried out in a variety of different contextual settings. Some linguists work **in-house** – that is, they are employed by and work within a specific company, institution, or non-governmental organisation (a good source to consult on institutional translation and interpreting is Prieto Ramos, 2020). The best examples of this professional model are major international organisations such as the European Union (EU), which hires large numbers of translators and interpreters to handle the day-to-day flow of content between languages. In 2017, the total number of in-house translators in the European Commission's Directorate-General for Translation amounted to roughly 1,500, covering the 24 official languages

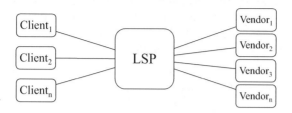

Figure 1.2 Outsourcing model

and translating over 2 million pages per year (Standvik, 2017). However, the vast majority of translations globally are farmed out to freelance translators by LSPs; this is referred to as **outsourcing**, which tends to be the default arrangement in the translation industry (Dunne, 2012, p. 144), and this is the primary focus of this textbook.

The outsourcing model (represented in Figure 1.2) is based around three key entities: clients, the LSP, and vendors. **Clients** are the initiators of projects: they are the companies, organisations, or individuals that need a particular document to be translated, or a meeting to be interpreted, or a video to be subtitled. Without clients, the translation industry would have no reason to exist. The **LSP** – language service provider – is the main intermediary between the end client and the linguists that provide the translation, interpreting, or subtitling services, for example. In most cases, an LSP is an independent company (often referred to in the industry as a translation agency, translation company, or language service company), but, in some cases, it might be a separate department (or even individual) within a larger company. This textbook is structured around the assumption that the LSP is an independent translation agency, as this is the most common arrangement in the outsourcing model. The final part of the outsourcing involves **vendors**. You will often hear translation agencies referring to their linguists as vendors and the process of managing them as vendor management. Etymologically, vendor means *seller*, the logic behind the use of this term being that outsourcing first assumes the sale of a service by a linguist to the LSP. While vendors can of course be referred to using more specific terminology depending on their role (e.g. translator, reviewer, proofreader, etc.), vendor is used as a hypernym to avoid this specificity, and, for the purposes of this textbook, this is ideal, as it helps us to conceive of translation as a broader and more far-reaching service than might originally have been considered. For the same reason, the term translation is used in this textbook as a hypernym to cover all forms of translation in the broadest sense.

We will now continue with the theme of terminology and start to turn our attention to ISO 17100:2015 and the specific terminology that it employs to describe the project management process, language, and content. It is important to have a clear understanding of terminology before we proceed to examine translation project management in more depth, especially when some terms are to be interpreted differently to their common meaning or when other terms are typically used imprecisely or interchangeably.

Projects and Project Management

The first terminology that we will turn our attention to sit at the very heart of translation project management. But before reading further, consider:

? How would you define a 'project'? What features does an activity or task need to have in order to be called a project?
? How would you define 'project management'? What specific tasks might project management comprise? And what is the role or underlying purpose of project management, or its *raison d'être*?

According to the PMBOK, a **project** is defined as 'a temporary endeavor to create a unique product, service, or result' (Project Management Institute, 2017, p. 542), and in the PRINCE2 framework it is defined as 'a temporary organization that is created for the purpose of delivering one or more business products according to an agreed business case' (Office of Government Commerce, 2018, p. 8). These are simple enough definitions, but they conceal many layers of complexity. To begin with, let us consider the two primary characteristics of projects: they are both *temporary* and *unique*. Firstly, a project is not open ended but has clear start and end points. Secondly, while projects may be similar to others completed in the past, every project is different (a different project team, a different client, a different period of time, etc.). Projects are generally recognised as bringing about some form of progress, advancing from a current state to a future state of being, often in the form of a new product or a specific service delivered to one or more stakeholders.

With that in mind, **project management** is concerned, first and foremost, with ensuring that the aforementioned unique product, service, or result is achieved successfully and in accordance with the defined specifications. As will become clear throughout this textbook, projects are shaped by a number of constraints – timescales, costs, scope, quality, benefits, and risk – and how these constraints are managed will ultimately determine the success of a project. All of these factors and more besides are part of project management and will be discussed in detail. Effective project management allows business objectives to be met (e.g. turning a profit), client expectations to be satisfied (which, in turn, generates business goodwill), problems and risks to be resolved in a timely manner, and failing projects to be recovered. Poorly managed projects can result in deadlines being missed, project budgets being exceeded, quality issues, loss of reputation, and dissatisfied clients (Office of Government Commerce, 2018, p. 9; see Project Management Institute,

2017, p. 10–11). Project management therefore includes 'identifying project requirements; addressing the various needs, concerns, and expectations of stakeholders; establishing and maintaining active communication with stakeholders; managing resources; and balancing the competing project constraints' (Project Management Institute, 2017, p. 542).

Of course, in the translation industry, we are talking about very specific types of projects: translation projects, or indeed other related forms of project such as subtitling, localisation, the interpreting of a specific conference, which would also fall under the category of a 'project', etc. The handling of such projects falls to the aforementioned **language service providers**. A more specific term is sometimes used – **translation service provider (TSP)** – and indeed this term is introduced and defined in ISO 17100:2015, but in this textbook, we will retain the use of language service provider, or **LSP**, as this tends to be one of the most common designations adopted in the industry alongside the related term 'language service companies' (LSC). While ISO 17100:2015 offers a rather vague definition of LSPs – 'person or organization who provides language-related services' (International Organization for Standardization, 2015, 2.4.1) – and an equally vague definition of LSPs – 'language service provider that provides professional translation services', also giving examples of 'translation companies, individual translators, or in-house translation departments' (International Organization for Standardization, 2015, 2.4.2) – in the main, in this textbook, we will be viewing LSPs as the intermediate companies that manage the translation process in the standard outsourcing model outlined above.

The **translation service** itself, managed and 'supplied' by these LSPs, is referred to in ISO 17100:2015 as an 'intangible product' resulting from 'interaction between client and TSP' (note that the ISO standard specifically uses TSP throughout, in contrast to this textbook) (International Organization for Standardization, 2015, 2.1.6). The service itself is borne from the **translation workflow** ('processes, or parts thereof, involved in achieving target language content', International Organization for Standardization, 2015, 2.1.3), which is a **process** (International Organization for Standardization, 2015, 2.1.4) typically aimed at delivering some form of **product** (International Organization for Standardization, 2015, 2.1.5) (noting, of course, that products can be intangible).

These processes and the products that result from them will all involve various different **stakeholders** (a term not defined in ISO 17100:2015). In this textbook, the term 'stakeholder' is used in a broad sense to refer to any individual person or corporate (or non-corporate) entity that has a stake in a particular project or process. In this sense, stakeholders can include clients, LSPs, and vendors, as well as wider interpretations including end users of the products, governments and institutions, and even the general public.

The elements that make up the aforementioned workflows, processes, and products are covered in much more detail in various chapters throughout this textbook. This now brings us to a point where we need to briefly consider what we are working with as our source and target materials.

Language and Content

ISO 17100:2015 specifically refers to **content** as 'anything representing meaningful information or knowledge' (International Organization for Standardization, 2015, 2.3.1). In the industry, especially in the context of producing new content, this is often referred to as **copy** (hence the terms 'copywriting' and 'copy-editing'). A **text**, therefore, which is typically what we are dealing with in many (but not all) forms of translation, is 'content in written form' (International Organization for Standardization, 2015, 2.3.4).

? In what ways is this focus on 'text' in ISO 17100:2015 potentially problematic in the translation industry?

This content, or the texts with which we deal, comes in different forms and exhibits different characteristics. All texts will employ different types of **language register**, defined as a 'variety of language used for a particular purpose or in a particular social or industrial domain' International Organization for Standardization, 2015, 2.3.7). Note that 'register' is not necessarily to be interpreted in the most common sense attributed to the term; we often think of register in terms of 'high' or 'low' (colloquial) register only, but the definition provided in the ISO refers to a specific form, style, and manner of writing used in a particular **domain**. The domain is what we might colloquially call the 'field' or 'subject matter' of a text: 'subject field, sphere of knowledge or activity having its own specialized culture, social context, and linguistic characteristics' (International Organization for Standardization, 2015, 2.3.10). An example of a domain might be 'medical', for instance, or even a more specialist subset such as 'cardiology', in which the text uses certain terminology and phraseology, and indeed certain text-type conventions.

These **text-type conventions** have been addressed in some detail in translation studies literature (among functionalist theories in particular), and this is a point where the overlap between theory and practice is quite important. Nord, for example, refers to genre conventions, which she argues to be 'culture-specific' (Nord, 2018, p. 51). A translator 'has to be familiar with the conventions of the genre to which the text belongs', which can include 'things like measurement conventions, formal conventions for numbering chapters or marking neologisms by italics, or conventions in graphic representations in technical texts' (Nord, 2018, p. 51). Nord also references 'general style conventions' and 'translation conventions' (Nord, 2018, pp. 54–56), among others.

? What role do you believe text-type conventions play in translation project management?

These conventions are in turn shaped by another important term: **locale**, defined as the 'set of characteristics, information or conventions specific to the linguistic, cultural, technical, and geographical conventions of a target audience' (International Organization for Standardization, 2015, 2.3.11).

? What role do you believe locales play in translation project management?

Sikes considers an understanding of locale to be critical to the concepts of localisation, internationalisation, and globalisation. As he writes:

> A locale is not simply a country nor a language, but rather a combination of the two, reflecting the fact that some languages are spoken in multiple countries and that not all countries are monolingual. ... The concept of locale also reflects the fact that significant cultural differences may exist within or between countries in which different languages are spoken. ... The notion of locale encompasses not only language, but also various types of data, such as date, time, numbers, currencies, weights, measurements, as well as rules for presenting and sorting these data in accordance with the cultural conventions of a given language and geographic area.
> [Sikes, 2011, p. 239]

Hence, it should be apparent that the ways in which locale and text-type conventions interact with, and are defined by, concepts such as domain and register, as well as even more fundamental notions of source and target, are critical to the ways in which translation projects are managed from start to finish. It is important that these terms (and indeed others throughout this textbook) are used consistently to refer to the same concepts, as one of the biggest problems in the translation industry is a lack of consensus surrounding terminology (one of the very aims that ISO 17100:2015 sets out to address, incidentally).

Now that terminology is suitably defined – with many more definitions to follow throughout this book – let us now turn to the structure of the textbook, with a brief overview of the content.

Structure

This textbook is split into two parts: the first addresses the workflow in detail, and the second explores some of the principles, theories, and approaches that are adopted to manage the diverse aspects of translation projects. The sub-sections below will explain briefly the content of each part.

Part 1. From Cradle to Grave: The Translation Project Lifecyle

Despite the somewhat morbid-sounding name for this section, the term 'cradle to grave' is widely used in project management circles and the business world more generally. The phrase is used to refer to the entire lifecycle of a project, and even beyond the project itself to encompass use of the product or service at the heart of the project. This is the very focus of Part 1: to consider, in considerable technical detail, the practicalities of how translation projects are managed from start to finish.

Chapter 2 looks at the first part of the project lifecycle: pre-production. It covers how project enquiries can be assessed in terms of their feasibility, and how quotations and schedules can be drawn up based on an analysis of the files to be translated, the client's needs, and the available human, technological, and technical resources. It also considers some of the preliminary steps carried out by a project manager prior to the launch of a project with a view to ensuring the subsequent success of the ensuing tasks carried out by the various parties involved in the process.

Chapter 3 moves to the production stage of the project. One of the important aspects of this chapter for readers is a thorough understanding of the key terminology used, especially in relation to often-confused terms such as 'revision', 'review', 'proofreading', and 'editing'. By focusing on the waterfall nature of translation projects, the chapter guides readers to an awareness of what each stage might involve and what some of the final 'sign-off' tasks of the project's production phase might comprise.

Chapter 4 rounds off the lifecycle part of the textbook by focusing on post-production. Particular emphasis is placed in this chapter on multidirectional feedback (between client, LSP, and vendors), as well as some of the more technical aspects of post-production such as invoicing, record keeping and file management, and the post-project 'post-mortem' meeting.

Part 2. Triangles, Diamonds, and Stars: Evaluating Translation Project Constraints

Part 2 moves away from some of the more rudimentary aspects of project management towards a more theoretically informed analysis of various project constraints. Since the focus and content of these sections are perhaps less apparent, it is maybe useful at this juncture to offer a little context on project constraints and their development.

In 1969, before project management even started to be conceived of as a discipline or organised practice, Martin Barnes, the founding member and president of the Association for Project Management (APM), devised what has now become one of the most fundamental elements of project management: the Project Management Triangle. This paradigm has come to be known under various names – *the Iron Triangle*, *the Law of Triple Constraints*, *the Project Pyramid* – but its elegance, simplicity, and, above all else, utility has meant that it has remained at the forefront of project management ever since, as well as being expanded and enhanced to incorporate new understandings of the project management process.

The original project management triangle was modelled with 'time', 'cost', and 'quality' in each corner, demonstrating, for the first time, that projects were not just managed in terms of schedules, but also in terms of costs and the quality of the outcome too. In Barnes's first mention of this concept (the story of which is described briefly in Barnes, 2006), he sketched this diagram on a piece of overhead projector acetate, moving a coin around the triangle to block out different constraints and show how one constraint influenced the other two. The logic behind this triangle was that it is impossible to change one constraint without having an impact on the other two:

- a project can be carried out quickly and to a high-quality standard, but it will be expensive;
- a project can be carried out quickly and cheaply, but quality will be low;
- a project can be carried out to a high-quality standard and cheaply, but it will take a long time.

The recognition of these inter-related constraints has given rise to a well-known adage in project management circles: 'pick any two: fast, good, or cheap'.

Confusingly, over time – it is difficult to ascertain precisely how and when – 'quality' came to be replaced in some diagrams by 'scope', and whichever was not on the outside of the triangle was shifted to the centre (for an example of 'scope' being in the centre of the triangle, see Dunne, 2011). Indeed, Barnes himself later changed 'quality' to 'performance', to confuse matters further (Barnes, 1988). The rationale for these changes was that the scope of a project – or rather, its specific *performance targets*, to use Barnes's updated terminology – alongside its budget and schedule would determine the overall quality of the output. The confusion surrounding which constraints should be situated outside the triangle was more than likely the reason for the later development of the diamond model, with either 'expectations' or 'client satisfaction' at the centre, on the grounds that the client's needs will dictate how cost, time, quality, and scope will be balanced. The precise origin of the diamond is unclear, but the first edition of *A Guide to the Project Management Body of Knowledge* (the 'PMBOK Guide') refers to 'balancing competing demands among: scope, time, cost, and quality; [and] stakeholders with differing needs and expectations' (Project Management Institute, 1996, p. 6), which may be the source of this design. Similar wordings remain in the second and third editions of the PMBOK Guide (Project Management Institute, 2000, 2006). With its fourth edition, the Project Management Institute (PMI) expanded its project constraints to 'scope', 'quality', 'schedule', 'budget', 'resources', and 'risk' (Project Management Institute, 2008, p. 6; also retained in its fifth edition: Project Management Institute, 2013, p. 6). Interestingly, the most recent PMBOK Guide (6th edition) omitted any clear identification of constraints, but it does refer to five of these six as *examples* of constraints (Project Management

14 Translation Project Management

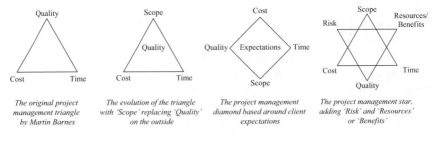

Figure 1.3 The evolution of project constraint models

Institute, 2017, p. 10). These six constraints are often conceptualised as a star, or more precisely, two overlaid triangles (see Figure 1.3), with project input/output factors on one triangle (scope, cost, time) and project process factors on the other (risk, resources, quality).

Alternative geometric shapes such as tetrads, tetrahedra, pyramids, and cubes have also been used to conceptualise these constraints (and others) in different ways (for selected references, see Vahidi & Greenwood, 2009, p. 928), but one complementary approach to that of the PMI is advocated in the PRINCE2 method of project management (Office of Government Commerce, 2018), which is the constraint model adopted in this textbook. The PRINCE2 method largely agrees with the PMI's identified constraints, referring to them as 'variables' or 'aspects of project performance to be managed', but makes one notable replacement among the six, introducing 'benefits' in place of 'resources'. The PRINCE2 framework defines the constraints as follows (Office of Government Commerce, 2018, pp. 9–10):

- **Timescales (Chapter 5)**: 'Closely linked to costs, and probably one of the questions project managers are most frequently asked, is: When will it be finished?';
- **Costs (Chapter 6)**: 'The project has to be affordable and, though we may start out with a particular budget in mind, there will be many factors which can lead to overspending and, perhaps, some opportunities to cut costs';
- **Scope (Chapter 7)**: 'Exactly what will the project deliver? … There must be agreement on the project's scope and the project managed needs to have a sufficient understanding of what is and what is not within the scope';
- **Quality (Chapter 8)**: 'Finishing on time and within budget is not much consolation if the result of the project does not work. In PRINCE2 terms, the project's products must be fit for purpose';
- **Benefits (Chapter 9)**: 'Why are we doing this? … The project manager has to have a clear understanding of the purpose of the project … and

make sure that what the project delivers is consistent with achieving the desired return'; and
- **Risk (Chapter 10)**: 'All projects entail risks but exactly how much risk are we prepared to accept? ... Is there something we can do about the risk?'

The underlying objective of Part 2 is to consider why these constraints matter and how they can be applied to the specific case of *translation* project management. Part 2 will explore some of the factors that influence these constraints as well as ways to manage these various factors, and, most importantly, we will discuss how and why these constraints are relevant to the translation profession and the role of a project manager. A number of preliminary discussion points are listed below to offer some initial prompts for discussion on the relevance of these concepts to the translation industry and translation outsourcing model:

? For each of the project constraints listed above – cost, time, quality, scope, benefits, risk – how might these constraints influence the ways in which a project is prepared, executed by freelance professionals, managed by project managers, and received by end clients?
? Which of these constraints do you believe to be the most influential (or restrictive) in translation project management? Why?
? Are there any project management constraints that you consider to not be covered by the six listed above? If so, what are they? And why do you consider them to be project constraints?

It may be beneficial to revisit these questions again after reading the remainder of the textbook to see whether your understanding has changed or whether new constraints or components of these constraints have come to light in your mind.

The book closes with **Chapter 11**, entitled **Post-mortem**. Echoing the project-management-specific meaning of a post-mortem, initially covered in **Chapter 4**, the aim of this chapter is to draw together all of the threads from the previous ones to consider the wider context in which translation project management operates. The chapter therefore draws on various strands of research into the sociology of the translation industry, as well as offering some pathways to future research into translation project management for those who would like to explore undergraduate and postgraduate dissertations or even doctoral research in this area.

Topics for Discussion and Assignments

1. What role does translation play in the world, and within this, what role does translation project management play?

2. What do you understand to be the primary reasons behind the dominance of the outsourcing model in the translation industry? Why does outsourcing exist? What benefits does it offer to clients and to freelancers?
3. Based on your limited knowledge so far, what do you believe to be the main challenges of translation project management?

Further Reading

Dunne and Dunne (2011a) provides an excellent overview of translation project management as a field of study and research, as well as summarising briefly the content covered in the remainder of the edited book that it introduces.

Angelone et al. (2020a) offers a short overview of the language industry, its growth, and research in this field, also summarising the content in subsequent chapters of the edited book.

References

Angelone, E., Ehrensberger-Dow, M., & Massey, G. (2020a). Introduction. In E. Angelone, M. Ehrensberger-Dow, & G. Massey (Eds.), *The Bloomsbury companion to language industry studies* (pp. 1–13). Bloomsbury Academic.

Angelone, E., Ehrensberger-Dow, M., & Massey, G. (Eds.). (2020b). *The Bloomsbury companion to language industry studies*. Bloomsbury Academic.

Barnes, M. (1988). Construction project management. *International Journal of Project Management*, 6(2), 69–79.

Barnes, M. (2006). *How it all began*. Retrieved 31 May 2020 from https://pmworldlibrary.net/article/how-it-all-began/

CSA Research. (2019). *Global market for outsourced translation and interpreting services and technology to reach US$49.60 billion in 2019* [Press release]. Retrieved 23 July 2020 from https://csa-research.com/More/Media/Press-Releases/ArticleID/546/Global-Market-for-Outsourced-Translation-and-Interpreting-Services-and-Technology-to-Reach-US-49-60-Billion-in-2019

Dunne, K. J. (2011). Managing the fourth dimension: Time and schedule in translation and localization projects. In K. J. Dunne & E. S. Dunne (Eds.), *Translation and localization project management: The art of the possible* (pp. 119–152). John Benjamins.

Dunne, K. J. (2012). The industrialization of translation: Causes, consequences and challenges. *Translation Spaces*, 1, 143–168. https://doi.org/10.1075/ts.1.07dun

Dunne, K. J., & Dunne, E. S. (2011a). Mapping terra incognita: Project management in the discipline of translation studies. In K. J. Dunne & E. S. Dunne (Eds.), *Translation and localization project management: The art of the possible* (pp. 1–14). John Benjamins.

Dunne, K. J., & Dunne, E. S. (Eds.). (2011b). *Translation and localization project management: The art of the possible*. John Benjamins.

International Organization for Standardization. (2015). *Translation services – Requirements for translation services (ISO 17100:2015)*. International Organization for Standardization.

Matis, N. (2014). *How to manage your translation projects*. Retrieved from www.translation-project-management.com/en

Matos, S., & Lopes, E. (2013). Prince2 or PMBOK – A question of choice. *Procedia Technology, 9*, 787–794. https://doi.org/10.1016/j.protcy.2013.12.087

Nimdzi. (2019). The 2019 Nimdzi 100 – Language services industry analysis. Retrieved 23 July 2020 from www.nimdzi.com/2019-nimdzi-100/

Nord, C. (2018). *Translating as a purposeful activity: Functionalist approaches explained* (2nd ed.). Routledge.

Office of Government Commerce. (2018). *Managing successful projects with PRINCE2 2017 edition* (6th ed.). The Stationery Office Ltd.

Prieto Ramos, F. (2020). *Institutional translation and interpreting: Assessing practices and managing for quality*. Routledge.

Project Management Institute. (1996). *A guide to The Project Management Body Of Knowledge (PMBOK® guide)* (1st ed.). Project Management Institute, Inc.

Project Management Institute. (2000). *A guide to the Project Management Body Of Knowledge (PMBOK® guide)* (2nd ed.). Project Management Institute, Inc.

Project Management Institute. (2006). *A guide to the Project Management Body Of Knowledge (PMBOK® guide)* (3rd ed.). Project Management Institute, Inc.

Project Management Institute. (2008). *A guide to the Project Management Body Of Knowledge (PMBOK® guide)* (4th ed.). Project Management Institute, Inc.

Project Management Institute. (2013). *A guide to the Project Management Body Of Knowledge (PMBOK® guide)* (5th ed.). Project Management Institute, Inc.

Project Management Institute. (2017). *A guide to the Project Management Body Of Knowledge (PMBOK® guide)* (6th ed.). Project Management Institute, Inc.

Rico Pérez, C. (2002). Translation and project management. *Translation Journal, 6*(4). Retrieved 25 July 2020 from https://translationjournal.net/journal/22project.htm

Risku, H. (2016). *Translationsmanagement: Interkulturelle Fachkommunikation im Informationszeitalter* [Translation management: Intercultural technical communication in the information age]. Narr.

Sikes, R. (2011). Rethinking the role of the localization project manager. In K. J. Dunne & E. S. Dunne (Eds.), *Translation and localization project management: The art of the possible* (pp. 235–264). John Benjamins.

Standvik, I. (2017). Evaluation of outsourced translations. State of play in the European Commission's Directorate-General for Translation (DGT). In T. Svoboda, Ł. Biel, & K. Łoboda (Eds.), *Quality aspects in institutional translation* (pp. 123–137). Language Science Press.

Toury, G. (1995/2012). *Descriptive translation studies – and beyond*. John Benjamins.

Vahidi, R., & Greenwood, D. (2009, 27 September). *Triangles, tradeoffs and success: A critical examination of some traditional project management paradigms* [Paper presentation]. CIB Joint International Symposium 2009, Dubrovnik, Croatia. Retrieved 31 July 2020 from www.irbnet.de/daten/iconda/CIB16214.pdf

Part I
From Cradle to Grave
The Translation Project Lifecycle

2 Pre-production

> **Learning outcomes:**
> - Understand the importance of thorough and careful project planning in pre-production
> - Identify and carry out the main stages of a project feasibility study, including a provisional schedule, and client quotation
> - Understand the content and role of a client–LSP agreement
> - Determine the tasks that need to be carried out to prepare a project for production
> - Design appropriate resources to gather information from clients, and catalogue project records

Pre-production is a critical stage in translation project management. There are two key perspectives to this argument. Firstly, there is the 'outward-facing' business case argument: a client approaches your LSP requesting a quotation and schedule for the translation of a lengthy legal contract. You, the project manager, need to convince that client that your LSP is the right business to handle their request by demonstrating that the service will be provided at a fair price, that the product will be delivered within a reasonable timescale, and that what is included in the service, and the quality of the service more generally, will be to the client's satisfaction. Accurate information and incentives need to be given to the client – without deception or false promises – to choose *your* LSP over others. If an LSP fails to secure projects on a regular basis, its very existence will come under threat. The second perspective is 'inward-facing': can the LSP manage this project successfully without excessive risk and deliver on the promises made to the client? Pre-production is the phase during which the project manager has arguably the greatest control over the project, and getting these preliminary stages right can make the difference between a project running smoothly and the project encountering bumps in the road.

Pre-production is therefore based around four key steps. Firstly, the **feasibility study**: is the project achievable in terms of the resources available

DOI: 10.4324/9781003132813-3

22 The Translation Project Lifecycle

to the LSP to complete the tasks? Second, the **client–LSP agreement** (and, later, purchase orders with vendors): can an agreement be reached with the client on the cost, the timescale for completion, scope and quality, and other specifications? Furthermore, are the terms of this agreement consistent with the findings of the feasibility study? For instance, how does the cost quoted to the client compare with the vendor charges, and the timescale quoted to the client with the vendor timescales? Third, **project preparation**: what tasks need to be completed by the project manager and/or vendors before work can begin in earnest on the project? And finally, **project administration**: how is this information and these pre-production stages recorded by the LSP to aid in the project being a success?

This chapter focuses on the higher-level, fundamental tasks that project managers might carry out during the pre-production stage, but without going into the intricacies of project constraints such as timescales, costs, scope, and quality, which are analysed in depth in Chapters 5 to 10. Before we start to look at the first steps of pre-production, note down your preliminary thoughts on the following questions:

? What tasks do you think the project manager will need to carry out to determine whether a project is feasible (i.e. as part of a feasibility study)?
? If a project is not deemed feasible, what should/could the project manager do?
? Why is it important to have a client–LSP agreement or purchase order with vendors?
? What steps might be involved in preparing a project for the production stage?
? What administrative tasks might need to be undertaken? Think about the sorts of data or information that might need to be collected, both in relation to the client itself and also the project.

Feasibility Study and Quotation

When a translation project enquiry arrives from a client, the project manager will need to handle and analyse the enquiry promptly but thoroughly. The feasibility study is arguably one of the most important stages of project management. Assessing whether a project is feasible means, by definition, assessing whether it is practical, workable, realistic, possible, and appropriate. ISO 17100:2015 (International Organization for Standardization, 2015, 4.2) delineates three aspects of this assessment:

- an analysis of the enquiry to identify the client's specifications for the services;
- an analysis of the enquiry to determine whether the LSP is capable of meeting the client's specifications; and

- an assessment of whether the necessary human, technical, and technological resources are available.

This chapter adapts the structure above and breaks the feasibility study down further into a project analysis, the drafting of a project schedule, an assessment of available resources, and the drafting of a quotation. Box 2.1 provides two examples of project enquiries ranging from the basic to the detailed.

Having read Box 2.1 and considered the two questions, some readers will have possibly identified close ties between this preliminary 'analysis' stage of the feasibility study and a well-known aspect of translation theory: **skopos theory**. Skopos is the Greek word for 'purpose', and in the case of this theory, it refers specifically to the purpose of the target text: 'translate/

Box 2.1 Project enquiries

Enquiries can take many forms and can differ vastly in the amount of information provided by the client. Below is an example of an enquiry at the very basic end of the spectrum (unfortunately not an uncommon occurrence in the translation industry):

Example 1
Dear [LSP],
I have a text that requires translating (see attached). Would you be able to organise this for me?

And another enquiry towards the more detailed end of the spectrum, which we will use throughout the remainder of this chapter:

Example 2
(Sent on 5 June)
Dear [LSP],
My company Global Web Design is planning to release a new brand name and logo, which we are due to launch in just under one month on 1 July. We will also be launching a new website that will require all content in Arabic, French, German, and Spanish. This might include a lot of translating and I am a little worried that this is going to be very last minute. The priority is to push the default English site and Arabic site on 1 July – ideally, we want to launch all languages, but Arabic is a priority. Do you have someone available that could potentially translate the content within a two-week window? I will, of course, try to send

> across content ahead of time, but everything is a little rushed. Let me know your thoughts.
>
> Based on these two enquiries:
> ? Carry out a preliminary analysis of the client's requirements in the basic and detailed examples above. What precisely do these clients want (timescales, languages, format, volumes, etc.)?
> ? What additional questions might you want to ask each client in each of the examples above?

interpret/speak/write in a way that enables your text/translation to function in the situation in which it is used and with the people who want to use it and precisely in the way they want it to function' (Vermeer, 1989, p. 20, in Nord, 2018, p. 28), but this raises questions of who decides 'in what way' the text should be translated. Determining the translation **brief** is an important part of reaching an agreement between client and project manager on the translation's purpose and how it will be translated. In some cases, however, no explicit brief is given by the client; the project manager (and in turn the vendor) simply infers the purpose from the context of the enquiry (i.e. a translation of a business letter originally drafted in German will be required to function and operate in the same manner and context in France but simply in the French language). Such assumptions frequently require an element of source text analysis on the part of the project manager: the source text can offer information on the communicative situation of the translation (who is the audience, what is the domain, what is the register, where was the ST published, etc.?). The resulting brief (assuming instructions to the contrary have not been given by the client) will therefore likely contain information on the purpose ('for information purposes', 'for publication', etc.), the TT addressee(s) (who will use the translation?), the time and place of TT reception (when is it required and how will it be disseminated?), the medium of delivery (hard copy, electronically, etc.), and the motive for the translation (why is translation needed?) (Nord, 2018, p. 29–30, 56–62). The project manager will also likely need to ask pertinent questions and guide the client towards the sorts of answers that are needed to analyse the project fully.

Let us return to our example of a basic enquiry in Box 2.1 (Example 1). What do we know from this enquiry? The obvious answer is 'very little'. We have an attachment, on which we could conduct an ST analysis and make *assumptions* about the purpose, addressees, and time and place of reception, but these assumptions would need to be checked with the client. We also have no information on which language(s) are needed or when the translation needs to be delivered (or the mode of delivery). We might assume, however, that the translation is not especially urgent, given the tone of the enquiry. In any case, there would be a lot of questions that need to be asked by the project manager before the feasibility study can begin.

Turning to the more detailed enquiry in Box 2.1 (Example 2), while it does contain substantially more information, it is still lacking in certain specificities. We know that the client is about to launch a company rebrand (*the motive*), meaning that the content (depending on the size and reputation of the company) will be in the public domain online (*the place of reception*) and will form an important part of its marketing and outreach to new and existing markets (*the purpose*). Part of this rebrand also involves the launch of a new multilingual website in four new languages (*the addressee(s)*, implicitly). Because of the public-facing nature of company websites, high quality will be important, as mistakes could tarnish the company's brand, making it appear careless in its presentation of published materials. We also know that timescales are problematic. We know that the brand launch is 'in just under one month' (*the time of reception*) and the translation will need to be completed within two weeks – 'very last minute' – presumably because the English content is not yet finalised. Furthermore, in terms of priorities, the Arabic translation is the most important, but in an ideal world, the client wants the French, German, and Spanish sites to be ready at the same time too. Some questions do still remain, however. The domain is not specified (but could be ascertained by visiting the company's existing website, if available); the locale needs to be clarified (for Arabic, in particular); it is not clear whether the website needs to be localised or simply translated; and there will need to be some discussion with the client about the level of quality assurance (revision, review, proofreading), which may also entail a degree of client education (a recurrent theme in this textbook).

We will continue to use the detailed example in Box 2.1 throughout this chapter to aid understanding, adding additional information at relevant points based on hypothetical responses obtained from our client.

Project Analysis

Moving to the project analysis, there are four key pieces of information that need to be gleaned from the enquiry and any files provided with the enquiry at this stage in order to start elaborating a schedule, assessing resources, and drawing up a quotation:

- source language and target language(s);
- domain (subject matter);
- number of 'units'; and
- levels of quality assurance required.

The first element of the content analysis is usually straightforward, mainly because the client will normally be able to inform the LSP of the

source language and the intended **target language**. There are some rare cases where a client has received a document in an unknown language and they are appealing to the LSP's expertise to determine the source language. There are various online tools that can be used to identify an unknown language, although many project managers start to become quite adept at recognising features of different languages over time, based on scripts (various forms of Cyrillic, Arabic, etc.) or certain grammatical features. The choice of target language(s), however, should only rarely pose a problem, as these are predetermined based on the client's needs (perhaps working into the client's native language, or working into one or more foreign languages determined by business with foreign companies, for example). Yet there are very rare instances where a client might be unaware of which specific language is required and they are again calling on the LSP to advise. Take a country such as India, for example, which has hundreds of different spoken languages. Constitutionally, Hindi is the official language of India alongside English, but there are also a further 21 official languages, including Bengali, Gujarati, Kashmiri, Nepali, Punjabi, Tamil, and Urdu, each of which is favoured in different parts of India. Hence, a client needing a translation for use in India, but with little knowledge of the languages of India, might ask the LSP for advice. In a similar vein, project managers should also be careful to ascertain which variety of the source and target language is required. French, for example, differs depending on whether it is French as spoken in mainland France, Belgian French, Swiss French, Canadian French (of which there are several sub-varieties such as Acadian and Quebec), Haitian French, Cambodian French, Vietnamese French, and a wide range of African varieties (e.g. as spoken in Algeria, Côte d'Ivoire, Djibouti, etc.), among others.

The second element – the **domain** or subject matter of the project – is also relatively easy to ascertain. Once again, the client will in most cases inform the project manager of the subject matter, or at least the general domain. The client might state simply that it is a 'legal' text but without further details; equally, they might offer more information and describe the text as 'a legal contract relating to the purchase of automotive spare parts'. If the client does not provide such information, it would be wise to ask the client, but, as with languages, the client may not know. If the project manager is familiar with the language, the task of ascertaining the domain will be relatively easy; if the project manager (or anyone else at the LSP) cannot read the language, sometimes the quickest solution is to use a free machine translation tool to generate a quick 'gist' translation (bearing in mind confidentiality and data privacy concerns, of course). Alternatively, for a more reliable assessment (or indeed if the source/target language is not available in the machine translation engine), the file can be sent to a friendly vendor for a quick review to ascertain the subject matter.

? How could you perhaps incentivise a vendor to carry out this preliminary review for you?

The third element is the most important of this initial content analysis: a count (or estimate, at least) of **the number of units** involved in the project. It is essential that this figure is as accurate as possible, as it will be used, firstly, to generate a provisional project schedule (which in turn feeds into an assessment of available resources) and then to draw up an estimate or quotation for the client. So what do we mean by 'units'? The term units is used here as a generic description of the quantitative assessment of a linguistic task's workload. The simplest example of this is a document's word count. Text-based tasks (translation, revision, review, etc.) are typically quantified based on the number of words (for alphabetic languages such as English), characters (for character-based or 'logographic' languages such as Chinese), lines (used sometimes for German and Finnish due to their extensive use of long compound words), or pages (usually only if a precise word count cannot be obtained). Interpreting tasks would typically be quantified in hours or days; audiovisual translation might be measured in reels (segments of audiovisual content lasting about twenty minutes) or simply minutes; and desktop publishing (DTP) – an added-value non-linguistic service – is usually measured in pages. In short, the type of unit used will depend on the task.

Calculating the number of units is normally straightforward. Microsoft Word files (.docx) can provide an instant breakdown into words, characters, lines, and pages with one click. Other file types can be more complex. Microsoft Excel, for instance, does not have a word count function, but content can be copied and pasted into Word to obtain a word count. Non-editable files, such as .pdf files, are far more problematic. A project manager might have to use an estimated word count (based on a crude metric such as 500 words per page, single spaced, or 250 words, double spaced), a manual word count (which is incredibly time consuming), or use optical character recognition (OCR) software to convert the file into an editable format (which comes with its own risks of inaccuracies). As a general rule, it is advisable to overestimate than to underestimate the unit count, as it is best to assume that a task will take longer or cost more than it actually does in reality, then reduce the corresponding quotation and schedule later.

Perhaps the most reliable method of generating a word (or character) count from a wide range of different file types, beyond the Microsoft Office suite alone, is to use CAT software. Importing a .docx or .xlsx file into Trados Studio or memoQ, for example, will allow the project manager to run an instant analysis of the total word count, but it will also reveal any repetitions and translation memory (TM) matches, which can reduce the time required and potentially the cost too (see later in this chapter). Figure 2.1 in Box 2.2, for example, shows a screenshot of an analysis report in memoQ, broken down into the number of new words, repetitions, and various degrees of fuzzy matches (for more on this feature, see Mitchell-Schuitevoerder, 2020, p. 33–36). These reports can also be exported and inserted directly into pre-existing templates in Excel or other tools to calculate rudimentary timescales and costs automatically.

The final step of this preliminary project analysis is to ascertain with the client how many levels of **quality assurance (QA)** are required. As previously noted from the basic overview of the project lifecycle, ISO 17100:2015 refers to translation, checking, revision, review, and proofreading as main linguistic tasks, each of which builds on the original translation stage to incorporate additional levels of checks and corrections. Each of these steps needs to be explained clearly to the client and a decision needs to be reached, perhaps jointly between the LSP and the client, depending on the project brief, as to what QA stages are required. The topic of quality will be addressed in greater detail in Chapter 8.

The next step of the feasibility study involves mapping out a provisional project schedule. As eminent project management consultant Peter Drucker once said, 'time is the scarcest resource, and unless it is managed, nothing else can be managed' (Drucker, 1967, p. 51).

Project Schedule

After the project (and relevant files) have been analysed, the project manager must elaborate a **provisional schedule**. Remember that it is merely an enquiry at this stage: to go beyond a provisional schedule (i.e. one that is likely to be adjusted later) may be superfluous and an unnecessary use of time if the client decides either not to proceed with the translation or to take their business elsewhere. The elaboration of a project schedule must come before an assessment of the availability and suitability of resources, as the project manager will need to know precisely how many translators, revisers, reviewers, proofreaders, and other human resources are needed for the project, not to mention any other technical requirements that might add time to the project's execution. After all, what use is there in asking if one translator is available when the client's deadline dictates that the project must be completed in a timescale that is too short for one translator alone?

This stage of the feasibility study uses the unit count from the preceding project analysis to compute a feasible timescale for each individual component of the project. It is therefore crucial that the number of units used in these calculations is as accurate as possible. When a vendor registers with an LSP, he or she will typically state his or her daily **throughput** (i.e. how many words/characters the vendor can translate, revise, review, or proofread per day). This volume will be dependent on a number of factors, such as the language pair, file type, domain, and individual idiosyncrasies (i.e. some vendors simply work faster or slower than others). A widely used but very crude – and not especially reliable – industry standard for translation throughput is 3,000 words per day. For ease, we will use this figure for discussion purposes in this section.

Box 2.2 Project analysis example

Continuing on from the detailed enquiry example in Box 2.1, let us assume now that the client (Global Web Design) has sent you their website content in a Microsoft Excel file, with each page in a new tab. In each tab, the original English is in Column A, and the client has asked you to insert the Arabic, French, German, and Spanish translations in Columns B, C, D, and E, respectively. You have now uploaded the Excel file into memoQ and have run a project analysis, yielding the breakdown shown in Figure 2.1.

Type	Segments	Source words	Source chars	Weight	Source tags	Percent	Chart
All	1846	45042 (43090.3)	251719 (240077.3)		2907	100	
X-Translated	0	0 (0.0)	0 (0.0)	0 %	0	0	
Repetition	128	521 (156.3)	3184 (955.2)	30 %	46	1	
101%	99	846 (0.0)	5073 (0.0)	0 %	75	1	
100%	11	42 (12.6)	219 (65.7)	30 %	4	0	
95-99%	118	290 (145.0)	2088 (1044.0)	50 %	117	0	
85-94%	58	1325 (1060.0)	7225 (5780.0)	80 %	70	2	
75-84%	77	1508 (1206.4)	8488 (6790.4)	80 %	77	3	
50-74%	395	7093 (7093.0)	40142 (40142.0)	100 %	470	15	
No match	960	33417 (33417.0)	185300 (185300.0)	100 %	2048	74	

Figure 2.1 Analysis report in memoQ

The weighted source word count – shown in brackets – is a useful tool to integrate repetitions and fuzzy matches into a simple single-unit metric. In the example above, there are 45,042 source words for translation, but, taking into account fuzzy matches and repetitions, this equates to 43,090.3 'weighted words', based on the percentages listed in the 'Weight' column.

? Given the nature of a website, which forms of quality assurance would you recommend for this client? You might want to refer to the QA definitions later in this book or in the glossary.
? What specific questions might you need to ask about each of the languages? Think about the countries in which Arabic, French, German, and Spanish are spoken.

Having asked these questions, and now having access to the content itself, you are able to ascertain the source and target languages, the domain (subject matter), the number of units needing to be translated, and the levels of quality assurance required. This information can then feed into the project schedule, resource assessment, and quotation.

Let us assume that a basic translation project (no QA required) comprises 15,000 words. A basic calculation tells us that 15,000 words can be translated in five days (15,000 words ÷ 3,000 words per day = 5 days). That is simple enough, but suppose that the client needs the translation sooner.

Two translators working on the project could translate 6,000 words per day, meaning that the translation could be ready in two and a half days (15,000 words ÷ 6,000 words per day [3,000 words per translator per day] = 2.5 days). In project management terms, these are forms of 'schedule compression' (specifically 'fast tracking' and, in some cases, 'crashing', see Project Management Institute, 2017, p. 215). However, having two translators work on a single file can cause consistency problems (different terminology and phraseology, contrasting styles, etc.). Sometimes an additional stage, referred to as **harmonisation**, is required to 'harmonise' the two translators' work, meaning 'to make the two translations consistent with one another'. This harmonisation stage would require less time than translation and would likely be more in line with the throughput of monolingual QA tasks (e.g. review and proofreading). The best approach to calculating throughput is to rely on translators' own assessments of their abilities (for more on this, see Chapter 5), but some LSPs make use of 'scheduling metrics'. Matis (2014, p. 83), for example, suggests that a translator could translate 2,500 words per day on a 'standard text' (in contrast with 2,000 words per day on a marketing text) and that a reviser carrying out 'simple revision' (which Matis uses loosely to refer to non-technical text) could revise 7,500 words per day.

If the client has not specified a deadline, this allows the project manager some freedom to plan the schedule as he or she sees fit, more than likely with as few linguists as possible to avoid the need for harmonisation stages. If a deadline has been specified, however, this places additional constraints on the project manager that will likely require more linguists in each stage, depending on the number of units involved. This topic is taken up in more detail in Chapter 5; for now, we will limit ourselves to the basic calculations above, based on throughput metrics either provided by the translator (the ideal situation) or determined by the LSP (far from ideal, but workable for the purposes of the feasibility study).

Resources

Once the provisional schedule has been drawn up, the project manager will have a much clearer idea of how many vendors are needed and what tasks will need to be carried out for each stage of the project, and he or she can then start to assess whether the necessary resources are available for the project.

ISO 17100:2015 breaks down resources into human resources (e.g. vendors, project managers, etc.), and technical and technological resources. **Human resources** (International Organization for Standardization, 2015, 3.1) are a fundamental ingredient in translation projects, even with the rapid growth of increasingly reliable machine translation (MT) systems, so it is important that project managers, and LSPs more generally, vet their human resources appropriately to ensure that they are properly qualified for the

Box 2.3 Project schedule example

Using the unit total in Figure 2.1 (in Box 2.2) – 45,042 source words – a single translator translating 3,000 words per day would require 15 days to complete the translation. However, recall from Box 2.1 that our client specified that the content needed to be translated 'within a two-week window'. And what about the QA stages? For a project like this, where the content is prominent and 'public-facing' and therefore reflects the company's image and reputation, it would be advisable to have a 'revision' stage, at the very least, and because multiple translators will have worked on the project, a harmonisation stage would be advisable to make the lexicon and style as consistent as possible. (The harmonisation could also double as a 'review'.)

? Can you devise a rough project schedule that fits within this two-week window? For translation work on the basis of 3,000 words per day per translator, for revision – 7,500 words per day per reviser, and for harmonisation – 15,000 words per day.
? Why should there ideally be only one harmoniser per language pair?

Let us now work through this example with one possible solution (there are other possible solutions too). First, two translators, who would deliver half of the content in seven to eight working days, would leave very little time for any QA. Therefore, perhaps the best solution in this case is to split the content three ways (3 × 15,000 words), with each batch ready in five business days. For the revision stage, we would still likely need three revisers (3 × 15,000 words, requiring only two business days), and this would leave three business days for harmonisation. This solution is *per language pair*, so this setup would be required for Arabic, for French, for German, and for Spanish in this example.

So, in summary:

- three translators per language pair, each translating 15,000 words of the total (five business days);
- three revisers per language pair, each revising 15,000 words of the total (two business days);
- one harmoniser per language pair, harmonising the full 45,000 words (three business days).

We have therefore managed to set up a project schedule to complete the translation, revision, and harmonisation within two weeks (ten business days), with the weekend days serving as additional leeway (for more on leeway, see Chapter 5).

32 The Translation Project Lifecycle

task assigned to them. Before we proceed any further, consider the following questions:

? Which agents might be involved in a translation project? Consider those that might be involved at the LSP itself and outside the LSP on the vendor side.
? What do you consider to be the necessary qualifications and skills (competences) of a translator?

You may wish to revisit your answers after reading the short section on recruitment in Chapter 3. However, competences and qualifications are only part of the equation when it comes to the feasibility study. In many cases, the LSP will have a substantial database of vendors who have already been vetted to verify their qualifications and experience. Occasionally, an unusual enquiry comes in from a new client requesting a different mode of translation to that frequently managed by the LSP (e.g. transcreation), or a niche area of expertise (e.g. in-situ uranium mining, space physiology, astroparticle physics, etc.), and this will then require the project manager to source one or more new vendors for the project. For the purposes of this chapter, we will assume that the LSP has a pre-existing database with sufficient vendors. Besides competences and qualifications, therefore, the project manager must ensure that appropriate, *suitably qualified* vendors are available *in sufficient numbers*, depending on the nature of the project. Hence, using the preliminary schedule discussed in the previous section, the project manager can determine the number of human resources required for each stage of the project and send out a preliminary enquiry to the vendors to ascertain their availability. This initial availability check is important; vendors in a database are no use to an LSP if they are unavailable at the time to take on work due to other projects or engagements.

The other dimension of the resources assessment is what ISO 17100:2015 refers to as **technical and technological resources**. Breaking this down further, it specifies certain requirements in terms of hardware and software, data and document handling, communications equipment, information resources and media, and 'translation technology tools' (International Organization for Standardization, 2015, 3.2). The project manager will therefore need to ascertain, for *all* agents involved in the project (not just the various vendors, but the LSP too), that the infrastructure required by each agent is available. Software and hardware would therefore include, depending on the agent, a working computer, backup servers, anti-virus software, and archiving software. Communications equipment relates to Internet access (ideally, high-speed Internet access, depending on the file sizes involved), telephones, fax (some people do apparently still use fax machines), instant messaging or video conferencing software (e.g. Microsoft Teams, Zoom, etc.), cloud-storage, etc. Information resources and media are rather vague but could comprise paper resources such as dictionaries and grammar books, and other electronic resources such as style guides and encyclopaedias, and standards, processes, and guidelines on various relevant topics. The final category – 'translation technology tools' – will likely be the most obvious to students and practitioners of translation and would naturally include CAT software such as Trados Studio and memoQ, but could also include machine translation engines, if used, and more basic (and generic) forms of translation software such as Microsoft Word.

On a practical level, what this means is ensuring that your translator has the correct version of memoQ to open up the project package that you, the project manager, created internally at the LSP. Many of the technical and technological resources identified above can be assumed by the project manager: the fact that the vendor is in contact with the LSP suggests that he or she has appropriate communications equipment, and the fact that he or she has good references from past clients or LSPs probably suggests that he or she uses appropriate information resources. Resources that are unique to a specific project – such as an encrypted file server for a highly sensitive project that cannot be sent via email, or remote interpreting using Microsoft Teams – would, however, need to be checked on a case-by-case basis.

Once the project manager has verified that the necessary resources are available, the feasibility study can move on to the quotation. However, in the interests of sharing real practices in the translation industry, an assessment of available resources is not a strict requirement for LSPs prior to sending a quotation to a client. Some LSPs would draw up a schedule and a quotation, then worry about sourcing the necessary resources only after the client has agreed for the project to proceed. There are pros and cons to each approach. A prior assessment of available resources allows for a more accurate check of the project's feasibility and reduces the risk of realising that the necessary human resources are in fact not available; that said, checking this before submitting a quotation further allows the LSP to ensure that the quotation covers the costs of the identified vendors. If no assessment of resources is carried out before the quotation is submitted, an LSP might later realise that their ideal vendors are not available and have to settle for a more expensive vendor, perhaps reducing or even eliminating the calculated margin.

Quotation

Before we progress to the process of drawing up a quotation, we first need to address an important terminological distinction between a **quotation** and an **estimate**. A quotation is a *fixed* price that cannot (or should not) change, except in very specific cases. An estimate is an *approximate* price that is subject to change depending on the actual work involved. Both quotations and estimates are used in the translation industry, depending on the circumstances. Quotations assume that all of the project tasks can be suitably identified and costed, while estimates would be used for projects with certain unpredictable elements. An example where an estimate might

Box 2.4 Resource assessment example

Using our preliminary schedule developed in Box 2.3, we established that we would need three translators, three revisers, and one harmoniser (doubling as a reviewer) per language pair (English into Arabic, French, German, and Spanish). Let us consider in more detail, beyond numbers alone, what we might require in terms of resources for this project:

? What sort of skills or expertise might we want our vendors to have specifically for this project?
? What technical and technological resources might be required for this project?

We will focus first on human resources and their skills and expertise. We need to ensure that each of our vendors works with the correct variety of each language. So, for the purposes of this project, we will assume that our client has informed us that the Arabic version is targeted at the United Arab Emirates but will be written in Modern Standard Arabic; the French version is aimed at mainland France (but to cater for Belgium and Switzerland too); the German version is intended for the market in Germany (but to cater for Austria and Switzerland too); and the Spanish version needs to be written in European Spanish. The vendors should also probably have expertise in marketing and business language, as there will be a mixture of business and financial terminology on the website; they should also have a good knowledge of information technology too, given that Global Web Design specialises in website design and hosting. Finally, we need to ensure that the required number of vendors with the identified expertise (correct language variety and relevant expertise) are available, either by using an availability tracker set up by the vendor or by sending a preliminary email to the vendors to ascertain their availability.

The technical and technological resources required for this project are relatively straightforward. In this case, we would want our vendors to have and be conversant with memoQ (since this was the CAT tool used to set up the project) and to have and be conversant with Microsoft Excel (since this was the original file format). The use of memoQ is important for this project, as it would be wise to set the project up on a project server so that the translation memories and term bases can be shared 'live' as each translator populates them with new segments and terms. Doing so will greatly aid consistency and facilitate the later work of the revisers and harmoniser. The other resources identified can be logically assumed (such as having access to a computer, the Internet, and information resources, etc.).

be used is a consultancy role, where a law firm has asked an LSP to supply a vendor on site to review documentation and make judgements as to which files need to be translated in full. The unpredictable element of this project is linked, firstly, to the amount of time that would be needed by the linguist to analyse the documentation, and secondly, to the amount of translation subsequently required, depending on which files are identified by the consulting vendor. Here, we will focus on quotations, as they need to be more carefully calculated given that they cannot be changed once agreed by the client and the LSP.

The main information required for a quotation will come from the earlier project analysis, which determined the number of units involved. This may have been the number of words to be translated, revised, reviewed, proofread, etc.; it may have been characters (for non-alphabetic languages); or it may have been hours or days for tasks such as interpreting. As noted above, additional value-added services such as desktop publishing would be quantified in pages. There are, however, other elements that are frequently overlooked. For instance, does a Microsoft Word document contain any images that cannot be edited (which would not have been included in the automatic word count) and would need to be 'overtyped' using text boxes? Do such images need to be localised to be made more appropriate for the target locale? For smaller projects, does the LSP operate a **minimum charge** policy? For example, a small 250-word email translation might bring in a very small amount of money for the LSP that is enough to cover the vendor costs, but it would make a minimal contribution to the LSP's overheads and other costs (let alone profit). Some LSPs may have a policy which states that any project costed for a client below the minimum charge value (which will differ from LSP to LSP) will be charged the minimum charge instead.

? Why might minimum charge policies exist (both for LSPs and freelance vendors)?
? Tricky question: how might you handle more 'multimodal' elements that require translation? (e.g. audiovisual media, illustrations that need to be adapted or localised more dramatically, etc.). And how might you handle something highly creative such as the 'transcreation' of a product advert?

There are three main approaches to drawing up a quotation. The first two are based around the assumption that the client does not have a maximum budget for the translation. The first is the simplest and involves **price grids** (see also Matis, 2014, p. 54–60). A price grid is an internal document drawn up by the LSP setting out the default charges for different linguistic services and for different language pairs. For example, the price grid might state that translation from English into Welsh costs £0.14 per word, English into French costs £0.12 per word, English into Hungarian costs £0.10 per word, and so on. It might then list charges for revision tasks, review tasks, proofreading, etc., each broken down by language. Sometimes languages are grouped into bands, depending on the different factors influencing their value (see Chapter 6). This price grid approach is very straightforward to implement, as it simply involves multiplying the relevant number of units by the correct figure in the price grid (depending on the task and language pair).

The second approach is to apply a **standard margin** determined by the LSP to the stated vendor cost. If a French into Ukrainian translator states that their standard rate for translation is €0.08 per word (many vendors will still adopt major currencies such as USD, EUR or GBP as their currency for rates, even if it is not the currency of their home country), the LSP might add a margin of 40% on top, taking their client charge up to €0.112 (rounded to €0.11). The actual percentage will differ depending on the LSP and will normally be decided by the senior management team to allow overheads such as costs for staff, utilities, premises, etc. to be covered, in addition to making a profit.

The third approach is the most complex from a project manager's perspective. A client might approach the LSP with a project and **strict budget** (e.g. £1,000). The project manager would need to work backwards from this figure, by first calculating the obligatory LSP margin (40% = £400). The remainder (£1,000 – £400 = £600) would then provide the maximum budget for vendor costs, and the project manager would need to find the required resources to carry out the work within this budget. It is at this point that effective vendor management truly comes into play. Having a well-organised and up-to-date database of vendors and their fees makes this task immeasurably easier, if not to find the ideal linguist for the job, then at least to identify those linguists who could be approached to negotiate their costs.

But what about the lauded benefits of CAT tools and their supposed cost-reducing properties? Many major CAT tool developers vaunt the ability of their software to reduce translation costs, so how can a project manager harness the power of translation memories to reduce costs? The main selling point of CAT tools is that they can recycle previously translated segments that are either identical or similar to the segment currently being translated. The theoretical benefit of this is that it saves the translator time (as well as improving consistency); but anything that saves time should also, in theory, save money. As such, it is very common in the translation industry to pay vendors less (and, in turn, charge clients less) for repetitions and higher fuzzy matches (a contentious issue for many vendors; see Mossop, 2019). For instance, the project analysis shown in Figure 2.1 already incorporates a 'Weight' column showing that 100% matches and repetitions are paid at 30% of the full rate, 101% matches (or 'Context Matches' in Trados Studio) are not paid at all, etc. The calculations involved are relatively straightforward, and most LSPs will have pre-made tools (e.g. an Excel spreadsheet) into which the relevant figures can be inserted to calculate the total vendor cost and client cost immediately. These weightings are not industry-wide;

Box 2.5 Quotation example

There are two components to drawing up a quotation for a prospective client. On the one hand, you need to work out what the project will cost you, the LSP, in terms of payments to vendors for their services (e.g. translation, revision, etc.), and, on the other hand, you need to calculate how much to charge the client so that the vendor costs are covered, any LSP costs are covered (staff costs, overheads, etc.), and the LSP makes a profit (the main aim of most businesses).

In the example calculations below, for ease, the project analysis (broken down into repetitions, fuzzy matches, and no matches) is simply divided by three for each of the three translators (see Box 2.3); the total word count is also split three ways for the three revisers. In reality, the actual segments to be translated or revised by each linguist would be analysed separately and might have different numbers of repetitions and fuzzy matches. The calculations below also assume that the charges are the same for all four languages, which may not be the case (see Chapter 6). To illustrate the three separate stages of this project, there are three tables to represent 'Translation', 'Revision', and 'Harmonisation' (see Table 2.1).

Table 2.1 Vendor costs calculation

Translation Match type	Source words (per translator)	Weight	Translator 1 Rate: £0.07	Translator 2 Rate: £0.09	Translator 3 Rate: £0.08
Repetition	174	30%	£3.65	£4.70	£4.18
101%	282	0%	£0.00	£0.00	£0.00
100%	14	30%	£0.29	£0.38	£0.34
95–99%	97	50%	£3.40	£4.37	£3.88
85–94%	442	80%	£24.75	£31.82	£28.29
75–84%	503	80%	£28.17	£36.22	£32.19
50–74%	2,364	100%	£165.48	£212.76	£189.12
No match	11,139	100%	£779.73	£1,002.51	£891.12
		Total:	£1,005.47	£1,292.75	£1,149.11
	Source words (per reviser)	Weight	Reviser 1 Rate: £0.04	Reviser 2 Rate: £0.04	Reviser 3 Rate: £0.05
Revision	15,014	100%	£600.56	£600.56	£750.70
	Source words	Weight	Harmoniser Rate: £0.04		
Harmonisation	45,042	100%	£1,801.68		

The total **vendor costs** (i.e. the amount that would be paid out to our envisaged three translators, three revisers, and one harmoniser) come to **£7,200.83 per language**, amounting to a grand total of **£28,803.32 for all languages**.

We now know what the cost to us – the LSP – will be, but we need to work out how much to charge our client in order to cover this cost and, importantly, make a profit, which is probably the main benefit of a translation project for an LSP (see Chapter 9). The margin charged by an LSP can vary considerably and will be determined by the LSP's senior management in most cases. In this example, we will use a 40% margin, which is relatively commonplace in the translation industry. There are two ways to approach the task of adding on the margin. The simplest is to simply add 40% to the total figure (i.e. £28,803.32 × 1.4 = £40,324.65), but the problem with this approach is that it is harder to provide a breakdown of where this figure comes from, and adding a large lump-sum 'Project Management' surcharge is likely to make many clients somewhat uneasy and question the rationale of this item.

It is therefore preferable to add this 40% margin to each component of the project. So we could add on 40% to the highest price of translation (£0.09 × 1.4 = £0.126, rounded to £0.12), add 40% to the highest price of revision (£0.05 × 1.4 = £0.07), and 40% to the price of harmonisation (£0.04 × 1.4 = £0.056, rounded to £0.06). We can then feed these numbers back into our original project analysis table (using the total word count, instead of the three-way split used above) as shown in Table 2.2.

Table 2.2 Client costs calculation

Match type	Source words	Weight	Translation Rate: £0.12	Revision Rate: £0.07	Harmonisation Rate: £0.06
Repetition	521	30%	£62.52	–	–
101%	846	0%	£101.52	–	–
100%	42	30%	£5.04	–	–
95–99%	290	50%	£34.80	–	–
85–94%	1,325	80%	£159.00	–	–
75–84%	1,508	80%	£180.96	–	–
50–74%	7,093	100%	£851.16	–	–
No match	33,417	100%	£4,010.04	–	–
Total count	45,042	100%	–	£3,152.94	£2,702.52
		Total per language:	£5,405.04	£3,152.94	£2,702.52
	Total for ALL languages (×4):		£21,620.16	£12,611.76	£10,810.08
		GRAND TOTAL:	£45,042.00		
		(Forecast Profit:)	£16,238.68		

? Why is it important to provide a breakdown of the total price for a client?

? Why did we add the 40% to the *highest* cost of translation and revision (and not the average or lowest)?

> The total quotation that we would send to our client – with a full breakdown of how this figure was calculated – would therefore be £45,042.00. This might seem like an eye-watering sum of money to some readers, but two things need to be borne in mind. Firstly, translation (and related services) is a professional service, requiring not only lengthy (and costly) training in the form of university degrees, accreditations, and continuing professional development, but also a wide range of skills and competences not that dissimilar to those required by lawyers, accountants, and other highly paid professionals (on this topic, see Tyulenev, 2014, pp. 67–69). Hence, the fees charged by vendors are (or at least should be) commensurate with this status. Secondly, from the perspective of our hypothetical client (Global Web Design), the company's aim is to expand their business into new international markets where Arabic, French, German, and Spanish are spoken. If every new client of Global Web Design pays £1,000 for their web design services (which is not unrealistic for such services and is actually at the cheap end of the spectrum), the company would only need to bring in forty-five new clients from these new markets to justify the investment in this translation.

they may differ for different vendors and for different LSPs (see also Mitchell-Schuitevoerder, 2020, p. 33–36 for more on this).

The maths involved in these calculations is very straightforward and will in many cases be automated, but project managers need to have a good understanding of how quotations are produced in case the specifics of a unique project dictate that a project has to be costed differently. Furthermore, it would not be uncommon for more senior project managers to be tasked with updating price grids from time to time, and they would therefore need to understand how the relationship between vendor costs and client costs is managed.

As with some of the calculations described above, drawing up the quotation itself may well be automated and require only the basic input of certain information by the project manager. In other cases, the quotation might need to be drafted in a more 'hands-on' manner. Certain information must be included on the quotation, including the full contact details of the client and the LSP, the name and reference number for the project, some details on the project itself (such as language pairs, QA tasks involved), the date on which the quotation was drawn up, the date by which it must be accepted, the proposed deadline, and any other relevant information that the client might need or request to make their decision. Beyond these pieces of information, the quotation itself – i.e. a breakdown of the full costs by task and by language pair, as well as rates per unit, etc. – is the key component.

This breakdown is essential so that the client can understand precisely how the project manager has calculated the total cost. Take the example in Box 2.5. If you, a project manager, were to simply send a sheet of paper stating 'Quotation for translation services: £45,042.00' to your client, would this be likely to convince the client that your LSP was the right company to handle the project (or that your LSP was trustworthy)? More than likely not. Clients like to understand how costs are calculated. They obviously do not need to know what you are paying your vendors (and, in fact, this information should *not* be disclosed to clients), but they do in most cases want to understand what the charge per unit is for translation, for revision, etc., and for each language pair. In part, this will help them to predict translation costs for future projects, but it also allows them to compare your services with other LSPs. Pricing transparency is also an important element of trust and building good relationships with clients.

Acceptance and Project Preparation

Once the quotation has been submitted to the client for review, the project is temporarily out of the project manager's hands. There are three possible outcomes once the client has reviewed the quotation. The first is **rejection**: the client may simply reject the quotation (or may not even respond at all). In such cases, it is important to contact the client and try to obtain some feedback as to why they have chosen not to accept your quotation. It may be that the quoted price was too high compared to other LSPs, perhaps the proposed schedule was too long, perhaps they did not have sufficient reassurances as to the quality of the delivered product, or any number of other reasons.

? Why is it important to seek feedback from a client if they decide not to accept your quotation?
? Are there any techniques available to you as a project manager to try and persuade the client to change their mind?

Any responses gleaned from the client need to be documented and fed back into pricing structures, scheduling processes, and various other aspects of the feasibility study stage; if too many clients turn down an LSP's quotations, it might suggest that there is a serious problem in some aspect of the quoting process that needs to be addressed as a matter of urgency. As a general rule, however, outright rejection of a quotation by a client is not especially common. As discussed in greater detail in Chapter 6, most clients requesting quotations are in the market to buy, and many will be reluctant to shop around for a cheaper deal, for various reasons.

The second possible response to the quotation is **negotiation**: the client might wish to negotiate its cost, its schedule, its scope (i.e. what services are involved), or its quality.

Pre-production 41

? What could you do to reduce the cost of a project quotation?
? How could you reduce the amount of time required to complete a project?

The client might ask for a discount or price reduction if the project is slightly more expensive than they anticipated, or they might try to have the project delivered sooner. Some of the factors that are involved in costs and timescales are explored in Chapters 5 and 6, and they may provide some ideas on techniques that could be used to cut costs or shorten timescales. A negotiation request might involve a reassessment of which human resources are used (those with cheaper rates, vendors based in a different location, etc.), but it may also involve a re-design of the main project workflow (e.g. the use of machine translation and post-editing). What is absolutely essential, however, is that the project manager does not make any promise that cannot be delivered: never offer a discounted price or a significantly shorter timeframe if achieving it will prove difficult or even impossible, and especially if it could risk compromising on the agreed quality. Finally, any 'counter-offer' that you do make should be subject to a new written quotation so that the offer is properly documented.

The final option – the desirable outcome – is **acceptance**: the client accepts the quotation, which means that the project can move to the next stage: project preparation.

Client–LSP Agreement

Assuming now that the client wishes to proceed with the project as per the terms stated in the quotation (perhaps with one or two minor adjustments), the LSP and the client need to sign some form of agreement to 'formalise' the terms and conditions stipulated in the quotation.

? Why is this contractual document necessary?

The client–LSP agreement is an important stage of pre-production, as it serves not only as the initial 'green light' for the project to proceed but also, and more importantly, as a legally binding contract between the client and the LSP. It documents the obligations of the LSP to provide translation services according to certain specifications, and it lays down obligations for the client to pay the LSP a certain amount of money by a certain date, subject to certain conditions being met.

Typically, the client–LSP agreement will take a form similar to the quotation (and may even be identical to the quotation) and will stipulate precisely the same terms and conditions set out in the quotation: the names, addresses, and contact details of the client and LSP, project reference numbers, delivery date(s), total fee (and currency), etc. However, the document title will no longer be 'Quotation' but will be labelled in such a way as to draw attention to it being a contract or agreement for certain services (e.g. 'Project Agreement'). In most cases, LSPs will attach a copy of their standard terms and conditions of business to this project agreement. The project agreement itself provides specific details unique to the project, while the terms and conditions of business lay down more general terms applicable to all projects.

ISO 17100:2015 provides an extensive list (International Organization for Standardization, 2015, Annex B) of the sorts of clauses that might be included in a client–LSP agreement. With regard to 'commercial terms', it offers the following examples, among others:

- confidentiality clauses and non-disclosure agreements (NDAs);
- copyright on deliverables (including the use of 'by-products' such as translation memories);
- payment terms (e.g. payment within 30 days);
- liability in law;
- complaints procedure; and
- applicable law (and jurisdiction).

In terms of the particular conditions of the project, it suggests that the following project specifications should be included:

- an itemised list of standard and value-added services;
- the location where the work will be carried out (if applicable);
- the project schedule and delivery date(s);
- the quoted price and currency;
- information on the source content, such as the number of units (words, characters, etc.);
- the languages involved (e.g. Romanian into French); and
- information that might be included in a translation brief (e.g. audience, purpose, style guides, register, etc.).

The standard also suggests that clauses could be included with additional specifications:

- the use of technology (e.g. translation memory tools, machine translation, etc.);
- how communications will be handled during the project (if the project is classified, for example);
- the format and layout of the target content (if different from the source);
- the delivery method (e.g. email, FTP, hard copy, etc.);
- the type of translation (e.g. localised, generalised, transcreation, etc.); and
- any recognition for the translator (if the translation is due to be published, will the translator be credited and, if so, where?).

ISO 17100:2015 states that the agreement should be documented in writing but can be given verbally provided that it is subsequently followed up in writing (e.g. by email) and shared with the client. If, for whatever reason, the terms and conditions of this agreement cannot be respected at any time, the LSP has to agree changes with the client; the project manager cannot simply do as he or she pleases without first obtaining written confirmation (and therefore a written change to this agreement) from the client (International Organization for Standardization, 2015, 4.4).

Once the agreement has been formalised, the project manager can move on to 'project preparation', which can be one of the most time-intensive stages of a project but is also the stage that, if done right, can greatly facilitate the smooth progress of a project throughout the lifecycle.

Administrative Tasks

As soon as the client–LSP agreement has been signed (or confirmed in writing), the project manager should collect any additional information on the project. Perhaps the client is already aware of specific difficulties in the source language content or formatting (e.g. specific terminology, uneditable images, etc.), or the client might have some additional documentation to pass on to the project manager, such as the client's in-house style guide. It is important that such information is collected as early as possible so that it can be passed on to all parties involved in the project; it is far easier to implement such requirements from the outset than to make changes later, once the content has already been translated or, worse, been through various stages of QA. Such information might also be subject to specific confidentiality requirements, such as only being disclosed to certain individuals involved in the project or being destroyed a certain period of time after the project is complete. It may even involve the signing of a separate non-disclosure agreement (NDA) supplied by the client. Once such information has been collected and any confidentiality issues have been resolved, the project manager can start to prepare the project in earnest.

On an administrative level, first of all, the project manager will need to log the project in a project tracking system. LSPs will have their own unique system of recording project information. It may be a piece of generic commercial software used for tracking project progress (e.g. Microsoft Project), commercial project management software specifically for translation projects (e.g. Trados Business Manager linked to Trados Studio, XTRF, Plunet, etc.), a bespoke database or piece of software designed specifically for, or by, the LSP (created using software such as Filemaker Pro or Microsoft Access, for example), or a more basic spreadsheet-based tool (using Microsoft Excel, for example). The project record will need to log information such as

- a unique project code or identifier;
- the client's name and contact information;

44 The Translation Project Lifecycle

- a reference number for the client–LSP agreement or client-prepared purchase order;
- the project volume (i.e. number and type of units);
- the project start date;
- the deadline (or deadlines, if the project is to be delivered in batches);
- the quotation (including currency and taxes, if applicable);
- any project specifications (including purpose, intended use, style guides, etc.);
- the composition of the project team (i.e. vendors assigned to the project – once assigned – and project manager(s) overseeing the project);
- the language pair(s) involved;
- links to files with existing terminology or previous translations (if supplied);
- any amendments made to the client–LSP agreement during the project; and
- the project status (allowing the project manager to monitor its progress through each stage of production).

This list is not exhaustive, and different LSPs will record this information in different ways depending on the configuration of their project tracking software. This system of recording projects is also adopted by many freelance vendors, who each develop their own method of logging project details for later invoicing.

The final crucial administrative task is to assign the project to the relevant vendors. In an ideal world, this will be as simple as contacting the vendors originally identified in the earlier resource assessment to confirm the project. If the identified vendors are unavailable, the project manager will need to source alternative vendors who satisfy the same criteria (language pair, expertise, etc.) and whose charges are still in line with the project budget. If the project has been costed on the basis of a translator charging £0.08 per word, it could be problematic for the project budget if the project manager then selects a translator who charges £0.10 per word. Sometimes this is unavoidable and the additional cost can be absorbed, but, under ideal circumstances, the project manager should attempt to find a vendor whose conditions are as close to the originally identified vendor as possible.

Normally, confirmation with the vendors will take the form of a project purchase order (PO), which is the vendor equivalent of the client–LSP agreement. The purpose of the PO is to provide a legal basis for the LSP's 'purchase' of the vendor's services. The contents of a PO will be essentially the same as the details included in a client–LSP agreement (project details, fees payable to the vendor, deadline, etc.), but with the appropriate fees and deadlines for the vendor in question, depending on their role in the project. The PO will also typically include standard terms and conditions explaining the LSP's payment practices (e.g. payment within 30 days of the invoice date).

Linguistic Tasks

There are two main linguistic tasks that will form part of a project's preparation. Firstly, a more in-depth content analysis might be carried out by the project manager. For instance, the project manager might – if a detailed breakdown of repetitions and fuzzy matches was not previously prepared – want to ascertain how much repetition there is in the document and how many matches there are from the LSP's existing translation memories. If repetition is virtually non-existent and there is little in the way of matching from pre-existing language resources, the project manager might decide to allow the vendors to translate the document in whatever format they please. Some vendors use CAT software religiously (with a view to continually building up their translation memories and term bases), while others prefer to use standard word processing software if there is no obligation to use CAT software.

Sometimes the content analysis might form part of the services offered by the LSP to the client. Since many clients are unaware of precisely what services they might require, some projects involve a preliminary analysis of the content by the project manager (or a vendor) to ascertain what needs to be translated. Some source files, for instance, might contain segments that are already in the target language. Court rulings are a good example of this: some international court cases use quotations from documents in other languages, so certain extended passages might not need to be translated, and appropriate instructions on which sections the vendors should or should not reproduce need to be drawn up. Similarly, in other multilingual documents, the client might not be clear on which sections are in which languages, and the project manager will need to split the file up into the relevant chunks to distribute among vendors working in different language pairs. Similarly, a client might have instructed the LSP to translate section 1 of a document into Chinese, sections 1, 2, and 3 into Japanese, and sections 2, 3, and 4 into Korean. These instructions need to be drawn up clearly for vendors, and files might need to be split (or sections deleted) for each language to avoid any confusion.

Another linguistic task that is quite common is the preparation of project terminology lists. Often this task is outsourced to a vendor – usually one of the translators assigned to the project – who will be paid to create a project glossary from the source text to improve consistency when multiple translators are working on the same project. In other cases, it might involve the project manager locating appropriate terminology lists online or compiling such lists personally. Clients can also be involved in this stage. Some clients have lists of approved terminology that they supply to the LSP for a project; in other cases, the project manager might identify key terminology in the source text and ask the client if they have any preferred translations that they want the vendors to use.

On a topic related to terminology, the project manager will also likely prepare clear guidelines on language use more generally. For languages spoken in various locales, this might include the specification of a certain variety (e.g. US or UK English) and associated spellings (e.g. colour or color, generalise or generalize). The guidance could also extend to the formatting of numbers (e.g. 1,200.05 or 1200.05), dates (e.g. December 1, 2020 or 1 December 2020), and currencies (e.g. £100.50, 100.50 GBP or GBP 100.50). The project manager might also include more specific rules on style more generally (e.g. the use of the serial comma, single or double quotation marks, the placement of punctuation around quotation marks, etc.).

In general terms, these tasks are aimed at optimising the production stage of the project as much as possible and could include any task that might facilitate the linguistic elements of the project and aid consistency among vendors.

Technical Tasks

ISO 17100:2015 refers rather vaguely to the need to carry out 'technical tasks' as part of a project's preparation (International Organization for Standardization, 2015, 4.6.2). In fact, these tasks are a very important part of the modern-day translation project, which will frequently involve close cooperation between multiple vendors and the use of CAT software.

If CAT software is chosen to be used in the project, this will form a major part of the technical tasks involved in a project's preparation. For instance, the project will first need to be set up in the CAT software (translation file(s), translation memory, and term base added to the project), together with any project settings on the handling of numbers and non-translatables. In some cases, some alignment work may need to be carried out by the project manager. If, for instance, the client has provided a previous translation and source text, the project manager could align the two texts and add the finalised alignment to the project translation memory. Similarly, any glossary previously prepared either by the project manager, the client, or a vendor entrusted with this task can be imported into the project term base.

Sometimes there are additional tasks involved in setting up a file for translation beyond merely 'adding' a file to a project in a CAT tool. Two examples include

- the conversion of a document in .pdf format (which cannot be edited) into an editable format (e.g. .docx) using optical character recognition software so that it can be processed by a CAT tool; and
- manually adding any text that is embedded in an uneditable image using text boxes.

Recall that the client is not an expert. The client will often have little or no knowledge of what tasks might be involved, and it is therefore the project manager's job to identify which technical tasks might be needed.

Once the project is set up as required in the chosen CAT software, the project manager will need to assign specific tasks to different vendors. Depending on the chosen workflow method, the relevant portion of the project can be exported as a project package (.sdlppx in Trados Studio, for example) and sent to the relevant vendor by email or FTP, or it can be assigned via a project server or Cloud server (as in Memsource, for example).

If a project is not being translated using CAT software, the technical tasks are often much more straightforward. For example, a .pdf document will not need to be converted, previous translations do not need to be aligned, terminology does not need to be added to the term base, etc. The vendor can simply work as they please and supply the translation in .docx format, for example, when complete.

* * *

The foregoing explanation of the stages that make up the feasibility study and project preparation is by no means exhaustive and may, in some cases, even be excessive. Different LSPs adopt different practices and attach greater importance to different aspects of the pre-production process. Many – not just in the translation industry but in other industries too – would agree that the pre-production stage should be handled as carefully and conscientiously as possible, as this is the stage when the project manager has the greatest control. Once the project has been outsourced to the various vendors, the project manager loses significant hands-on control over the project; during this preparation stage, however, the project manager still has close control over what is taking place. It is certainly no exaggeration to argue that the care with which pre-production is approached can determine whether a project is carried out successfully or not. The next chapter moves on to the production stage, when the project is firmly in the hands of the vendors and the project manager is forced to take a slightly more 'hands-off' approach.

* * *

Topics for Discussion and Assignments

1. Debate the advantages and disadvantages of the use of CAT software for translation projects. Consider the topic from the perspective of the client, the project manager, and the vendors. Also consider the contentious subject of cost reductions for TM matches.
2. Prepare a feasibility study presentation on one of the case studies on the TS Portal. In particular, conduct an analysis of what the project involves, devise a provisional schedule, assess the resources that you would need, and draw up a formal quotation. Consider also which technological tools you might use to facilitate the project.

3. Discuss the importance of pre-production in the project lifecycle, addressing factors such as timescales, costs, and resource management.

Further Reading

Chapter 1 of Mitchell-Schuitevoerder (2020) offers a high-level overview of the project management workflow, but, more importantly, it also offers cross-references to a number of key CAT concepts and tools and how they can feed into the project workflow.

Sections I to V of Matis (2014) provide a complementary overview of pre-production processes, including project analysis, quotations, and schedules.

References

Drucker, P. F. (1967). *The effective executive*. Harper & Row.
International Organization for Standardization. (2015). *Translation services – Requirements for translation services (ISO 17100:2015)*. International Organization for Standardization.
Matis, N. (2014). *How to manage your translation projects*. Retrieved from www.translation-project-management.com/en
Mitchell-Schuitevoerder, R. (2020). *A project-based approach to translation technology*. Routledge.
Mossop, B. (2019). Subjective responses to translation memory policy in the workplace. *TTR, 32*(1), 309–339. https://doi.org/10.7202/1068023ar
Nord, C. (2018). *Translating as a purposeful activity: Functionalist approaches explained* (2nd ed.). Routledge.
Project Management Institute. (2017). *A guide to the Project Management Body Of Knowledge (PMBOK® guide)* (6th ed.). Project Management Institute, Inc.
Tyulenev, S. (2014). *Translation and society*. Routledge.
Vermeer, H. J. (1989). *Skopos und Translationsauftrag* [Skopos and translation commission]. Universitat.

3 Production

> **Learning outcomes:**
>
> - Understand each stage of the standard translation project workflow model
> - Identify the key components of a translation brief and the importance of a brief for a successful project
> - Distinguish between the closely related terms check, revision, review, and proofreading (as well as monolingual and bilingual editing)
> - Understand the role of post-editing, including the distinction between light and full post-editing, and the related term pre-editing
> - Appreciate the broader educational role of the PM in terms of advising the client and managing expectations

In the production stage of a translation project, the primary objective of the project manager is to ensure that the project progresses in accordance with the client–LSP agreement from the moment the project is confirmed until the moment the project completes production (and beyond, arguably). The project manager is therefore responsible for satisfying all of these requirements during the production process, following internal LSP procedures in terms of scheduling and notifying vendors, and complying with any other client requests (e.g. relating to DTP or similar) and industry or other specifications or standards (including ISO 17100:2015 for ISO-certified projects). It is also important that the project manager has a way of verifying and documenting that certain workflow stages have been carried out by vendors, whether this be in the form of checklists or more specific technical procedures (e.g. QA logs in CAT tools).

While many would argue that the project manager's role is *most important* during pre-production, the role is still critical during the production stage to ensure that the project is properly coordinated, following on from the effective planning in the pre-production stage. Despite the fact that the production stage lies largely outside the project manager's hands, it is obviously essential that he or she remains in control of the whole process.

The exact point at which a project moves from pre-production to production is hard to define, as the lines are blurred between planning the availability of vendors and other resources and the actual *assignment* of work to those vendors, and, indeed, whether such assignment constitutes production or pre-production. ISO 17100:2015, for instance, considers the assignment of vendors to fall under production. This conceptual definition is followed in this textbook, according to which any task carried out with a direct view to the subsequent performance of translation or related processes is considered to fall within the production stage of the workflow.

According to ISO 17100:2015 (International Organization for Standardization, 2015, 5.2), the project manager has the following responsibilities in production:

- assigning competent translators and revisers to the project;
- distributing information and issuing instructions for the assignment and management of the project to all parties involved;
- monitoring compliance with the agreed schedule and deadlines;
- reporting, documenting, and overseeing any changes in project specifications (where applicable);
- monitoring compliance with the client–LSP agreement and project specifications, and communicating with all parties involved in the project (including the client);
- ensuring that translation and any other queries are answered and fed back to relevant parties;
- managing and handling feedback during the production process (e.g. between revisers and translators); and
- verifying that the translation specifications have been followed before approving the translated content and clearing it for delivery to the client.

Project management during the production stage may also include:

- assigning competent reviewers and proofreaders to the project, if required;
- implementing any corrections and/or corrective action;
- ensuring that the project does not run over budget; and
- any other tasks and activities agreed with the client.

Key themes that persist in all of these items are risk management (i.e. avoiding problems with costs, time, quality, and other factors before they occur), communicating clearly with all parties involved in the project, and ensuring that the client–LSP agreement is respected and followed at all times. In short, as should be evident from Chapter 2, it is a question of balancing project constraints – time (see Chapter 5), cost (see Chapter 6), scope (see

Chapter 7), quality (see Chapter 8), benefits (see Chapter 9), and risk (see Chapter 10) – and managing human, technical, and technological resources. It will also include managing client expectations, client education as to what the translation process involves, and advising on and supplying additional value-added services as required.

The production process is largely set up around a **waterfall** workflow model, whereby one step is completed before another project step is initiated. Waterfall models are based around fairly linear sequential steps, and while this is broadly true of most translation projects in simple terms, it betrays some of the complexity involved in managing time constraints in translation projects (see Chapter 5). For the purposes of this chapter, we will look at the production stage from this waterfall angle alone. According to ISO 17100:2015, production comprises the following steps: **Translation, Check, Revision, Review, Proofreading,** and **Verification and Release**. Some of these steps are obligatory for ISO 17100:2015-certified projects (translation, check, revision, and verification and release), while others are optional (review and proofreading). For specific projects that do not follow the ISO 17100:2015 standard (just because an LSP is ISO-certified, not all projects have to be completed in this way), there is much more flexibility in the stages that will be selected. Nonetheless, the simple waterfall model is represented schematically in Figure 3.1.

The addition of **post-editing** to the ISO 17100:2015 production process in Figure 3.1 reflects current developments in translation industry practices. Post-editing itself is only mentioned once in passing in ISO 17100:2015, as this topic is treated in much more detail in a dedicated ISO standard: ISO 18587:2017 'Translation services – Post-editing of machine translation output – Requirements' (International Organization for Standardization, 2017). In many cases where post-editing takes place, it actually *replaces* the

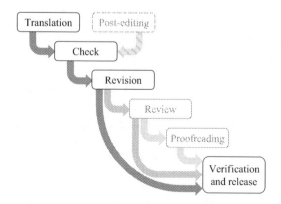

Figure 3.1 ISO 17100:2015 waterfall production workflow

translation step of the production workflow before other production steps (if required) are carried out as normal. This will be discussed in more detail under the 'Post-editing' section below.

Recruitment

Following up on the feasibility study in Chapter 2, it is worth addressing the recruitment of vendors briefly in terms of the skills and competences that the various vendors are required (or expected) to have. ISO 17100:2015 states that 'the TSP shall have a documented process in place to ensure that the people selected to perform translation tasks have the required competences and qualifications [and] shall keep a record of the evidence upon which [such competences] have been demonstrated' (International Organization for Standardization, 2015, 3.1.1). 'Competence' is a somewhat vague term, but it generally refers to an individual's ability to carry out a task successfully or efficiently; in a language context, we often speak of 'language competence' in relation to knowledge of rules and norms (e.g. grammar, vocabulary, etc.). These requirements laid down in the ISO are especially important in light of the outsourcing model widely practised in the translation industry, as the ISO further stipulates that if a task is sub-contracted (i.e. outsourced to another LSP), which happens more frequently than might be imagined, the original LSP will still be responsible for ensuring that these standards are met (International Organization for Standardization, 2015, 3.1.2).

The ISO focuses on three main 'linguistic' agents and one more general agent: translators, revisers, reviewers, and project managers. If an LSP seeks or wishes to maintain compliance with ISO 17100:2015 for a given project, its translators and revisers are required to have the following competences:

- **Translation competence**: the 'ability to translate' and to 'address the problems of language content comprehension and language content production' in accordance with the project's specifications;
- **Linguistic and textual competence in the source language and target language**: the 'ability to understand the source language, fluency in the target language, and general or specialized knowledge of text-type conventions';
- **Competence in research, information acquisition, and processing**: the 'ability to efficiently acquire the additional linguistic and specialized knowledge necessary to understand the source language content and to produce the target language content'. Research competence also involves 'experience in the use of research tools and the ability to develop suitable strategies for the efficient use of the information sources available';
- **Cultural competence**: the 'ability to make use of information on the behavioural standards, up-to-date terminology, value systems, and locale [of] both source and target language cultures';

- **Technical competence**: the 'knowledge, abilities, and skills required to perform the technical tasks in the translation process'; and
- **Domain competence**: the 'ability to understand content produced in the source language and to reproduce it in the target language using the appropriate style and terminology' (International Organization for Standardization, 2015, 3.1.3).

There are three possible pathways for translators and revisers in relation to qualifications: (1) they must have a graduate qualification in translation from a higher education institution (e.g. a BA in French with Translation or, more commonly, a postgraduate MA in Translation Studies); (2) they must have a graduate qualification in another field (e.g. law, chemistry, history) in addition to two years' professional experience working as a translator or reviser; or (3) they must have five years' professional experience working as a translator or reviser (but no specific qualifications). Some might wonder how the cases described in (2) and (3) above are possible, and how such experience might be gained if the individual does not have a relevant qualification to start working as a translator or reviser. In many cases, people falling under this category tend to work in-house at a company with an international presence; they may be bilingual (working, for example, as a bilingual secretary) but have a more general qualification in another field, and they may have been asked to translate documents on a regular basis for the company. Over time, this experience can count towards these minimum criteria to work as a translator or reviser on an ISO 17100:2015-certified project.

While we have not yet discussed the distinction between revision and review (the former focusing on bilingual editing and the latter on monolingual editing, by way of a brief summary – see later in this chapter), the competences of a reviewer differ substantially. ISO 17100:2015 states only that reviewers should be 'domain specialists and have a relevant qualification in this domain' from a higher education institution or relevant experience. Since review focuses only on the target language content, no knowledge of the source language is required. Many reviewers are therefore monolingual and may have accumulated in-depth expertise in a specific field, such as economics, international law, or clinical psychology. They will likely hold a qualification (e.g. university degree, diploma, etc.) in the relevant field or will have worked as an economist, lawyer specialising in international law, or clinical psychologist before a change of career to work in the translation industry. Equally, domain specialism and 'relevant qualifications' or experience need not necessarily be specifically tied to that domain; translators who have developed expertise or a specialism in economics, international law, or clinical psychology, for example, can still satisfy these criteria.

What about project managers, incidentally (the very people that are responsible for overseeing the project)? Many students of translation are often surprised to learn that some project managers working in the translation industry have no specific training or qualifications in translation and, in some rare cases, no or very little knowledge of another language. This fact alone does not make them bad project managers(!), but there are certain instances where a better knowledge of the processes involved in translation or even in the use of foreign languages more generally can aid project managers in anticipating and resolving certain problems that can arise. That notwithstanding, ISO 17100:2015 is somewhat vague in its description of the competences required of project managers, mentioning only that they should have 'appropriate documented competence to support the TSP in delivering translation services to meet client and other project specifications' (International Organization for Standardization, 2015, 3.1.7). It further states that such competence can be acquired through 'formal or informal training', referring to a specific training course (diploma, degree, etc.) on project management, on-the-job training (perhaps the most common occurrence in the industry), or prior industry experience (sometimes in a different industry). It is therefore entirely acceptable, and not at all uncommon, for many 'junior' project managers to be thrust into a position of responsibility in managing projects without any substantial knowledge or experience of the translation industry. This very phenomenon is part of the rationale behind the drive to promote project management training as part of degrees in translation (see, in particular, the initiatives behind the European Masters in Translation framework), as well as being a key motive behind the drafting of this textbook.

Let us now turn to the main production stages of a translation project, beginning with translation.

Translation

Translation is, without a doubt, the stage of the workflow with which readers will be most familiar, but it also sits at the very heart of the work that LSPs carry out. Therefore, it should not be overlooked in terms of understanding precisely what steps need to be considered during the translation stage of a project. This stage (broadly defined) comprises two separate components: translation itself and checking. These components should be considered one and the same in truth, as both stages, according to ISO 17100:2015, are to be carried out by the translator and both are a requirement of all ISO-certified projects, as well as simply being good practice for any conscientious translator.

Translation

>   **Definition:** render source language content into target language content in written form.
>
>   [International Organization for Standardization, 2015, 2.1.1]

The definition of what translation is needs no explanation, but it is also important to remember that translation is an extremely broad hypernym comprising a wide variety of specialist *forms* of translation, some of which may be interlingual, some intralingual, and some involving different modes (e.g. different forms of audiovisual translation). The instructions associated with translation itself are defined in ISO 17100:2015 as follows and bring to light a number of important considerations:

> The translator shall translate in accordance with the *purpose* of the translation project, including the *linguistic conventions* of the target language and relevant *project specifications* [emphasis added].
> [International Organization for Standardization, 2015, 5.3.1]

Firstly, the translation must be produced in accordance with the **purpose** of the project itself. As noted in Chapter 2, for students of translation studies, this should bring to mind *skopostheorie*, or the theory of applying the notion of *skopos* (the Greek word for 'purpose') to the act of translation. This theory argues that actions are governed by intention, and that the intention is oriented towards the underlying aim of a particular action, i.e. the purpose for which the translation is needed or assumed to be needed. For a conceptual discussion of these and related terms, see Nord (2018, p. 27–30).

A common tool used – certainly in academic settings, but to a lesser degree in the professional world – is the translation **brief** (also referred to as a commission, assignment, specifications, or instructions). The role of the brief is to clarify for all parties concerned what purpose the translation is intended to serve in terms of who will use the translation, when and where it will be used, and the manner (or medium) in which it is to be produced, among other things (see Box 3.1 for an example). In most professional contexts, however, clients rarely provide all (or even any) of such information, and the brief tends to be negotiated between the project manager and the client.

In the outsourcing model, the importance of this step should not be overlooked. The LSP itself is not normally the entity producing the translation; it is the vendor that produces the translation. It is essential, therefore, that the vendor is fully apprised of any information that could dictate *how* the document should be translated, which in turn helps to govern translation strategies and individual micro-level choices. The brief can also serve an important purpose before the vendor even agrees to translate the document: he or she may read the brief and realise that it is beyond his or her expertise. In many contexts, however, no explicit translation briefs are drawn up, and, if they are, they are not shared as a matter of course with vendors. Despite being widespread, this is bad practice and, returning to the principles of good project management set out in Chapter 2, if the project manager wants to inculcate fulfilment of the project brief from the

Box 3.1 Example of a translation brief

Translation briefs can take on many different forms, ranging from a simple set of instructions embedded within an email to formal documents with a clear breakdown of fields and information. Some briefs will also focus more on technical instructions (e.g. relating to the use of CAT tools), while others (more rarely, sadly) will also include information on genre, audience, and intended purpose. Many briefs, such as the example below, fulfil the combined function of a translation brief and purchase order to document project-related information such as deadline, payment amount, and payment terms.

Project ID	20211025_0255
Files	• "App 4_13.case no 41195" • "App 5_14.appeal no 11-11570"
Word count	3196 words (with TM matches and repetitions, see below)
Language pair	French (France) > English (United Kingdom)
Domain	Law, Court, Case Law
Context	This translation is for a large law firm involved in an international legal dispute. The document is a French court ruling on jurisdiction when foreign companies and foreign contracts are involved in a business transaction. The translation will not be published or used in court; it is solely for research purposes for the law firm.
Instructions	• Use Trados Studio 2021 (Project Package provided) • Ensure that all placeables and tags are correctly positioned in the target text and run tag check • Deliver to the Partner Portal • Use concordance function for consistency check in Translation Memory • Deliver Return Package with 100% progress • Overwrite source text with translation • Translate and proofread all match ranges • Read and edit (where necessary) all 100% Matches • Perform spellcheck • Adhere to all style guides and terminology provided • Ensure formatting matches source where possible • Confirm all segments to 'Translated' and update TM
Deadline	25 October 2021 at 13:00 (UK time)
Payment breakdown	1819 Words Translation No Match at 0.08 GBP = 145.52 GBP 679 Words Translation 50–74% Match at 0.08 GBP = 54.32 GBP 28 Words Translation 75–84% Match at 0.048 GBP = 1.34 GBP 394 Words Translation 85–94% Match at 0.04 GBP = 15.76 GBP 276 Words Translation 95–99% Match at 0.024 GBP = 6.62 GBP

Total payment	223.56 GBP
Payment terms	30 days from receipt of invoice
Invoicing	Submit invoice via Partner Portal. Log into your profile and ensure that your payment details are up-to-date. Upload your invoice under the 'Invoicing' tab. Please contact your Project Manager if your PO needs to be updated or you need further instructions to submit your invoice.

start, appropriate project documentation needs to be prepared so that every party involved is aware of the requirements, and any misunderstandings in instructions can be rectified as soon as possible (avoiding unnecessary costs and further risks).

The definition given in ISO 17100:2015 also refers to **linguistic conventions** and **project specifications**, which can relate to a wide range of different high- and low-level requirements that a client or project manager might have requested from a vendor. In broad terms, these concepts relate to matters such as appropriate spelling, grammar, syntax, style, and register, as well as more technical requirements imposed by the client in terms of style guides, terminology, and delivery formats, among a host of other possible requirements. The ISO offers details on what some of these conventions and specifications might include. These are summarised, with examples, in Table 3.1.

The act of translation itself is, of course, beyond the direct control of the project manager, but the way in which these conventions and project specifications are communicated to the vendor, via either the translation brief itself or other supplementary documents, is critical to the success of the project. The project manager is responsible for producing, or at least sharing, this content with the vendor prior to work starting and drawing the vendor's attention to it, as well as being available to resolve any problems during the translation process. The ISO importantly states (International Organization for Standardization, 2015, 5.3.1): 'The translator shall raise any uncertainty as a query with the project manager'. The vendors need to be made aware of the importance of raising queries, but the project manager may also need to seek advice from the client or other individuals to resolve a query if it cannot be resolved internally.

Check

Definition: examination of target language content carried out by the translator.

[International Organization for Standardization, 2015, 2.2.5]

58 The Translation Project Lifecycle

Table 3.1 Linguistic conventions and project specification examples

Types of linguistic conventions and project specifications (ISO 17100:2015, 5.3.1)	Specific examples
Complying with domain and client terminology and/or any other reference material provided	Use of *agreement* instead of *contract* when translating the French *contrat*
Ensuring terminological consistency throughout	Using the example above, translating *contrat* as *agreement* in some places, but *contract* in others
Ensuring semantic accuracy of TL content	Mistranslating the French word *police* as *police* instead of *policy* in an insurance document
Using appropriate syntax, spelling, punctuation, diacritical marks, and other orthographical conventions	Correct and accurate use of spelling and accents in post-spelling reform French: *oignon* becomes *ognon*, *coût* becomes *cout*, etc.
Ensuring lexical cohesion and phraseology	Checking use of anaphoric references: e.g. 'The man...' (Has a man been mentioned previously?), 'He' (Has a 'he' just been mentioned?), 'As stated previously...' (Has this already been stated?)
Complying with proprietary and/or client style guide	Use of US versus UK English; use of currency symbols with figures ($150.00) but currency name with spelled out numbers (one hundred and fifty dollars)
Respecting the locale and any applicable standards	Are there any taboos or local customs that need to be respected?
Replicating formatting (where relevant)	Ensuring that words appearing in bold in the ST are also in bold in the TT
Keeping in mind the target audience and purpose of the TL content	In an accounting document, writing negative figures in brackets instead of with a negative symbol preceding the figures

The check (or the process of checking) is one of a cluster of words that are often used synonymously (and inconsistently) in the translation industry and in pedagogical settings (namely checking, revision, reviewing, editing, and proofreading). It is precisely for this reason that an ISO standard on translation services is a useful construct to attempt to standardise the meanings of different concepts across the industry.

Checking is explained in more detail in ISO 17100:2015 as follows:

> This process shall at least include the translator's overall self-revision of the target content for possible sematic, grammatical and spelling issues,

and for omissions and other errors, as well as ensuring compliance with any relevant translation project specifications. The translator shall make any corrections necessary prior to delivery.
[International Organization for Standardization, 2015, 5.3.2]

It is therefore a process carried out by the translator *after* the initial translation process has been completed and is sometimes referred to as 'self-revision' (Mossop, 2014, Chapter 13). It is intended to pick up fairly high-level errors, often with the benefit of automated tools such as spellcheckers and grammar checkers (where relevant), as well as fairly obvious problems such as omissions of sizeable chunks of text from the source text. This stage also offers the translator an opportunity to undertake a preliminary review of compliance with project documentation and consistency of terminology, as in the basic example in Box 3.2.

Translators should carry out this check stage as a matter of course and will not need to be reminded of the need to check work prior to delivery, but it is still an important stage that needs to be stipulated in any handover documentation passed on to vendors. If this stage is not explicitly stipulated by the project manager in such documentation, the vendor has a legitimate reason to not carry out this stage (even if it does somewhat call into question their professionalism in terms of what should in theory be an automatic step in any project). It should also go without saying that, if the translator detects any problems in the translation, these issues should be resolved prior to delivery, as explicitly noted in ISO 17100:2015. Vendors will often need to

Box 3.2 Checking example

Source text (French): La notion de "Contrat" recouvre, aux termes des présentes, le présent contrat et ses annexes, ses éventuelles renouvellements et/ou ses éventuelles prolongations…

Translation (English): The term "Contract" covers, for the purposes hereof, this contract and its appendices, any potential renewals and/or any potential extensions…

Checked translation: The term "~~Contract~~Agreement" covers, for the purposes hereof, this ~~contract~~agreement and its appendices, any potential renewals and/or any potential extensions…

Note that the 'Track Changes' appearance above would not be used in practice given that the translator is revising his or her own work directly. It is used here for demonstration purposes alone. Track Changes is, however, typically used in later stages of quality assurance where requested (revision, review, and proofreading).

complete a checklist upon delivery of the translation to verify that they have carried out certain procedures such as spell checks, numbers checks, and the like. This is usually in the form of a self-certification by the vendor but can, on occasion, be backed up by QA logs from a CAT tool, for example. Similar processes may also be requested for subsequent steps in the workflow too.

Post-editing

> **Definition:** edit and correct machine translation output.
> [International Organization for Standardization, 2017, 3.1.4]

Post-editing does not feature in ISO 17100:2015, as the practice is distinct from that of (human) translation. However, it deserves to be mentioned in the same workflow stage as translation because, based on current trends, the post-editing of machine-translated output is becoming a common approach to the translation of text with a view to saving both time and money in the initial production of the target text and improving quality with the intervention of a human post-editor. Cronin notes that, in the past, post-editing was 'largely for the purpose of making the translated text minimally comprehensible' (2013, p. 128). However, 'full post-editing is now encroaching into areas that had been dealt with up to now by translation assisted by TM' (Garcia, 2011, p. 218).

With this in mind, it is helpful to turn to ISO 18587:2017, which not only addresses post-editing in detail but can also be read in conjunction with ISO 17100:2015 to understand how post-editing could be integrated into a standard project management workflow by replacing or supplementing the translation stage with post-editing of one form or another. ISO 18587:2017 describes the post-editing stage as follows:

The LSP shall ensure that the following tasks are performed by the post-editor:

a) reading the MT output and evaluating whether a reformulation of the target language content is necessary;
b) using the source language content as reference in order to understand and, if necessary, correct the target language content; and
c) producing target language content either from existing elements in the MT output or providing a new translation (International Organization for Standardization, 2017, 4.3.3).

From these definitions, we should therefore see post-editing as a substitute for (human) translation in the project workflow, with the post-editor acting as translator in the sense that he or she is editing the MT output to generate a text that fulfils the required level of functionality in the relevant context. Post-editing would also then typically be followed by a checking stage carried out by the post-editor, as reflected in Figure 3.1. Automatic post-editing is also mentioned in ISO 18587:2017 (see International Organization for Standardization, 2017, Annex E), but since this is not currently particularly effective, uptake among LSPs seems to be relatively low at the present time. There are still, however, different approaches to the way in which post-editing takes place, in terms of both editing the MT output itself ('light' or 'full' post-editing) and preparing for the MT ('pre-editing'). The project manager will first need to make a decision about the extent to which it replaces or supplements (human) translation, as well as to how the post-editing will be carried out. Will the post-editing take place in a CAT tool, for instance? If not, will it be carried out in a word processor? In both cases, will the Track Changes function be used to highlight the post-editing changes? The obvious advantage of using a CAT tool is that post-editing MT output offers a faster method than 'regular' human translation for increasing the size of translation memories (and term bases, if the post-editor is instructed to add to them at the same time). CAT tools also offer ready-made statistics such as edit distances, which show how many edits (quantified in words or as a percentage, usually) the post-editor had to make from the original MT output in each segment or across a project as a whole. Such data can then be used in the future to weigh up the potential time- and cost-savings of post-editing against human translation as alternative workflow stages.

Pre-editing

> Pre-editing refers to modifying the source language content before machine translation (MT) to facilitate the process, improve raw translation output quality, and therefore reduce the post-editing workload, especially if one document is to be machine translated into several languages.
>
> [International Organization for Standardization, 2017, Annex C]

As the above definition explains, pre-editing takes place before the content is passed through the MT engine. While pre-editing can function on a fairly basic level of checking for spelling and grammar mistakes (e.g. often involving commonly mistaken homophones such as *ou* and *où* in French, *its* and *it's* in English, etc.), it can also delve into more complex matters of avoiding ambiguities and simplifying sentence structures. Several examples are given in Box 3.3.

In some contexts, pre-editing can edit source texts so that they use Controlled Language. Controlled Language is a form of language that restricts grammar and vocabulary to reduce ambiguity and simplify sentence structures, thereby facilitating processing by MT engines and, in theory, improving MT output and reducing post-editing time. A project is currently under way to draw up

> **Box 3.3 Pre-editing example**
>
> **Source text (French):** N360 sauvegarde les fichiers en plusieurs répertoires, ce qui peut parait abscons, mais c'est correct.
>
> **Back-translation:** N360 saves files in several directories, which may seem complicated, but it is correct.
>
> **Pre-edited ST (French):** N360 sauvegarde les fichiers en plusieurs répertoires~~, ce qui~~<u>Ceci</u> peut parait abscons, mais c'est correct.
>
> **Back-translation:** N360 saves files in several directories~~,~~<u>.</u> ~~which~~<u>This</u> may seem complicated, but it is correct.
>
> In this example (adapted from Bouillon et al., 2014), the longer, more complex sentence structure involving the relative pronoun *ce qui (which)* is replaced with a simpler two-sentence structure, which will be easier for the MT engine to process more reliably.

an ISO standard on Controlled Natural Language (an update to ISO 24620-1:2015) with a view to standardising these principles. However, some general principles – often broken down into lexical, syntactic, and semantic rules – can be offered by way of instructions to pre-editors if formal guidelines are unavailable (adapted from O'Brien, 2003, Appendix A):

- keep sentences short (less than 23 words);
- use only the active voice instead of the passive;
- use dictionary-approved words and use them in accordance with their dictionary-approved meaning;
- use commas to separate a subordinate clause at the start of a sentence, as well as between list items;
- avoid metaphor, slang, jargon, or irony; and
- avoid noun clusters exceeding three nouns.

Pre-editing is not common practice in the translation industry at present, but there is scope for it to grow in prevalence in the future to some degree. For our purposes, the project manager will need to decide whether paying for *pre*-editing will significantly affect the amount of time taken to *post*-edit the MT output. Unfortunately, there are no hard and fast rules for this, and in many cases such insight will come from experience of past projects. ISO 18587:2017 recommends, for instance, that pre-editing is a worthwhile venture if the document is to be translated into more than three languages, as 'it is more cost-effective to invest time in extensive linguistic pre-editing to ensure the best possible MT output, and hence lesser post-editing expenditure in each target language' (International Organization for Standardization, 2017, Annex C). It also particularly recommends carrying out pre-editing if a document is to be machine translated into another language and then translated onwards into different languages based on the initial target language output (i.e. a pivot translation or indirect translation).

Pre-editing is not nearly as widespread as post-editing at the present time. In most cases where it is carried out, the pre-editor should be a native speaker of the source language and should ideally be conversant with how MT engines work and the output that they tend to produce (i.e. common errors and traps).

Light Post-editing

> **Definition:** process of post-editing to obtain a merely comprehensible text without any attempt to produce a product comparable to a product obtained by a human translation.
>
> [International Organization for Standardization, 2017, 3.1.6]

Light post-editing, unlike full post-editing below, has limited applications in the wider commercial world, but it is still widely used for the purposes of internal documentation and, more generally, any documents that need to be translated for comprehension purposes but are not likely to be public-facing. As such, the amount of work involved in light post-editing is relatively small compared to full post-editing and will therefore be much cheaper and faster to carry out – at the expense of quality, of course. A full description of the process from ISO 18587:2017 is as follows:

> In this level of post-editing, the output shall be comprehensible and accurate but need not be stylistically adequate. ... Post-editors should focus on:
>
> a) using as much of the raw MT output as possible;
> b) ensuring that no information has been added or omitted;
> c) editing any inappropriate content;
> d) restructuring sentences in the case of incorrect or unclear meaning.
>
> [International Organization for Standardization, 2017, Annex B]

A brief example of light post-editing is given in Box 3.4.

The decision to employ only *light* post-editing will be entirely dictated by the translation brief and the specific instructions given by the client, as laid down in the client–LSP agreement. The project manager also needs to make clear to the post-editor that he or she is only being paid for light post-editing,

> ### Box 3.4 Light post-editing example
>
> **Source text (Russian):** Сторона, для которой создалась невозможность исполнения обязательств по настоящему договору, должна известить об этом другую Сторону в течение 72 (семидесяти двух) часов с момента наступления обстоятельств форс-мажора, а также должна подтвердить наступление форс-мажорных обстоятельств актом регионального отделения Торгово-промышленной палаты Российской Федерации в течение 20 (двадцати) рабочих дней с даты наступления, указанных обстоятельств.
>
> **MT output (Google Translate, English):** The Party for which the impossibility of fulfilling obligations under this agreement has been created must notify the other Party about it within 72 (seventy two) hours from the moment of occurrence of force majeure circumstances, and must also confirm the occurrence of force majeure circumstances by an act of the regional branch of the Chamber of Commerce and Industry Russian Federation within 20 (twenty) business days from the date of occurrence of the specified circumstances.
>
> **Light PE output:** The Party ~~for which the impossibility of~~ unable to fulfil~~ling~~ obligations under this agreement ~~has been created~~ must notify the other Party ~~about it~~ within 72 (seventy-two) hours from the moment of occurrence of force majeure circumstances, and must also confirm the occurrence of force majeure circumstances by an act ~~of~~ issued by the regional branch of the Chamber of Commerce and Industry of the Russian Federation within 20 (twenty) business days from the date of occurrence of the specified circumstances.
>
> As can be seen in the example above, the original MT output is functionally accurate and understandable, but some very minor edits can help to clarify the meaning further and avoid any ambiguity. For instance, 'an act of the regional branch' does not make it clear that this 'act' is, in fact, a document and is also issued or drawn up by the regional branch of the Chamber of Commerce and Industry; rather, it could be interpreted as an *action*, ownership of a particular document, or indeed a requirement to produce such a document (the correct meaning). Evidently, however, this MT output is not on a par with human translation, which is the level that would be expected in full post-editing (see Box 3.5).

and that extensive modifications to the MT output are not required. A clear set of instructions to the post-editor are therefore essential to avoid scope creep (see Chapter 7). This is also another reason why translation briefs and client instructions must be shared openly with vendors, so that all parties are fully aware of the context in which the work is being carried out and the specific requirements of the output. There may be some language pairs, however, where, due to significant structural differences in syntax and word order, or poor MT performance more generally, more extensive post-editing simply cannot be avoided. In these cases, a higher charge for even light post-editing would likely be requested by the vendor to reflect the amount of work involved.

Full Post-editing

> **Definition:** process of post-editing to obtain a product comparable to a product obtained by human translation.
>
> [International Organization for Standardization, 2017, 3.1.5]

Full post-editing is intended to be a like-for-like substitute for human translation, and the level of semantic and stylistic adequacy and accuracy is therefore much higher than light post-editing, where the emphasis is on low-cost, quick-turnaround, purely functional output. The full description given in ISO 18587:2017 is given below:

> On this level of post-editing, the output shall be accurate, comprehensible and stylistically adequate, with correct syntax, grammar and punctuation. The aim of this level of post-editing is to produce an output which is indistinguishable from human translation output. Nevertheless, it is recommended that post-editors use as much of the MT output as possible.
>
> [International Organization for Standardization, 2017, Section 6]

Like light post-editing, there is still a strong focus on using as much of the MT output as possible, as the reason for choosing a post-editing approach over a direct (human) translation approach is to save time and money while still achieving (via post-editing) the same quality that would be expected of a human translation. As such, if the post-editor is in effect re-translating each sentence from scratch, the time savings are lost, and the vendor himself or herself is not being paid an appropriate amount of money for the service that is being provided.

Box 3.5 Full post-editing example

Using the same source text and MT output as in Box 3.4:

Full PE output: ~~The~~Whichever Party ~~for which the impossibility of~~finds itself unable to fulfil~~ling~~ its obligations under this agreement ~~has been created~~ must notify the other Party ~~about it~~accordingly within 72 (seventy-two) hours ~~from the moment of occurrence~~of the onset of force majeure circumstances, and must also confirm the ~~occurrence~~onset of force majeure circumstances by means of ~~an acta~~ a document ~~of~~from the regional branch of the Chamber of Commerce and Industry of the Russian Federation within 20 (twenty) business days ~~from~~of the ~~date of occurrence~~ onset of ~~the specified~~ such circumstances.

Clean PE output: Whichever Party finds itself unable to fulfil its obligations under this agreement must notify the other Party accordingly within 72 (seventy-two) hours of the onset of force majeure circumstances, and must also confirm the onset of force majeure circumstances by means of a document from the regional branch of the Chamber of Commerce and Industry of the Russian Federation within 20 (twenty) business days of the onset of such circumstances.

In this example, the focus not only incorporates the basic functionality of light post-editing (e.g. spelling, lack of omissions, etc.) but also integrates a need to achieve stylistic adequacy and, arguably, adherence to text-type conventions. In this case, as an extract from a contract, appropriate legal terminology and phraseology has been added to the MT output (whichever party, by means of, such circumstances, etc.). The ultimate aim of full post-editing, as per the ISO, is to aim for a translation that is 'indistinguishable from human translation output'.

ISO 18587:2017 offers a list of instructions for post-editors when undertaking full post-editing. This list can of course be copied and adapted as necessary to provide a template set of instructions to post-editors for projects requiring this workflow stage. Post-editors are recommended to focus on:

- checking that no information is added or removed from the source text;
- editing any inappropriate content;
- adjusting the sentence structure if the meaning is incorrect or unclear;

- producing target language content that is grammatically, syntactically, and semantically correct;
- following any client-supplied and/or domain terminology;
- applying any spelling, punctuation, and hyphenation rules;
- checking that the style is appropriate for the text type and that any style guides supplied by the client are followed; and
- applying any specific formatting instructions.

Full post-editing is starting to become more popular with LSPs and clients alike for the considerable time and cost benefits it offers to both parties while still upholding a high-quality standard that is suitable for public-facing documentation. It is not, however, without its controversy and is not widely accepted or liked by vendors across the industry due to the strong downward pressure that it is exerting on prices and turnaround times. The project manager needs to bear in mind the impact on vendors of the decision to favour post-editing over translation and remember the *human* element of the translation workflow. If vendors are dissatisfied with working conditions, pay, or unnecessary pressure from powerful LSPs, the project manager may in future find it difficult to find the human resources to accept work. A careful balance therefore needs to be struck between maximising cost and time savings for the client and LSP and the vendors' need to generate a sustainable income. It is also worth stressing that any decision to include post-editing instead of translation should always be discussed with and made explicit to the client. It goes without saying that it would be wholly unethical to charge the client for a (human) translation service and then provide the translation by means of post-editing MT output in order to maximise LSP profits.

Quality Assurance

Once the initial stage of producing a target text is complete – whether by translation or by post-editing – and once the preliminary checking has been done by the translator (and arguably by the post-editor too), the workflow progresses to the next stage of the waterfall: one or more stages of quality assurance. **Quality assurance** should not be confused with the term **quality assessment**, or, more specifically, translation quality assessment, which is discussed in greater detail in Chapter 8. Quality assurance is a term referring to the process of ensuring quality, or 'the provision in a company's activities to take care of quality' (Vandepitte, 2017, p. 17). (Translation) quality assessment is a more product-oriented term and refers to judgements as to the quality of a specific text in a specific context, often using forms of qualitative and even quantitative feedback.

This stage of the translation project is one where the project manager can play an important educational role in his or her dealings with the client. Because clients often have little understanding of what translation and related services involve, the project manager will not only need to explain to the client on many occasions what additional services are on offer, but also why they may or may not be needed depending on the nature of the project itself. The important question here, to be discussed and agreed with the client, is 'how much' quality is needed in this particular project? Does the translation need to be publishable standard, or does it need to be merely functional?

Gouadec (2010, p.273) distinguishes three main levels of translation quality: '(1) rough-cut, (2) fit-for-delivery (but still requiring minor improvements or not yet fit for its broadcast medium), and (3) fit-for broadcast translation (accurate, efficient, and ergonomic)', as well as identifying another grade – 'fit-for-revision' – to recognise the fact that some translations could be produced efficiently and subsequently revised with little time, cost, and effort. While it may seem counter-intuitive to strive for anything less than excellent quality, it is always essential to bear in mind from a project management perspective that with quality comes cost, and if a client is working to a tight budget, excellent quality is simply not affordable and may not even be required.

However, this raises another philosophical question. How do you define quality? Mossop argues:

> [There is] no such thing as absolute quality. Different jobs will have different quality criteria because the texts are meeting different needs. In one job, a reviser must improve the readability of the text to a very high level; in another job, a lower degree of readability will suffice.
>
> [Mossop, 2014, p. 22]

Mossop, in a similar vein to Gouadec, also distinguishes between 'information-quality' and 'publication-quality' levels of quality (Mossop, 2014, p. 23). For ISO 17100:2015-certified LSPs, the choice of whether to revise or not to revise does not exist: it is a requirement of ISO-certified companies in all translation projects. But the stages that follow – review and proofreading – are optional and may be added to or removed according to the unique specifications of the project. Hence, as is becoming a recurrent theme in this textbook, it is a question of balancing competing constraints: cost, time, scope, quality, benefits, and risk, all with a view to satisfying the client's needs and expectations and maintaining a successful translation business.

Revision

> **Definition:** bilingual examination of target language content against source language content for its suitability for the agreed purpose.
>
> (International Organization for Standardization, 2015, 2.2.6)

[Note: The term **bilingual editing** is sometimes used as a synonym for revision.]

As noted above, revision is an essential stage of the project workflow for ISO 17100:2015-certified projects. That is not to say that an ISO-certified LSP must carry out all projects in this way, but if a project has specifically been sold as 'ISO-certified' then it needs to be delivered in this way. Clients may prefer cheaper options, though, and provided it is made clear to them that a project is not ISO-certified, there is no requirement that *all* projects are conducted in this way for a certified LSP. That being said, there are ISO-certified companies that admit to not carrying out this essential stage of the workflow in ISO-certified projects (Schnierer, 2021). However, this stage exists and is stipulated as a requirement for such projects because it aims to uphold quality standards in translation service provision. Hence, by having a self-checked translation then revised by another independent vendor, it raises the likelihood of quality issues being spotted and corrected prior to delivery to the client. The process is described in ISO 17100:2015 as follows:

> The reviser, who shall be a person other than the translator … shall examine the TL content against the SL content for any errors and other issues, and its suitability for purpose. … As agreed upon with the project manager, the reviser shall either correct any errors found in the target language content or recommend the corrections to be implemented by the translator.
>
> [International Organization for Standardization, 2015, 5.3.3]

Hence, the translation must be revised by a 'person other than the translator'. This 'four-eyes principle' is an important principle of revision. Many readers of this book will appreciate that it is easy to miss errors in your own work, as you, the writer, know what you *intended* to write, even if the reality turns out differently. The original translator, therefore, is likely to miss at least some aspects of his or her own work when undertaking the initial check stage. A fresh pair of eyes will read the text anew from a different perspective and will be drawn more readily to errors. Furthermore, unlike the check stage, this is a *bilingual* examination of SL and TL content (hence the synonym **bilingual editing**), meaning that the revision focuses on the semantic transfer of information (including additions and omissions), alongside other key criteria such as the TL content's *suitability for purpose* (referring back to the translation brief).

If the reviser detects any problems in the TL content:

> Any errors or other issues affecting target language quality should be corrected and the process repeated until the reviser and LSP are satisfied.

The reviser shall also inform the LSP of any corrective action he/she has taken.

[International Organization for Standardization, 2015, 5.3.3]

The project manager must provide clear instructions to the reviser as to how such corrections are to take place and who will have responsibility for approving and/or implementing them. In terms of the technical act of proposing corrections firstly, the project manager will need to decide if the Track Changes function is to be used in a Microsoft Word (or equivalent) version of the TL output, or whether the reviser is able to make the proposed revisions in a particular CAT tool (with or without Track Changes). Instructions will

---

Box 3.6 Revision example

Source text (French): Par ailleurs, il nous appartient, le cas échéant, de vous communiquer les informations prévues à l'article R. 226-02 du Code de commerce relatives à l'exécution, au cours de l'exercice écoulé, des conventions déjà approuvées par l'assemblée générale.

Translation (English): In addition, it is our responsibility, where applicable, to communicate to you the information set out in article R. 226-02 of the Commerce Code relating to the performance, during the past financial year, of agreements already approved by the general meeting.

Revised translation: In addition, it is our responsibility, where applicable, to communicate to you the information set out in article R. 226-02 of the ~~Commerce~~Commercial Code relating to the performance, during the past financial year, of agreements already approved by the general meeting.

Note, in the example above, that revision is not necessarily about smoothing out the translation 100%, as this can drastically increase the workload of the reviser to an extent that is not strictly necessary. The only 'error' in this translation was the use of the word 'Commerce' as opposed to 'Commercial', and even this was hardly critical. All other aspects, such as rephrasings or the restructuring of certain elements, do not need to be carried out at this stage. We should also bear in mind that the ISO states that the reviser is checking for 'suitability for purpose', so this may dictate in part the level of detail and depth of the revisions. All other stylistic changes arguably fall under 'Review'.

also need to be given as to whether comments are permitted in the revision stage, either to explain certain choices or to raise questions with the project manager and/or original translator. In extreme cases, the revision stage can also include the **retranslation** of specific sentences, paragraphs, or even larger chunks of text.

Once such corrections have been made and any comments added (if applicable), the project manager will sometimes solicit general feedback from the reviser on the translator's performance. This may be numerical scores against certain criteria or a general one- or two-sentence overview. For more detail on this feedback and monitoring quality, see Chapter 8. This feedback should, as a matter of course, be shared with the translator so that he or she can improve practices if required.

More importantly, however, a decision needs to be made as to who is responsible for producing the final version of the translation. In some LSPs, a reviser's edits will be sent back to the translator, who will then proceed through each change item by item, accepting or rejecting the proposed revisions and responding to comments if required. Some comments may require input from the project manager, who may in turn need to liaise further with the reviser if a dialogue between the two vendors needs to be established with a view to finding the best solution.

Clear instructions from the project manager are essential throughout the revision stage, not solely to establish the technical means by which revisions are to be proposed and responsibility for the final decision on those revisions, but also – and equally importantly – to avoid the risk of 'over-revising' the TL content. A study by Nitzke and Gros (2021) on preferential changes in revision and post-editing involved a series of experiments to explore vendors' urge to improve texts in pursuit of 'perfect quality' even when it is not required, thereby making the process less efficient and more costly. They referred to this phenomenon as 'over-editing'. The results showed that over-editing tended to be observed in relation to lexical or stylistic preferences, despite guidelines specifying that only necessary changes should be implemented. In the two tasks involving post-editing, 28% and 60% of 'over-editing instances' were in relation to style alone (the highest proportions in both tasks, followed by 22% and 24% for lexicon). For the revision task, lexical over-editing was the most prominent (43%), followed by style (15%) and additions (12%). Nitzke and Gros hypothesised that vendors found it difficult to 'adhere to guidelines that prescribe quality requirements lower than [their] own quality standards and stylistic preferences, which they had to suppress' (Nitzke & Gros, 2021, p. 31). Indeed, as discussed in Mellinger and Shreve (2016), vendors will actively search for issues in the TL content because their task is perceived as 'improving' an existing text. This causes a conflict between the existing text and the vendor's own competing translation in his or her mind, leading them to 'prefer their own translation, and they then decide to change target text units that do not need any corrections' (Nitzke & Gros, 2021, p. 31).

72   The Translation Project Lifecycle

Hence, guidelines need to stress the importance to vendors of suppressing personal preferences and only correcting *problems*. As Mossop summarises: 'Your aim is not to make changes; it's to find problems, which is very different' (Mossop, 2014, p. 115). A clear itemised list of what is and is not included in revision should be produced for vendors so that they only focus on those aspects of language that are important to the revision task and do not make unnecessary or preferential changes to TL content that will ultimately slow down the translation workflow with further proposed revisions to accept/reject and a lengthier revision process overall.

For particularly large projects, another often overlooked dimension of the revision stage is a role that is sometimes referred to as **harmonisation** (first introduced in Chapter 2). Imagine a 100,000-word project that, due to time constraints, has had to be split between ten translators (10,000 words each). Even with good coordination of terminology in the form of a glossary and clear style guides, the written style and certain non-specialist terminology will inevitably differ between the translators. Where time allows, a single **harmoniser** (who may or may not also act as reviser at the same time) would review the entire translation (or series of translated files) in order to try to standardise terminology and phraseology as much as possible. This role is quite common in the industry and is widely used to improve the consistency of delivered translations where files or projects as a whole have had to be split across multiple vendors due to time constraints. Of course, it only makes sense to use a harmoniser if the number of harmonisers can be as low as possible (ideally just one); there is little point in employing harmonisers if there are as many harmonisers as there were translators.

Review

> **Definition:** monolingual examination of target language content for its suitability for the agreed purpose.
>
> [International Organization for Standardization, 2015, 2.2.7]

> *[Note: The term **monolingual editing** is sometimes used as a synonym for review.]*

Review is an optional stage of ISO 17100:2015-certified translation projects. In contrast with revision, which is sometimes described as bilingual editing, review is often referred to as **monolingual editing**. As noted at the start of this chapter, the professional competences and qualifications of a reviewer are different to those of a reviser according to the ISO, and this reflects the differing focus of review work and the monolingual context in which it is undertaken. ISO 17100:2015 describes the work of the reviewer as follows:

Production 73

> **Box 3.7 Review example**
>
> **Previously revised translation:** In addition, it is our responsibility, where applicable, to communicate to you the information set out in article R. 226-02 of the Commercial Code relating to the performance, during the past financial year, of agreements already approved by the general meeting.
>
> **Reviewed translation:** In addition, <u>where applicable,</u> it is our responsibility~~, where applicable,~~ to ~~communicate to~~<u>provide</u> you <u>with</u> the information ~~set out~~<u>provided for</u> in a<u>A</u>rticle R. 226-02 of the <u>French</u> Commercial Code relating to the performance <u>of agreements</u>, during the past financial year~~, of agreements~~<u>which had</u> already been approved by the general meeting.
>
> **Clean reviewed translation:** In addition, where applicable, it is our responsibility to provide you with the information provided for in Article R. 226-02 of the French Commercial Code relating to the performance of agreements during the past financial year which had already been approved by the general meeting.
>
> Comparing the 'Review' with the 'Revision' stage in Box 3.6 above, the extent of the changes is clear to see. None of these changes are errors; rather, they reflect changes to address suitability for the designated purpose and, more importantly, 'domain accuracy' and 'text-type conventions'. For instance, 'provided for' is more commonly used in legal documents of this nature, the capitalisation of 'Article' reflects English-language conventions for references to legislation, the addition of 'French' clarifies the source context before the name of the legislation, and the restructuring, more generally, aids readability.

> The reviewer [shall] carry out a review to assess the suitability of the TL content for the agreed upon purpose and domain and recommend corrections to be implemented by the LSP. The LSP can instruct the reviewer to make corrections. The review includes assessing domain accuracy and respect for the relevant text-type conventions.
> [International Organization for Standardization, 2015, 5.3.4]

Being a monolingual stage of quality assurance, the SL content is entirely put to one side, and the reviewer does not need to be supplied with the source text at all. Indeed, providing the source text to an unsuitably qualified reviewer could even detract from the underlying purpose of the review stage. As noted in the quotation above, the focus lies on the *suitability* of the TL content given its *purpose* (as laid down in the translation brief and agreed with the client) and the *domain* in which the TL content will be used. In particular, this involves some consideration of *domain accuracy* and *text-type conventions* specific to the domain. Hence, in a text on nuclear power plant management, the reviewer (who should ideally have domain expertise) will check for and revise in line with the jargon and terminology typically found in such documents.

By dispensing with the SL content and ideally having a native speaker of the TL review the TL content only, it allows a more in-depth focus on TL expression, style, and phrasing, with a particular focus on the end use of the product. If it is to be published or public-facing, at least, it would typically need to read well and fluently, be free of mistakes, and satisfy common expectations of similar TL documents.

As with revision, the project manager will need to communicate a clear set of instructions as to what aspects of language the reviewer should focus on, and they should also relay precisely how proposed amendments should be added to the document (e.g. using Track Changes, directly via a CAT tool interface, etc.), as well as instructions on raising queries or logging comments. The project manager will again need to decide who has responsibility for deciding on the proposed changes (e.g. translator, reviser, reviewer, or project manager).

Proofreading

> **Definition:** examine the revised TL content and applying corrections before printing.
>
> [International Organization for Standardization, 2015, 2.2.8]

Proofreading is the final optional stage of the ISO 17100:2015 translation project workflow. There is some confusion as to the specific differences between the review and proofreading stages, but one helpful way to look at proofreading is to view it as a final stage of checks often focusing on very technical (and sometimes visual) issues in the TL content.

Unlike other vendors, the profile of the proofreader is not explicitly stated in ISO 17100:2015 in terms of the competences, skills, and qualifications that he or she should have. In many instances, proofreading falls to the project manager, to a designated 'proofreader' working in-house at the LSP, or, sometimes, to an external vendor. If the proofreading is carried out internally, corrections will simply be added to the document and implemented (accepted) immediately; if the proofreader is external to the LSP, the same process of using Track Changes and the Comment tool (if required) will typically be followed so that the project manager can see the level and nature of the changes proposed. Where complex DTP and typesetting work is involved, the document may be sent back to the original translator for

Box 3.8 Proofreading example

Figure 3.2 Example of proofreading comment in final PDF

As shown in Figure 3.2, many proofreading tasks are carried out in PDF documents where the text is in its 'final location' following translation. In the simple example above, one of the numbers ('2018') has been split across two rows due to the text box being too small. The proofreader has flagged this for the attention of the PM, who will in turn pass this on to the DTP team to correct.

the final proofreading stage to check that the final content is approved for release.

Proofreading would also typically take place in the final typeset version of a document just prior to printing or release, so it can therefore hone in on very visual elements of the document (as well as obvious linguistic errors). In terms of the focus of proofreading activities, it could cover such aspects as

- the presence of both parts of paired punctuation marks (e.g. "…", '…', ¿…?, etc.);
- the correct transfer (and localisation, if appropriate) of figures (i.e. thousand separators and decimal points);
- correct use of date formats as per the style guide (e.g. long date format instead of DD/MM/YYYY);
- general adherence to the style guide and brand image (if applicable);
- checks for missing sentences, missing paragraphs, etc.;
- adjusting pagination so that ST page breaks and TT page breaks match up, if requested by the client;
- adjusting line breaks and hyphenation, where appropriate, especially where the TL content ends up being much shorter or longer than the SL content;
- final spellcheck and checks for common typos (e.g. 'of' and 'off'); and
- checking layout and appearance in terms of paragraph indents, equivalent use of bolds, italics, and underlines, correct transfer of symbols (e.g. superscripts) or special characters (i.e. checking that there are no 'empty boxes' when characters are not properly displayed).

Because of the context of proofreading (often with a DTP focus, as noted above), many proofreading edits will be added to PDF documents in the form of Comment balloons or markers for deletion and insertion. The one benefit of this approach is that the comparative difficulty of marking changes (e.g. compared to direct changes in a Microsoft Word document) helps to reinforce the message to the proofreader that this stage is focused on a very limited number of aspects and should not include any elements that are stylistic or preferential in nature.

As with all other QA stages, it is important to specify clearly and to all concerned parties who, exactly, will be responsible for implementing any changes identified during proofreading. Since proposed changes during proofreading will often take the form of Comment bubbles (as opposed to Track Changes), particular care needs to be taken when implementing them. In some cases, it may be worth the project manager building in an additional stage of proofreading so that the final version (post-proofreading) can be examined once again by the proofreader to ensure that his or her changes have been implemented correctly.

Final Checks

Once all of the main production stages have been completed, it is important for the project manager to take the time to carry out enough final checks to be confident of the end quality of the files to be delivered to the client. In simple projects, this may be a simple and relatively quick process, but as project complexity increases, so too will the scope of the final checks. In ISO 17100:2015, this process is referred to as 'Verification and Release'.

Verification and Release

The 'Verification and Release' stage is defined in ISO 17100:2015 as: 'a process ... for final verification of the project against specifications by the project manager before delivery to the client' (International Organization for Standardization, 2015, 5.3.6). A finite list of checks that should be carried out for all projects is not possible, of course, due to their changing nature and the differing scopes and client demands of each and every project, but a non-exhaustive list of checks could include the questions listed below.

- *Are all of the required files present?*
  This may not seem like an onerous task for a small project, but when the number of source files extends into the hundreds, it is easy to not provide the required files on delivery, potentially causing delays in the end use of the translations and, ultimately, client dissatisfaction.

- *Are the files to be delivered all in the target language?*
  If the first question may have seemed trivial, this question perhaps appears even more so! However, if appropriate file management and naming conventions are not properly adhered to, it is not uncommon to deliver one or more source files back to the client at the end of a project, especially in large projects with many complex files. A quick check that the documents are in the expected language is not particularly time consuming, but it once again avoids any disgruntlement on the part of the client.

- *Are the files to be delivered in their final 'deliverable' form?*
  In essence, this is a check to ensure that no Track Changes or Comment balloons are still showing in the document, or any other editorial highlighting or queries. The deliverable files should be ready for use, without any further action being required by the client.

- *Have all of the required QA steps been carried out?*
  This is perhaps the easiest of the questions to answer, as it is a simple workflow check: if the client–LSP agreement specified revision and proofreading, for example, have the revision and proofreading stages actually been carried out? If not, this needs to be remedied as a matter of urgency before delivering anything to the client.

- *Are the files compliant with the project specifications?*
  Again, with reference to the client–LSP agreement, have any special requirements been taken into account during the production process? For instance, as per the translation brief in Box 3.1, have the style guides and terminology lists been adhered to (based on a short-sample check, of course, as opposed to a full check of all text within all documents). Furthermore, on a technical level, the project manager needs to ensure that the file delivery format is as requested. If the client has requested a .pdf, the deliverables need to be in this format as opposed to, say, .docx or another format.

- *Which files need to be delivered?*
  Sometimes a client will request other deliverables besides the translations themselves. For instance, some clients will specifically request that translation memories and term bases be returned to them, since they constitute, according to some agreements, proprietary data belonging to the client. In many instances, the rationale for this is that clients may wish to take their services to another LSP in the future but still want to harness the leveraging of TMs and TBs. Hence, if such a request is made, the project manager needs to ensure that these files are delivered, and that they are delivered in the correct formats (e.g. .tmx for a TM, .xlsx or .xml for a TB).

78 The Translation Project Lifecycle

- *Has the client specified a particular naming convention for files?*
  Many clients are quite particular in their requests regarding file management and will specifically request a naming convention for files to help them to distinguish files in different languages. In many cases, this is simply the addition of a suffix such as '_en-GB' or '_fr-FR' to denote, in this instance, a file in British English and one in French for Mainland France, respectively.

- *Does the client require a special delivery method?*
  Last, but by no means least, the client may specify a particular method of delivery. Some documents might be delivered as hard copies and need to be posted (or even delivered in person in rare cases) and others may need to be transferred via a cloud-based server; but the majority of projects will simply be delivered by email. As with all of the checks above, whatever has been agreed with the client is of paramount concern here.

Only once the project manager is satisfied that all of the deliverables meet the conditions of the client–LSP agreement and are ready to be delivered to the client should the delivery take place.

* * *

As should have become clear from this chapter, there are a number of compulsory and optional stages that make up the translation project lifecycle, some of which will be familiar to readers and some of which will be less familiar, or may at least be known under different names. Figure 3.3 offers an enhanced version of the previous waterfall diagram presented in Figure 3.1, with some additional annotations to clarify the key responsibilities at each stage. It also shows how, when, and where the various stages are typically carried out and how, in some cases, each stage might relate back to a previous one. Note that the diagram refers specifically to ISO 17100:2015-certified projects; for 'non-certified' projects, any combination of stages can be followed.

The key theme underpinning this chapter is the need for clear and precise instructions to all parties involved in the translation project. The project manager therefore plays a critical role in drawing up these instructions, negotiating expectations and responsibilities with all parties (including the client), and – most importantly of all – ensuring that these instructions and responsibilities are followed and respected throughout the project. It may seem that much of the project manager's work takes place in the pre-production stage, but, in fact, the production stage involves just as much work for the project manager but in a totally different capacity. Since much of the work during the production stage takes place beyond the project manager's direct control (i.e. the work may be largely in the hands of external vendors), this is

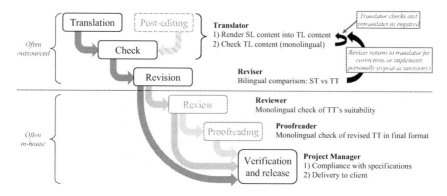

Figure 3.3 Annotated translation production workflow

where effective project management practices such as communication skills, time management, meticulous planning, attention to detail, and responsiveness to problems that may occur are essential to the smooth operation of a project during production.

* * *

Topics for Discussion and Assignments

1. Do you consider post-editing to be a form of quality assurance (i.e. carrying out quality checks and implementing corrections on a translation produced by a machine) or a form of translation (i.e. machine translation plus post-editing is holistically equivalent to translation by a human)? In other words, does translation require *solely* human input to be considered translation?
2. Design and carry out a short experiment to test the impact of vendor instructions on revision practices. Prepare a translation (or even a machine translation) of a short 250-word text. In small groups distribute the ST and translation to 2–3 people with no instructions apart from to 'revise' the translation; give them to another 2–3 people with a precise list of instructions covering which elements should be checked and which should be ignored. When complete, compare the revision practices of the two groups. How do they differ? Is the level of editing different between the groups?
3. Using what you have read in Chapter 2 and in this chapter, select one of the Case Studies on the TS Portal and design a 15-minute group or individual presentation – or write a short two-page report – to outline your approach to managing the project. Present a detailed quotation and a detailed schedule, and outline your rationale for selecting or not

selecting certain project stages (e.g. revision, review, etc.), as well as any other important decisions that you have made.

Further Reading

Mossop (2014) is an excellent resource on quality assurance processes. Mossop refers specifically to 'editing' and 'revising' (defined in the book), but the principles and examples provided throughout the book provide an accessible overview of what goes into the various stages after translation. For those with little time, Chapters 1 and 2 are the key chapters to read for a general overview. Chapters 9, 12, and 14 also offer perspectives on revision specifically, including procedures and revising others' work (including MT).

For an interesting discussion on the application of functionalist translation theories to translation processes, Calvo (2018) explores the relationship between functionalist concepts, translation briefs, and translation industry standards such as ISO 17100:2015.

References

Bouillon, P., Gaspar, L., Gerlach, J., Porro, V., & Roturier, J. (2014). *Pre-editing by forum users: A case study* [Paper presentation]. Proceedings of the 9th Edition of the Language Resources and Evaluation Conference (LREC), CNL Workshop, Reykjavik, Iceland.

Calvo, E. (2018). From translation briefs to quality standards: Functionalist theories in today's translation processes. *The International Journal for Translation and Interpreting Research, 10*(1), 18–32.

Cronin, M. (2013). *Translation in the digital age*. Routledge.

Garcia, I. (2011). Translating by post-editing: Is it the way forward? *Machine Translation, 25*, 217–237.

Gouadec, D. (2010). Quality in translation. In Y. Gambier & L. van Doorslaer (Eds.), *Handbook of translation studies* (Vol. 1, pp. 270–275). John Benjamins.

International Organization for Standardization. (2015). *Translation services – Requirements for translation services (ISO 17100:2015)*. International Organization for Standardization.

International Organization for Standardization. (2017). *Translation services – Post-editing of machine translation output – Requirements (ISO 18587:2017)*. International Organization for Standardization.

Mellinger, C. D., & Shreve, G. (2016). Match evaluation and over-editing in a translation memory environment. In R. Muñoz Martín (Ed.), *Reembedding translation process research* (pp. 131–148). John Benjamins.

Mossop, B. (2014). *Revising and editing for translators* (3rd ed.). Routledge.

Nitzke, J., & Gros, A.-K. (2021). Preferential Changes in Revision and Post-editing. In M. Koponen, B. Mossop, I. S. Robert, & G. Scocchera (Eds.), *Translation revision and post-editing: Industry practices and cognitive processes* (pp. 21–34). Routledge.

Nord, C. (2018). *Translating as a purposeful activity: Functionalist approaches explained* (2nd ed.). Routledge.

O'Brien, S. (2003). *Controlling controlled english: An analysis of several controlled language rule sets* [Paper presentation]. Proceedings of EAMT-CLAW 03, Joint Conference Combining the 8th International Workshop of the European Association for Machine Translation and the 4th Controlled Language Applications Workshop, Dublin, Ireland.

Schnierer, M. (2021). Revision and quality standards: Do translation service providers follow recommendations in practice? In M. Koponen, B. Mossop, I. S. Robert, & G. Scocchera (Eds.), *Translation revision and post-editing: Industry practices and cognitive processes* (pp. 109–130). Routledge.

Vandepitte, S. (2017). Translation product quality: A conceptual analysis. In T. Svoboda, Ł. Biel, & K. Łoboda (Eds.), *Quality aspects in institutional translation* (pp. 15–29). Language Science Press.

4 Post-production

Learning outcomes:

- Understand the importance of post-production stages in terms of continuous improvement and 'feed-forward' into future project execution
- Appreciate the importance of feedback and how and why feedback can be collected, as well as how best to undertake corrective action
- Understand the features of invoices and how and when to issue invoices to clients
- Develop an awareness of the types of documentation kept by LSPs and its role with regard to current and future operations
- Consider when to hold a post-mortem and what some of the typical outcomes of a project post-mortem might be for future projects

As the name suggests, the post-production stage of a project is concerned with all elements that take place after the core production processes are complete. Hence, after the 'Verification and Release' of deliverables to the client is complete and no further deliverables are due (and no further production-related processes need to be undertaken), the project can finally move to the post-production stage, when the project manager can start to think about closing a project. Having a clear end to a project may sound obvious, but it is important to understand at what point a project can be considered complete. Indeed, as the PRINCE2 framework notes:

> [A] clear end to a project is always more successful than a slow drift into use [of the deliverables] as it is a recognition by all concerned that: the original objectives have been met (subject to any approved changes); the current project has run its course; ... project costs should no longer be incurred; [and it] provides an opportunity to ensure that all unachieved goals and objectives are identified; [as well as] transfer[ring] ownership

DOI: 10.4324/9781003132813-5

of the products to the customer and terminat[ing] the responsibility of the project management team.

[Office of Government Commerce, 2018, p. 260]

The PMBOK adopts a similar stance, stating that the main focus of post-production (or 'closing a project', as PRINCE2 and PMBOK would define it) is to 'confirm that the project has delivered what is defined in the project product description, and that the acceptance criteria have been met' (Project Management Institute, 2017, p. 262). There is of course some overlap here with the 'Verification and Release' stage itself, as part of this stage (at the end of 'Production') is to check that all of the deliverables are present and any outstanding issues have been resolved, but the post-production stage of the project is more focused on confirming delivery and confirming formal acceptance of the deliverables, alongside general administrative tasks such as invoicing, file management, record keeping, and feedback. These aspects are the key focus of this chapter. Before proceeding to address these points, first consider the following questions:

? What tasks would you consider to be essential in the post-production stage of a project?
? Which of those tasks are internal to the LSP itself and which involve liaising with the client?

Feedback

One of the most critical stages of post-production in terms of the future success of the LSP and enhancing the prospect of repeat business from clients is feedback. Indeed, ISO 17100:2015 stipulates that feedback is a required component of an ISO-certified LSP's project workflow:

> The LSP shall have a process in place for handling client feedback, for assessment of client satisfaction, and for making appropriate corrections and/or corrective action. If there is a need to implement any corrections, the work will be redelivered to the client. It is good practice for the LSP to share feedback from the client with all the parties involved.
>
> [International Organization for Standardization, 2015, 6.1]

There are a number of elements to unpack from this seemingly straightforward provision of the ISO standard, which will be the focus of the first part of this chapter. This sub-section is divided into further sub-sections on 'Client–LSP Feedback' (i.e. feedback provided by the client to the LSP) and on 'LSP–Vendor Feedback' (i.e. feedback provided by the LSP or passed on by the LSP from the client to the vendor). The latter part of the ISO quotation above ('shar[ing] feedback from the client with all the parties involved') is all-too-frequently overlooked by LSPs and, as will become clear in the relevant sub-section below, is an essential workflow stage for any conscientious LSP looking to maintain high service standards.

As an aside, before we turn to the specifics of feedback collection and handling in translation, it is worth drawing on an example of performance management in an entirely different context so as to demonstrate how even seemingly small improvements (or declines) can have a significant impact. The principle known as the aggregation of marginal gains (see Box 4.1) has useful applications across a wide range of disciplines, not least project management, where it has been likened to the more widely known manufacturing principle called *kaizen*, which is also based on the principle of continuous improvement.

While the example presented in Box 4.1 is highly theoretical, what it does show quite convincingly is that even slightly poor performance, if allowed to endure, can have a significant negative impact on overall performance in the long term, while small improvements, consistently applied, will result in a sizeable change for the better over the course of a year. Of course, 'performance' is difficult to measure in an area such as translation, but this is where LSPs tend to draw on notions of quality and linguistic quality assessment in particular (see Chapter 8). But one approach that is easy to implement in post-production and is, in many ways, more important than fine-grained linguistic criticism is seeking feedback from the client in order to gauge their satisfaction with the end product and service provided. All of the information received through feedback collection can then be used to improve internal LSP processes and to aid vendors in improving their own practices.

Client–LSP Feedback

Once a project is complete and all deliverables have been sent to the client, the first step is to ensure that all of the required deliverables have indeed been received and that there are no obvious problems that the client would like the LSP to address on a superficial level (e.g. missing files, untranslated text, unlocalised images, etc.). Such a check is necessarily superficial and will often be sought very quickly after submitting the deliverables, meaning that confirmation from the client that the files are 'okay' does not signify that no further problems are likely to be identified. In order to check client satisfaction on a wider scale, the client first needs time to review the files properly. Depending on the size of the project, the request for more substantive feedback may be made within a matter of days, weeks or even a month or more after the project is complete.

In terms of what the LSP might ask of a client, this will depend entirely on what the LSP wants to ascertain. Some LSPs will simply ask for feedback in very general terms and not pose any specific questions at all to guide the feedback, while others will have a specially designed feedback form asking questions about different stages of the project, the deliverables

Box 4.1 The aggregation of marginal gains

In the run-up to the 2008 Olympic Games in Beijing, the British Cycling team famously implemented a principle called the **aggregation of marginal gains**. This approach was best explained by the cycling team's performance director Dave Brailsford, who stated at the time that 'if you broke down everything you could think of that goes into riding a bike, and then improved it by 1%, you would get a significant increase when you put them all together'. Such was the success of this philosophy, which included measures ranging from improving hygiene (to stave off illness) and encouraging mindfulness techniques through to the more obvious elements of bike ergonomics and fitness training, that the team won a record haul of cycling medals at the Olympics that year. The success has even prompted disciplines beyond sports science to adopt similar principles in their work.

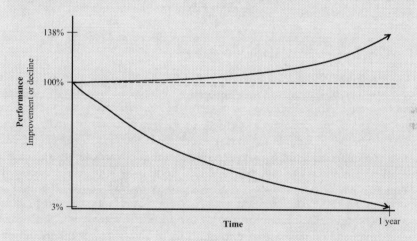

Figure 4.1 Aggregation of marginal gains over one year

Looking at the short-term picture, it's all too easy to dismiss the impact of a 1% improvement in some aspect of a project's performance. But in the long term, a consistent 1% improvement in the project's overall performance can make a significant difference to project successes and company operations more generally. If we assume that an LSP carries out one project every day for a year and that, through changes to the way in which projects are managed and adjustments to certain processes, the performance of those projects improves in some way by 1% each time, this will lead to a 38% improvement in performance over the year ($1.01^{365} = 37.783$). Conversely, if standards are

> allowed to slip – by erroneously assuming that minor shortcomings in each project's performance 'don't matter' very much – and therefore decline by 1% each day over the course of a year, performance will drop by approximately 97%(!) to a performance level of under 3% ($0.99^{365} = 0.025$) relative to the starting point (see Figure 4.1).

themselves, and even broader questions such as PM communication and repeat custom. The decision as to which approach to adopt will often be made on a higher level by senior management, but, in simple terms, a decision needs to be made quite clearly as to whether to try and guide clients towards specific types of feedback that the LSP wants to hear about (e.g. to identify ways to improve very specific internal processes) or whether it is quite content to hear if there are any problems with the deliverables (i.e. to fix one or more specific problems and anything else that the client happens to mention).

Handling Feedback and Corrective Action

The processing of feedback is a very important part of the project lifecycle for a number of reasons. For instance, if a client observes that the translation has not used preferred domain terminology, this raises the question of whether the client could in fact provide a glossary or whether the LSP could enlist a vendor to compile a glossary and have it checked by the client with a view to improving the use of preferred terminology in the future. Such a proactive approach in response to a fairly common, and legitimate, criticism can then help to reduce the amount of '**corrective action**' required in future. ISO 17100:2015 defines 'corrective action' as 'action taken to eliminate the cause of a nonconformity or errors in the translation process or target language content' (International Organization for Standardization, 2015, 2.5.5). Hence, it not only refers to specific errors in the translation (e.g. incorrect terminology), but it also relates to the *causes* of such errors in the content itself (e.g. the absence of a domain-specific and/or client-specific glossary) and in the translation process (e.g. failure by the reviser to note the incorrect use of a term, perhaps caused by the aforementioned lack of a glossary).

The ISO further notes that corrective action not only involves identifying what went wrong, but also what can be done to avoid the error/issue occurring again in the future. In the simple example above, the creation of a domain- or client-specific glossary would be a clear step towards mitigating this sort of problem. Looking at the bigger picture, though, it is all too easy to simply correct errors and move on to the next project, but attention to detail in the wider service provided to the client is important: repeated errors from one project to the next for the same client will quickly become tiresome, however minor they may be, and will soon develop into an overwhelming case to seek translation services from another LSP. Recall from Box 4.1 how even a small 1% decline in performance can translate into a significant drop in performance over time if the same mistakes are repeatedly made.

Many clients are quite forthcoming when they spot errors, but in some instances the feedback provided is not actionable and requires clarification. For instance, consider the following – unfortunately very common – comments provided by clients in terms of general feedback on a project:

- 'The translation is poor.'
- 'The glossary was not used.'
- 'I didn't like the style in which it was written.'

Sometimes, these curt and largely enigmatic remarks can even constitute the entirety of the feedback provided to an LSP. It is worth considering how best to respond to such comments.

? If your client were to email you with any of the criticisms above, how would you respond?

Clearly, in order to translate these comments into corrective action, as defined by ISO 17100:2015, and to make them actionable (i.e. having practical value), the PM needs more details. In what aspects is the translation poor? Can you offer specific examples where you are unhappy with the translation? Why does the translation not satisfy your intended purpose or needs? In some cases, the responses can be more revelatory about the LSP's processes than about the product itself. For instance, if it transpires that the client was in fact looking to publish the translation on its public-facing website and the LSP had only provided a 'good enough' translation 'for information purposes', perhaps by leveraging MT and PE to speed up the process and keep costs down, who is really at fault here? A fairly recurrent theme throughout this textbook is that of client education: many clients do not understand translation or have misconceptions about what it involves. Part of the PM's job is to fill in the gaps in the client's knowledge and help the client to understand what he or she actually needs. Hence, if the translation was in fact intended to be published on a public website and the PM did not check this, there is a case for saying that the client can be forgiven for not considering it necessary to specify the intended use.

However, even once the client has provided examples or more detail on the feedback, the PM might feel that the criticism is unjustified (or simply subjective in nature). How such criticism is handled, however, can be an important factor in the on-going relationship with the client, and the approach adopted might even (cynically) be determined on the basis of how important that client is to the LSP.

? If the client's criticism is unjustified, what would you do?
? In terms of payment, would you ask for additional payment to cover the costs of the corrective action?

The PM first needs to ascertain whether corrective action is needed. If the criticism is wholly unjustified, the stance adopted can shape the future relationship, as it can set a precedent as to what the client expects the LSP to do in future. It is therefore important to choose the course of action carefully: overreacting and going to great lengths to appease the client – while it might seem like the best choice – may simply create a rod for the LSP's back in future; inaction, on the other hand, could frustrate the client, who might take their services elsewhere in future. Then comes the question of cost. If the requested changes are unreasonable and subjective (and particularly extensive in scope), the PM might want to consider charging extra for non-essential corrections. If the changes are small and easy to implement, the PM could consider doing so free of charge in order to build further goodwill with the client.

If the criticism is justified, the case is in many ways simpler, but more frustrating, from a PM perspective, as it means that there has usually been a failing either internally (within the LSP) or on the part of one or more vendors. The cost of changes in this case will almost always be borne by the LSP (and/or passed on to one or more vendors in the form of a reduction in their invoice, depending on who is at fault). But if a vendor is at fault, this raises more questions: can the PM trust the original team to carry out the corrections? If the issue is much broader – e.g. consistent misunderstandings, poor written style, etc. – it would be wise to re-assign the task to another vendor; if the issue has a very clearly defined solution – e.g. replace term X with term Y, which is the correct term in the domain – assigning the task to the same vendor is unlikely to pose any problems. Throughout the process, however, the PM needs to be transparent with the client and with the vendors to clarify any additional costs (or indeed any deductions) that may be incurred as a result.

In some cases, clarity is even needed to ascertain what the client would like to have done. There are cases where clients supply files showing edits using Track Changes, but it is not clear whether these files have been provided for information purposes only (i.e. to show the PM what changes the client has made to the translations internally), or whether they expect the PM to check (or arrange for a vendor to check) the proposed changes and either accept or reject them. In such cases, it may be that the PM has the required expertise, or the queries may need to be passed on to a vendor. In either case, clarity is key to determine the client's expectations.

Client Satisfaction

The client's feedback and the nature of the feedback itself are usually the first step on the road to gauging how happy the client is with the products and services provided. It follows, therefore, that the way in which client feedback is handled, and the extent to which it is implemented, will then be a strong determinant of client satisfaction. If the request for corrective action is handled fairly and in good faith, client satisfaction will likely be higher.

It makes a lot of sense for LSPs to collect more general feedback from clients to ascertain their overall satisfaction. This might be relatively informal, such as asking for general comments and feedback via email; it may also be based on a formal document that the PM sends to the client on completion, asking pointed questions about specific aspects of performance. Whichever approach is taken, the responses need to be documented and stored so that any persistent patterns of client dissatisfaction (either from the same client across multiple projects or from different clients) can be detected and acted upon promptly before problems start to snowball.

Unfortunately, some LSPs do not follow up with clients upon completion. There seems to be a blanket assumption among some LSPs that 'no news is good news'. Sometimes this may be the case: the client is 100% satisfied and has no reason to contact the LSP again with any comments. However, many experienced PMs – and indeed freelance professionals for that matter – would argue that 'no news' can often mean 'bad news'. Matis (2014, p. 200) suggests that there are several reasons why a client might not contact the LSP. Firstly, the client may not have the time, budget, or staff to review the translations, perhaps due to insufficient knowledge of the language(s) and/or subject matter. Secondly, it may be that the client carried out only a cursory check initially and did not realise until much later that there were far more extensive problems in the translations but had left it too late to follow up with the LSP. Finally, in the worst case, the client may be so dissatisfied with the translations that they have already resolved to never go back to that LSP again. In all of these cases, until the PM actually makes contact with the client, everything is based on assumptions, mostly revolving around the assumption that the translation is indeed fit-for-purpose.

Overall, seeking feedback from clients is important to arrive at a better understanding of client expectations in the future, especially in terms of quality, but also in terms of cost, time, and other project constraints. It is also important to gather information on expectations and satisfaction so that the PM's client education role can be appropriately tailored in the future to avoid unrealistic expectations on the part of the client. On a more practical level, feedback also helps to reveal persistent errors in the deliverables and in the process itself. Reducing the likelihood of errors in the future will likely result in a happier client and therefore a stronger prospect of more work in the future. However, all of this feedback also plays an important role for the vendors too, as discussed in the sub-section below.

LSP–Vendor Feedback

Given the importance of feedback for the LSP, the relevance of *vendor* feedback is all too often overlooked. A great deal of what the client has to say about the project is usually extremely relevant to the vendors that worked on it. As with the LSP, awareness of errors can help to reduce the likelihood of such errors occurring again in the future. It can also help to improve the standard of future submissions through a better understanding of what specific clients want for specific projects.

Feedback should always be provided to the vendor, even if it is only a cursory note from the PM to say that everything was fine with the project. Vendors too will often assume that 'no news is good news', so, if they fail to hear from the LSP upon completion of a project, they will assume that no problems were identified. However, if, after a period of several weeks or months, no future work has been sent in their direction, they will start to wonder whether they did something wrong during the project. Once again, the vendor is forced to make assumptions as to the reasons for no feedback and, in certain cases, an LSP not going back to the vendor with future work.

The LSP can of course also draw on very detailed feedback from LQA scores or macro-level LQA feedback from the reviser and/or reviewer (see Chapter 8). Certain trends in the types of errors detected might be identified from the data, meaning that some very specific and actionable feedback can be passed on to the vendor to improve their performance in the future. Some of the LSP–vendor feedback might not relate specifically to the translation product itself though. It can – and arguably *should* – also focus on how well the vendor worked in their particular stage of the project workflow, how well they followed specific instructions, their adherence to deadlines, their rates, and any specific issues in terms of files delivered (both in relation to the translation itself and additional files such as translation memories, term bases, and even administrative documentation).

In summary, feedback is a crucial element of post-production but, importantly, should not focus solely on *client* feedback. The process of giving and receiving feedback needs to involve all parties in the project. Feedback needs to operate bidirectionally between the client and the LSP, and between the LSP and vendors. The vendors may even have specific feedback to pass on to the client (via the LSP). The more feedback is shared, the greater the improvements in the translation products and production processes will be in the future.

Closing Administration

When it is clear that the project has come to a logical end and, ordinarily, there are no further outstanding issues to be resolved (noting some of the provisos discussed under invoicing below), the project will then progress to closing administration. This stage typically involves invoicing and various forms of record keeping and file management, ranging from administrative documentation to task-specific files and resources, including translation memories and term bases. Before reading on, consider the following preliminary questions:

? At what stage before, during, or after a project should the invoice be raised?
? In general terms, what sorts of documentation will need to be stored once a project is complete?
? What are some of the practical and other challenges associated with record keeping and file management in the context of translation projects?

Invoicing

As a general rule, most projects are invoiced on completion, i.e. the translation and all other workflow stages are finished, files are verified and delivered to the client, and the invoice is then raised for payment. However, there are instances where invoicing might take place differently and may not technically fall under the typical temporal definition of *post*-production. Here, we will discuss three main invoicing practices, which all take place at different times during the project:

- invoicing upon project completion;
- pre-payment for the project or a project deposit invoice combined with a subsequent project completion invoice; and
- invoices for payment instalments throughout a project.

When to Invoice

In the simplest case (invoicing upon project completion), the decision as to when specifically to invoice the client will likely be dictated by an internal workflow policy, but it could potentially fall at three points in time:

- the invoice is sent at the same time as the final project deliverables;
- the invoice is sent once the client has confirmed receipt of the project deliverables; or
- the invoice is sent once the client has confirmed their satisfaction with the project deliverables.

Some LSPs will simply issue the invoice at the same time as all the project deliverables are sent to, or made available to, the client. Others (one of the more common practices, arguably) will first wait for confirmation from the client that all the files have at least been received and are correct in terms of the number and format but saying nothing of translation quality at this stage. Such a check may simply take the form of a request in the email accompanying delivery, e.g. 'kindly confirm safe receipt of all the (attached) files and I will arrange for the invoice to be raised and sent over'. Some LSPs will go one step further than this cursory check and wait for full confirmation that the client has not only received all of the files in the required format (remembering also that it is not necessarily only translations that are supplied, but also translation memories and term bases for some projects), but also that the client is 100% satisfied with the quality of the delivered translations. Evidently, such an approach is a signal of a strong customer-satisfaction focus at the LSP (and such a commitment should be commended), but waiting for confirmation of 'full' satisfaction incorporates an element of risk into the invoicing procedure.

The latter approach can cause significant delays in the raising of the final invoice, as it can be very difficult (in admittedly rare cases) to fully determine what 'satisfaction' actually is and how it might be measured. As noted already, the very reason that a client approaches an LSP for translation services is precisely because he or she does not have the necessary in-house expertise to carry out the translation or to procure and manage the translation services. Hence, this begs the obvious question: what exactly are we expecting the client to check? Indeed, this is where problems can creep into the post-production workflow. Clients, all too aware of their lack of source language skills, for example, may pay heightened (and arguably unnecessary) attention to target language expression, pointing to various minor errors in the translation as examples of bad practice. Of course, all LSPs would like their translations to be free of errors, but even with the best will in the world, some errors do inevitably evade the QA processes. Such errors, which could range from simple typos to bigger issues with sentence-level expression, can at times turn into sticking points, causing unnecessary back and forth between the client and LSP – and, in turn, between the LSP and vendors – to resolve relatively negligible issues, all the while delaying the raising of the final invoice. Such a delay, in turn, affects the LSP's cash flow, which could then have an impact on its own ability to pay the vendors, whose invoices may well have already been raised and submitted, meaning that the payment countdown has started.

Strictly speaking, there is nothing wrong with the client-centred approach of ensuring complete satisfaction with the deliverables prior to invoicing, but it has to be managed very carefully to avoid giving the client the impression that the invoice may be reduced due to what could, in fact, be incredibly minor and subjective issues. Of course, major issues can (and, in some cases, *should*) give rise to a discount of some form, but the risk is that offering an opportunity for clients to find errors does precisely that: it suggests that it is their responsibility or duty to find problems. This is similar to the 'over-revision' phenomenon mentioned in Chapter 3: to paraphrase Mossop (2014, p. 115) again, the idea is not to *find* elements that *could be* changed, but to spot genuine problems only.

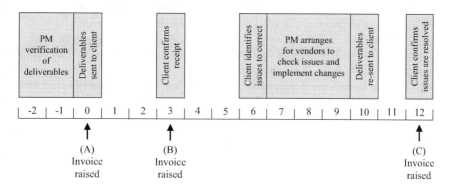

Figure 4.2 Example of different post-delivery invoicing approaches

Figure 4.2 provides a summary of the above approaches to post-delivery invoicing by drawing on a hypothetical example. If we assume the industry standard practice of requiring invoice payment within 30 days of the invoice being raised, and if we assume that the project deliverables are sent to the client on, say, 1 October, Approach A (see (A) in Figure 4.2) involves sending the invoice to the client at the same time as the deliverables. The invoice would then be paid before the end of October (31 October, to be precise). The second approach (B) assumes that it takes three days for the client to even confirm safe receipt of the deliverables (not an uncommon occurrence) and that the invoice is then raised on this date (4 October). This three-day delay then pushes back the invoice payment deadline to 3 November. The final approach (C) assumes a certain amount of back and forth with certain changes being identified, implemented, then approved by the client, resulting in final confirmation that the client is satisfied and the resulting invoice being raised on 13 October. This would then push back the payment deadline to 12 November, nearly 1.5 months after the initial delivery of the project deliverables.

For a large LSP, none of these invoicing approaches are particularly problematic (assuming that the project is relatively small, at least; see discussions below). But for a smaller LSP, where cash reserves might not be so plentiful, Approach C can be quite problematic when the vendors themselves will often invoice upon delivery or very soon after delivery. Of course, there is no 'correct' way to approach invoicing, and, in many cases, the approach to invoicing clients will need to be decided upon after careful consideration of how the LSP expects its own vendors to invoice for their work. If its vendors are allowed (or indeed encouraged) to submit invoices upon completion or upon confirmation of receipt of the project deliverables, then the LSP also needs to ensure that its own invoice is issued promptly after completion. Some LSPs, however, adopt a practice of asking vendors to only submit one single invoice at the end of the month, which is the point at which the (usually) 30-day payment term begins, thus granting the LSP some grace. It should be said, though, that this 'invoice at the end of the month' procedure is not well-liked among vendors, as this method in turn reduces freelancers' cash flow. In short, the approach to invoicing clients requires some careful thought and needs to be viewed in conjunction with other LSP post-production processes on the client side and the vendor side.

Other Common Approaches to Invoicing

Three other approaches to invoicing are also worth mentioning here, as they are relatively common across the industry. They are strongly connected with a desire to manage the payment risks associated with translation projects (see Chapter 10) and include

- the invoice being sent for **full payment prior to any work commencing**;
- an invoice for **part payment** being sent **prior to any work commencing** (a 'deposit'), with the remaining sum invoiced on/after completion; and
- a series of invoices being raised **before, during and after production** to establish a staggered payment schedule.

In the first case, some LSPs have a simple policy of demanding payment for the service up front (i.e. an immediate payment deadline for the invoice) before any work is carried out. This approach has the obvious advantage of considerably mitigating the risk of non-payment, but it has obvious downsides from the client's perspective. The client may well view such a practice as risky, as the service is being paid for before any evidence of work is provided. To obviate this problem with client perception, most LSPs would only adopt this approach for first-time clients. Some clients may in turn impose their own conditions for a payment procedure, with appropriate guarantees and cover in the event that they are dissatisfied with the resulting service.

This leads us nicely to the second invoicing approach listed above: the 'deposit' invoice. For new clients and for especially large projects, it is not uncommon for an LSP to raise an invoice before the project starts for either the entire project cost or for a percentage of the total cost. Again, this approach is taken to mitigate the risk associated with non-payment. With new clients, there is always a risk that they are untrustworthy and might not pay for the services after delivery. For larger projects, this risk is all the more acute as non-payment could lead to serious problems in paying the vendors' invoices. While legal avenues do exist to enforce payment via debt-collection agencies, these are time consuming and require a lot of effort to pursue. In this regard, prevention is better than cure, so to speak. Hence, deposit invoices will again have an immediate payment deadline, and no work will commence until the deposit has been paid. Once the project is complete, a standard 30-day payment deadline may then be applied for the final balancing invoice, if applicable.

The final approach of staggered payments is again concerned with risk management. Some LSPs may feel less comfortable invoicing for tens of thousands of pounds up front, for example, due to the client rightly wondering whether it will indeed receive the service after a number of weeks. As such, a common alternative is to arrange a certain number of staggered payments tied to staggered deliveries. Each of these staggered payments will usually be invoiced and due at a pre-determined time. Work will then not normally progress to the next stage until the corresponding payment instalment has been received.

Figure 4.3 provides an example of staggered payments being tied to project milestones. In the example, the project is a 150,000-word translation to be delivered in stages over a 15-week period. To keep matters simple, we shall assume a simple £0.20 per word fee is being applied to this project and that this rate includes translation, revision, and the LSP's margin, giving a total sum payable of £30,000. In this case, the LSP has decided to deliver the translation in 40,000-word batches at the end of each four-week period (resulting in three deliveries of 40,000 words over 12 weeks and a final delivery of 30,000 words after the remaining three weeks). Prior to work commencing, an invoice is raised for 50% of Batch 1 (£4,000), payable immediately, followed by invoices for the remaining 50% of the delivered batch and 50% of the forthcoming batch, again payable immediately. The advantage of this approach should be fairly evident: it offers good cash flow to the LSP and a degree of payment security to protect against unscrupulous buyers. If the client does not pay promptly, the project's progress is suspended and batch deliveries can even be withheld if necessary. Such conditions would need to be written into the client–LSP agreement and stated clearly on the corresponding invoices. In terms of vendor management, this improved

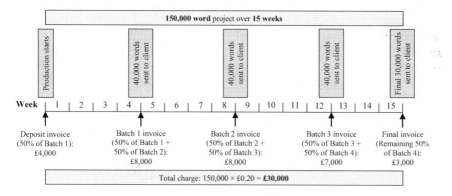

Figure 4.3 Example of staggered payments tied to project milestones

cash flow also helps to manage specially negotiated payment conditions for vendors. If we assume that a single translator is working on this project over 15 weeks, he or she will likely be unable to take on (much) other work given that the weekly throughput is expected to be approximately 10,000 words. Freelance vendors, therefore, will also want to protect their own cash flow so that they can pay regular bills and other day-to-day living costs. This project would occupy the translator for over 3.5 months with no other substantial income, so it is reasonable to expect that the vendor would ask for similar payment practices to be in place. For a large LSP, this is easier to accommodate without, in turn, requiring staggered payments from the client; for a smaller 'boutique' LSP, this could be quite problematic.

Invoice Content

The content of invoices is typically laid down by law, but a simplified set of guidelines (based loosely on guidelines in the United Kingdom) – some of which are usually obligatory and some of which are optional – might be as follows:

- **Invoice number.** The invoice number must be unique and, in some countries, sequentially numbered;
- **Invoice date.** The invoice date is important, as it marks the start of the 'countdown' to the payment deadline where this is expressed in a specific number of days as opposed to a date;
- **Name, address, and contact details of the LSP.** In some countries, it is also a requirement that the LSP's business ID number is included, if the LSP is a registered company. Some countries even require the company name, legal form of organisation, and identifying numbers to be written in a particular format;
- **Name, address, and contact details of the client.** As above, the client's name, address, and contact details need to be stipulated, in accordance with local legislation;
- **VAT numbers, if applicable.** Where relevant legislation requires it, the LSP and the client (or in some cases only the LSP, if the client is not VAT registered) typically need to include their VAT number;
- **A clear description of the products/services.** The title of the invoice may refer to 'Invoice for Translation Services', for instance. Most countries also require a detailed breakdown of the products/services, with an itemised list of quantities (e.g. word counts, number of hours) and unit prices;
- **A sub-total of charges, excluding VAT.** This item provides the sub-total of each individual item on the invoice before any taxes are added;
- **Additional charges or deductions.** In some cases, an LSP may charge a supplement for a project (e.g. an urgency surcharge on the whole project) or may offer a general discount (e.g. a 'first project discount' for new clients);

- **VAT (or equivalent)**. If applicable, the VAT is itemised separately depending on the rate in force in the country where the service is being provided;
- **Grand total**. The grand total is the sum of the sub-total of charges and VAT, plus or minus any additional charges or deductions;
- **Payment deadline**. The payment deadline may be expressed in a certain number of days (e.g. 'within 30 days of the invoice date') or as a precise date (e.g. 'by 1 January 2023'); and
- **Payment method**. The client and LSP will have typically agreed on a particular payment method such as bank transfer, debit/credit card, or some other means during the pre-production stage as part of the client–LSP agreement. This method is then usually repeated on the invoice with relevant payment details.

An example of an invoice incorporating these elements is also provided in Figure 4.4, but it is worth stressing again that requirements differ from country to country.

It is also incredibly important, especially in an industry where cross-border transactions are so common, to stipulate clearly and unambiguously in which currency the invoice is denominated. To avoid any ambiguity, currency symbols should not be used in isolation (e.g. £, $, etc.), as there are of course many variants of dollars, pounds, and other currencies around the world, and some symbols are not so well known – the Russian rouble (₽) and the Ukrainian hryvnia (₴), for instance, being two good examples. Three-letter currency codes are recommended as a minimum, accompanied, if necessary, by the currency in writing (e.g. 'pounds sterling / GBP').

Record Keeping and File Management

ISO 17100:2015 explicitly states in Section 6.2 that the LSP should 'have a process in place to ensure full project archiving', as well as pointing to any legal and/or contractual obligations that may be associated with such archiving, in particular with regard to the deletion of data and data protection more generally. It is generally expected that an LSP will have a clearly defined information management system to manage the vast amounts of project-related data in motion.

? What sorts of files will likely be generated before and during the course of a translation project?
? What sorts of files will a PM need to store after a project and why?
? What sorts of files will a PM likely be able to delete once a project is completed?
? Are there any files that a PM may be *required* to delete in certain circumstances?

Invoice for Translation Services

Client and invoice details

Client		Invoice	
Name:	Mr Hugo Escargot	Invoice no.:	20220131A
Address:	92, rue de Paris	Date:	**31 January 2022**
	Bordeaux	Project:	GWD20220101
	France 33999	PO no.:	20220101_HE
		Currency:	**Pounds sterling / GBP**
Phone:	+33 93 123 4567		
Mobile:		PM:	Jane Smith
E-mail:	h.escargot@snailmail.fr	Revision no.:	1

Breakdown of charges

Service	Files (List)	Languages	Units	Unit Type	Weight	Rate	Amount
Translation	Website_GWD.xlsx (Delivered: 20/01/22)	EN > FR	174	Repetition	30%	0.036	£6.26
			282	101% match	0%	0.000	£0.00
			14	100% match	30%	0.036	£0.50
			97	95-99% match	50%	0.060	£5.82
			442	85-94% match	80%	0.096	£42.43
			503	75-84% match	80%	0.096	£48.29
			2364	50-74% match	100%	0.120	£283.68
			1139	No match	100%	0.120	£136.68

Sub-total	£523.66
Discount/surcharge	£0.00
Tax value (VAT @ 20%)	£104.73
TOTAL	**£628.39**

Payment details

Term: within **30 days of invoice date**
Method: **Bank Transfer** (details below)

Account name:	Axle Translation Ltd.
Account number:	12345678
Sort-code:	12-34-56
IBAN:	GB29 ABCD 1234 5612 3456 78
BIC:	ABCDGB12

Figure 4.4 Specimen invoice

As the prompts above reveal, there is a large quantity of data produced during the course of a project. While no official categorisation of resources is proposed in the ISO, it is reasonable to assume that most files will fall under two broad categories: files related to the translation itself (including the source and target files, as well as other linguistic resources such as style guides, TMs, glossaries, etc.), and files relating to the management of the project in broad terms (including agreements, financial documentation such as purchase orders and invoices, and general project records). For the purposes of discussion here, let us name these records **task documentation** and **administrative documentation**, respectively.

Administrative Documentation

Beginning with **administrative documentation** – arguably the easier of the two to deal with in terms of file management – all LSPs will have systems to track and store project documentation. In some cases, on the 'boutique LSP' end of the spectrum, these will range from a system based on spreadsheets and carefully organised folder structures to store relevant files all the way up to complex and often bespoke content management systems. Much of the detail in terms of what is stored in these systems has already been covered indirectly through many of the considerations set out in Chapter 2 on pre-production. For instance, the client–LSP agreement, purchase orders, email threads, invoices, remittance advices (documenting payments made by one party to another), payment receipts, and other administrative documentation will all likely be preserved for a certain period of time depending on the relevant accounting and administrative regulations in the country of operation. In the UK, for instance, financial documentation must be kept for six years from the end of the last company financial year to which the records relate. Data security is another consideration here: processes, repositories, and policies need to be in place with regard to the storage and protection of all project-related documentation (including task documentation below).

The project management system (which might be an off-the-shelf system such as Plunet or XTRF, for instance) will also preserve information on the project itself, such as project identification codes, client names, details on instructions, files and file types, language pairs, the linguists involved in each stage, QA logs and other quality-related documentation, etc. The system will also likely have a financial module that covers not only the charges invoiced to the client, but also the charges invoiced by the vendors to the LSP itself, therefore enabling the LSP to arrive at a 'balance' (i.e. profit or loss) for the individual project. Email management and communications may also be integrated into the system, or indeed handled in a completely separate system such as a Microsoft Exchange Server in Outlook. All of these information systems will be present in all LSPs to some degree, but it is impossible to be specific about the details in a textbook such as this, as the processes and IT systems will differ with each LSP.

? Why is it important to keep such documentation?

There are, however, some common features and a – hopefully obvious – rationale as to why this is common practice and, in fact, mandated in ISO 17100:2015. It all ultimately boils down to accountability and traceability. As per the PRINCE2 framework, record keeping 'permit[s] any future audit

100 *The Translation Project Lifecycle*

of the project management team's decisions, actions and performance' (Office of Government Commerce, 2018, p. 268). If a client comes back to the LSP with a complaint about a project, an LSP representative (e.g. another PM, perhaps even after the PM who handled the project has left the LSP) can locate the details of the project in the records (using the project code) and find out exactly what processes the project went through (via the work breakdown structure records), who did what (via the task assignments), what was said to whom (via email threads), what monies changed hands (via the financial records), and even whether a similar complaint had been made about a previous project (via records on previous projects for the same client), and therefore whether the same vendors had already been forewarned about the same issues re-occurring (again via email threads and translation guidelines). Such complaints (and feedback more generally) or other unexpected problems that might have occurred during a project should be fully documented and even added to the risk register, if relevant and if maintained at the LSP (see Chapter 10 on risk).

Task Documentation

Turning to **task documentation**, translation projects are necessarily messy in nature. Even the simplest of projects can generate a large quantity of task and administrative documentation. As projects increase in size, however, the number of task-related files also increases considerably (as do the concomitant security concerns, as mentioned above). Such task-related files can include

- source texts and target texts;
- different ST versions;
- different TT versions, such as revision, review and proofreading files, and sometimes more than one of each;
- client feedback and vendor feedback (e.g. reviser' feedback on the translator);
- reference files;
- translation memories;
- term bases and glossaries in other formats;
- style guides;
- task-specific instructions; and
- other miscellaneous linguistic resources.

To touch briefly on each of these bullet points, in addition to there potentially being numerous STs and TTs within a multi-file project, there can also be numerous versions of the ST(s) too, as the client may decide to update sections or correct mistakes once the translation process has already been set in motion. Likewise, such updates may also need to be made to the TT after the initial translation has been submitted. There is then the question of all the various revision, review and proofreading files, not to mention the fact that these tasks (and indeed the translation itself) could be split between multiple vendors before being stitched back together into one or more final documents. As noted at the start of this chapter, different forms of feedback will also be collected during and after a project from, and for, different parties. The other bullet points pertain more to resources: reference files of various types, translation memories and term bases (or other glossaries), style guides, instructions and other resources, all of which can be many and various.

There are of course benefits to retaining all such documentation, again for the purposes of traceability, but decisions will need to be made by PMs (or potentially by senior management) as to which files need to be retained and which do not. In terms of the files specific to the translation itself (namely the ST, TT, and all versions thereof), it may be wise to retain all such documentation in the short term, but then have a clear policy whereby certain documents are deleted after a certain amount of time (subject to any specific obligations; see sub-section below). It is likely that any queries or problems with a translation are likely to arrive in the PM's inbox within a short time of its submission to the client (likely within a matter of days, or weeks at most). In rare cases, some problems are identified later, but such cases are the minority. To offer some indicative figures, it would be wise to retain all ST and TT versions for six months as a minimum, after which point some of the extraneous 'version history' documentation could be deleted (while still retaining the final translation and source text, of course). For many LSPs, however, documents tend to be stored for much longer and then deleted as a batch after a pre-defined (relatively long) period of time following project completion (e.g. five years) – again, notwithstanding any specific obligations in this regard.

For linguistic resources, these offer a different set of possibilities (and challenges). As will be widely known to both students of translation and seasoned practitioners alike, the main purpose of **translation memories (TMs)** is to allow the user to 'recycle' or 'leverage' a previous translation unit, either where it offers an exact match (a 100% match or even a context/ 101% match, depending on the software) or some degree of similarity (a fuzzy match) (Bowker, 2002, p. 92–107ff). In theory, if the same client were to return in the future with a similar text on a similar subject matter, the TM could be leveraged not only to speed up the translation process and improve quality, but also – potentially – to reduce costs (although there are some ethical questions that arise in connection with this practice). Therefore, ensuring that TMs are fully updated with the final (approved) version of a translation upon completion of a project is very important to the future functioning of the LSP. For projects hosted on a server, this process is relatively straightforward. But in addition to updating the TMs, there also needs to be regular maintenance or 'cleaning' of the translation units stored within the TMs to ensure that they operate as smoothly and efficiently as possible.

102 *The Translation Project Lifecycle*

Figure 4.5 Example of 'cleaning' a TM

Such cleaning typically involves removing duplicate entries from the master TM (especially if the entries offer inconsistent translations), removing 'junk' entries such as solitary numbers or URLs, clearing tags from the TM units, and carrying out spot checks on translation quality (e.g. checking consistency of US versus UK spelling). Regex (or regular expression) coding can prove very useful for this task, if the PM is conversant with it.

The aim of these tasks is to ensure that the TM returns accurate matches quickly and does not offer 'false positive' matches where possible. All of this is possible with appropriate TM management (on all of these points, see Mitchell-Schuitevoerder, 2020, p. 45–48). Figure 4.5 provides a simple example of how a TM could be cleaned. The two highlighted segments (6224 and 6260) can be removed from the TM entirely, given that they are URLs only, and the top five segments (1269, 1271, 1277, 1280, and 2924) all include URLs within the segment body, none of which need to be present in the TM, as this could in fact inhibit fuzzy-level matching. The initial section numbers (5, 6, 7, and 8) can be removed, and the segments could even be split so that there is only a single unit for Главная страница / Main page, then four separate entries with the subheadings (Press centre, Database on currency rates, Interbank market rates, Statistics). Doing so may prove more effective for sub-segment matching and fragment assembly in particular. In the example, taken from memoQ, there is also a button to remove all tags, which would be strongly advisable in units such as these.

The discussion of how to manage TMs also raises the question of *how many* TMs should be maintained. On an LSP level, it may seem attractive to combine all smaller TMs in a single language pair into one giant, master TM in order to maximise the chances of TM matches. However, there is considerable benefit also to maintaining smaller, domain-specific and client-specific TMs. A master TM could prove to be very large in terms of file size and searchability (slowing down CAT tool performance) and will inevitably offer a large number of 'false positive' matches where the solution is not appropriate in the relevant context. It is at this point that CAT tool functionalities allowing users to prioritise certain TMs over others, and to specify certain TMs as 'read only', can prove extremely useful in terms of the way in which TMs are managed and subsequently allocated to other projects. TM management can be a time-consuming process, and different LSPs will have their own processes to address this concern. For some, it will be a task to be undertaken after every project; for others, it may be undertaken on a periodic basis (e.g. monthly, quarterly); and for a small number, it may not even be undertaken at all.

The above discussion on TM management is equally applicable to **term bases (TBs)**, which allow users to harmonise and re-use frequently occurring terminology within and across projects for the same client and for different clients. While TBs do not offer the same degree of benefits in terms of speed of translation and cost, they certainly aid quality and, if managed appropriately, can contribute to a substantial reduction in errors and client complaints, especially in highly specialist domains. Just like TMs, at the end of a project, or on a periodic basis, the TB needs to be collated into one master version (if applicable) or, at the very least, to be cleaned and checked. Checks on TBs are often more straightforward, as, unlike TMs, entries are typically added to TBs manually, either during translation itself or prior to translation, by a dedicated project terminologist. Therefore, issues relating to the storage of numbers and URLs do not apply, but there are wider consistency issues, especially if multiple vendors have been contributing to the TB throughout a project (and even more so if the TB is hosted on a project server). The most common inconsistencies that are likely to require correction involve

- the capitalisation of terms (non-capitalisation being preferable unless there is a specific linguistic reason);
- nouns being stored in their 'root' form (i.e. typically singular and nominative case, for case-inflected languages);
- verbs also being stored in their infinitive form (i.e. 'play' instead of 'played'; however, many TB tools allow multiple entries to be stored, allowing for the storage of irregular forms, e.g. 'sell' alongside 'sold');
- the use or non-use of wildcards in certain tools (e.g. 'roj|o' ['red' in Spanish] allowing 'rojo' [masculine singular], 'roja' [feminine singular], 'rojos' [masculine plural], and 'rojas' [feminine plural], as well as other less desirable matches due to the nature of wildcards); and
- the storage of metadata (e.g. part of speech, definition, example of use, etc.).

Some LSPs may stipulate a minimal level of TB entry, requiring not only the source and target term but also the part of speech (e.g. noun, adjective, verb, etc.) and even relevant sources or context. In most cases, this is not likely to be necessary, but the range of options open to LSPs in terms of what is stored in a TB, and the linguistic form in which it is stored, will all have a bearing on the utility and usability of the TB itself in future projects. Decisions therefore need to be made by PMs (and senior management too) – formally or otherwise – on what might constitute a permissible entry in a TB. The cleaning of the TB itself will then use these as a guide to ensure, for instance, that terms are not capitalised and do not use wildcards, and that nouns and verbs are in their root form, in order to standardise the widely varying practices among vendors themselves. Standardised entries mean more predictable matching within CAT tools, both for TBs and for TMs too.

The points above all raise a number of ethical questions, none of which can be addressed at any length here, sadly, but are important to note in passing at least. For instance, who has ownership of the entries within a TM or TB? Can a TM or TB entry produced as part of a project for Client A be used for a project undertaken for Client B without Client A's consent? Should the vendor who produced the TM or TB entries be paid for any subsequent use? These debates essentially boil down to questions of copyright and intellectual property rights, which have been subject to relatively little attention in translation studies literature, despite the prevalence of TM and TB use, sharing, and re-application to future projects in the industry at large. However, some indicative reading in this regard can be found in Topping (2000), Gow (2007), and Moorkens and Lewis (2019). What is important for LSPs, however, is that a clear policy is in place as to how linguistic resources are used for future projects and, more importantly, that this policy is communicated clearly to vendors and clients and, if necessary, built into any terms and conditions or contractual agreements between the various parties.

Needs and Wants

All of the records and documentation noted above need to be maintained in an organised manner across the various information systems, such that they can be searched easily and relevant project details brought up quickly to resolve any potential difficulties. However, records should also not be kept forever (and the merits of keeping some types of records long term are questionable, too, as alluded to when discussing the 'version history' of TTs). That notwithstanding, from a pragmatic perspective, first of all, LSPs all have a process in place for project archiving, whereby projects are relocated from the 'main' repository for active or recently completed projects into a long-term storage repository. Such repositories will also take many forms.

In terms of the more administrative types of documents, such records do not often need to be actively archived, as the data tend to be text based and therefore occupy very little storage space. If the database also integrates .pdf versions of key administrative documents such as purchase orders, signed agreements, and invoices, for example, these too are often compressed when added to the database and only decompressed when they need to be opened. As such, these records rarely need any active archiving. For the task documentation, however, and STs and TTs in particular, these files will often be either left in a carefully managed folder structure or relocated to a separate repository built on an equally well-managed folder structure. In either case, clear file naming and folder management practices are essential so that all LSP employees know how to find relevant files quickly if needed. For resources (including entire projects) based primarily in CAT tools, these present different challenges for archiving. Some tools, such as memoQ, even offer a dedicated archiving function that compresses all files relating to a project into a single file (in memoQ, this is a .mqarch file). For resources such as TMs and TBs, whether these are archived for long-term storage is very much dependent on how they may be used in future. If they will not be used again (or indeed cannot be used in future due to some contractual arrangement, see below), one might question the utility of long-term storage. However, if long-term storage is required, it would be advisable to convert them first into a widely compatible file format, in case file compatibility changes in the future or even if the LSP decides to stop using a particular tool. For instance, instead of storing Trados Studio TMs in .sdltm format, it would make more sense to convert them to the industry standard (and smaller, in terms of file size) .tmx format; likewise, a memoQ TB in .mtb format would be better stored as a .tbx file for the same reasons.

From a different, practical perspective, it is always worth bearing in mind the importance of regular backups. On the one hand, on a local level, CAT tools in particular tend to be prone to corrupting files (TMs and TBs especially), so regular backups are important for this purpose alone. But on the other hand, looking more long term from a post-production angle, backups in various forms (on-site servers, cloud backup, and off-site servers) are essential to protect what are essentially vast assets compiled and maintained by LSPs on the back of however many years of translation projects. To lose such assets due to fire or hacking, for example, would be a significant loss that could take a large amount of time to recover from.

While all of the above are technically optional – there is, after all, no obligation to maintain archives of past projects – there is often one aspect of record keeping and archiving that is mandatory. In particularly sensitive projects, typically in the legal domain, many client–LSP agreements will specify certain confidentiality and data protection clauses, an example of which is as follows:

> [Party A] agrees to keep all Restricted Access Confidential Information under the highest practicable level of internal security, which at a minimum shall include keeping such information in locked drawers or files with and in password protected documents or computer files, in each case accessible only by Authorised Recipients.

Such agreements can even specify certain obligations regarding data archiving and deletion:

[Party A] agrees to return to [Party B], and to cause its Representatives to return to [Party B], not later than the end of the Projects, all Confidential Information received or created in the course of the Project, without retaining any copy thereof, including, to the extent practicable, expunging all such materials from any computer, word processor or other electronic storage device containing such information.

Such clauses are legally binding, of course, but raise interesting questions for PMs surrounding future work for a particular client and, in particular, the use of resources such as TMs and TBs. If it is the LSP's practice, for instance, to make use of master TMs and TBs within broad domains and language pairs, the PM will have to strip out any units added to the TMs and TBs during the project. This is one of the benefits of adopting a TM/TB usage model whereby master TMs/TBs are maintained for certain projects and then supplemented by project- or client-specific TMs/TBs as required. Such an approach makes it easier to manage the long-term use and storage of such data and compliance with any contractual arrangements. That said, there is a case to be made for PMs discussing with clients the advantages of retaining linguistic data longer term, and this is yet another instance where client education forms an important part of a PM's work.

In summary, effective record keeping and archiving practices are essential to the smooth operation of an LSP. Due to the vast amounts of data handled by LSPs on a daily basis, ranging from administrative documentation through to highly specialised linguistic resources such as TMs and TBs, each of these documents needs to be handled differently and stored in different ways not only according to practices and processes determined by the LSP's senior management but also by contractual arrangements with the client and even, sometimes, with vendors. Nonetheless, good file management is fundamental and helps to guarantee the provision of a high-quality service by facilitating the traceability and transparency of the pre-production, production, and even post-production processes within an LSP.

Post-mortem

The final stage of a translation project is optional, and whether it is necessary or not would depend mainly on the size and importance of the project. A **post-mortem** (literally *after death* in Latin) is an analytical exercise conducted to retrospectively assess the good and bad aspects of one or more recently completed projects (Matis, 2014, p. 206). The PRINCE2 project management framework refers to 'evaluat[ing] the project' in terms of 'an assessment of the results of the project against the expected benefits in the business case', 'a review of team performance', 'a review of the project's products', and 'a review of what went well, what went badly and any recommendations', as well as evaluating risks and quality issues and documenting any 'lessons learned' (Office of Government Commerce,

2018, pp. 266–267). The PMBOK also refers to updating operational and support documentation and fully documenting any 'lessons learned' (Project Management Institute, 2017, p. 128).

Project post-mortems will usually take the form of a meeting, either in person or remotely, between a number of stakeholders involved in the project. Typically, this will include the project management team (any PMs involved in managing the project, plus any direct line managers) and one or more client representatives, but it can also include vendors in certain cases as well as LSP senior management, depending on the nature of the project and the likely 'mood' of the post-mortem (i.e. positive or negative). Clients may specifically request a post-mortem, especially if the project was unsuccessful or they were particularly dissatisfied with the end results. Likewise, an internal post-mortem can be held between LSP senior management and the PM team if, for example, the project failed to cover its costs or the required profit margin was not secured.

The aim of the post-mortem is to identify both the positives and negatives of a project, to make those involved in the project aware of any errors or issues that occurred (and could have been prevented), and to delineate ways to prevent such problems re-occurring in the future. In short, as the quotations from PRINCE2 and the PMBOK show above, it's about 'lessons learned'. That notwithstanding, it is crucial to understand that a project does not have to be a failure for a post-mortem to be carried out; indeed, highly successful projects can also result in a post-mortem meeting precisely with a view to trying to identify *why* it was so successful and to promote similar good practices in future projects.

Once the post-mortem is complete, the meeting may or may not be documented in writing (e.g. minutes) or written up as a report, again depending on the circumstances. However, regardless of whether the meeting itself is formalised, it is always good practice to note down specific lessons learned in, for example, a risk register, or to build good practices into the standard operating procedure for PMs, or indeed to implement more specific improvements to project glossaries, for example. If no action is carried out after a post-mortem, then it calls into question the very purpose of holding the meeting in the first place.

* * *

To summarise, the aggregation of marginal gains concept, presented in Box 4.1, is a useful conceptual tool to keep in mind throughout the post-production process. While the tasks and purpose of post-production may not be nearly as apparent as those of the pre-production and production stages, there is a strong case for arguing that post-production is equally important to the longevity of an LSP's operations by highlighting good practices to continue in future projects and identifying problems that need to be eliminated from the LSP's processes. Much of this stage

108 *The Translation Project Lifecycle*

boils down to effective communication (as with many things in project management, it could be argued). On the one hand, the success of the PM in educating the client as to what services are required in the early stages of the project will likely be judged in the post-production phase once the production is complete and the PM can look back on the various stages of the project to determine their success or otherwise. These evaluations need to be carried out by PMs themselves, but insights should also be collected from the clients and vendors so that feedback can be shared in all directions with a view to identifying both good and bad practices for future operations.

As with all things in project management, the end of one project will typically signal the beginning of another or the shifting of attention to another in-progress project. So begins the endless cycle of pre-production, production, and post-production to satisfy the persistent demand for translation services.

* * *

Topics for Discussion and Assignments

1. Using the aggregation of marginal gains principle, try applying this to your own translation practice in practical translation classes and assignments. In your next piece of formative assessed work (e.g. weekly translation homework), identify one very tangible and actionable error that you have made (e.g. comma splicing) and make sure that you understand how to avoid the error in future. In your second piece of work, ensure that you do not make the same error again. When you receive the feedback for the second piece of work, select another tangible and actionable error to eliminate from your third piece of work and so on, each time adding one more error to the list of errors to eliminate. Are you ever criticised for the same error again? Do your marks improve (even if only slightly)?
2. With the help of your instructor, organise a short, simulated translation project where each student performs specific roles (project manager, translator, reviser, etc.). Complete a simple (or complex) translation project set by your instructor and managed by the project manager(s) using the principles in Chapters 2, 3, and 4. At the end of the project, hold a post-mortem meeting. What went well? What could be improved?
3. Look at the feedback provided to you for some of your practical translation homework or assessments. How have your instructors written the feedback? In what tone is it written? Have they categorised or described your mistakes in a certain way? Are there any good practices that you could carry over into project management practice or into your practice working as a reviser, for instance?

Further Reading

Section VIII of Matis (2014) provides a general overview of the 'project completion' stage, from delivery of the files to feedback, invoicing, the post-mortem, and archiving, offering similar (and in some cases contrasting) perspectives to the content in this chapter.

Looking ahead to a topic that is touched upon later in this book, Risku et al. (2016) is a fascinating article on how views between clients and translators differ and how they communicate. While it addresses project management indirectly, much of the article relates to the communication process and how different parties have different expectations and perspectives on the translation process and end product and how these discrepancies are handled. It therefore offers some unique perspectives, based on primary research, which can play directly into project management and the negotiation of feedback between clients and vendors.

References

Bowker, L. (2002). *Computer-aided translation technology: A practical introduction*. University of Ottawa Press.

Gow, F. (2007). You must remember this: The copyright conundrum of "translation memory" databases. *Canadian Journal of Law and Technology*, 6(3), 175–192.

International Organization for Standardization. (2015). *Translation services – Requirements for translation services (ISO 17100:2015)*. International Organization for Standardization.

Matis, N. (2014). *How to manage your translation projects*. Retrieved from www.translation-project-management.com/en

Mitchell-Schuitevoerder, R. (2020). *A project-based approach to translation technology*. Routledge.

Moorkens, J., & Lewis, D. (2019). Copyright and the reuse of translation as data. In M. O'Hagan (Ed.), *The Routledge handbook of translation and technology* (pp. 469–481). Routledge.

Mossop, B. (2014). *Revising and editing for translators* (3rd ed.). Routledge.

Office of Government Commerce. (2018). *Managing successful projects with PRINCE2 2017 edition* (6th ed.). The Stationery Office Ltd.

Project Management Institute. (2017). *A guide to the Project Management Body Of Knowledge (PMBOK® guide)* (6th ed.). Project Management Institute, Inc.

Risku, H., Pein-Weber, C., & Milošević, J. (2016). 'The task of the translator': Comparing the views of the client and the translator. *International Journal of Communication*, 10, 989–1008.

Topping, S. (2000). Sharing translation database information: Considerations for developing an ethical and viable exchange of data. *Multilingual Computing and Technology*, 11(5), 59–61.

Part II
Triangles, Diamonds, and Stars
Evaluating Translation Project Constraints

5 Timescales

Learning outcomes:

- Draw up work breakdown structures for a project to identify key project stages and milestones
- Sequence project stages appropriately and evaluate the approximate duration of different tasks
- Use appropriate tools to draw up and visualise project schedules
- Understand some of the factors that can have a positive and negative impact on timescales in project management
- Consider the role of time more generally in translation project management

As discussed in the Introduction to this textbook, a project is defined as a 'temporary endeavour undertaken to create a unique product, service, or result' (Project Management Institute, 2017) or a 'temporary organization that is created for the purpose of delivering one or more business products according to an agreed business case' (Office of Government Commerce, 2018, p. 8). The evident foregrounding of the word **temporary** is noteworthy in both the PMBOK Guide and the PRINCE2 method: it is an endeavour that is limited in time. The entire operation of an LSP from the moment of its founding to the day of its wind-up would not be described as a project, but the succession of individual, unique endeavours with clearly defined start and end points that make up its *raison d'être* are precisely that: projects. Hence, the strict management of time between that start and end point is an essential component of a project manager's work and a fundamental constraint on other factors such as cost, quality, and risk.

'Time waits for no man', or so goes the old adage. Time is widely recognised to be the most critical aspect of translation project management (Dunne, 2011, p. 120), as we can neither slow nor stop the steady ticking by of the second hand, nor rewind time if we find ourselves in need of additional hours in the day. We will have all likely seen examples in the press of large-scale, chronically overdue projects – typically megaprojects in the civil engineering sphere.

And while the scale is vastly different in the translation industry, the costs and implications of delay can be just as severe, if not more so in terms of business goodwill. We can add or remove costs in a project, we can change the scope or quality of a project, and benefits and risks can be balanced in various ways, but time is the one constraint over which we have zero *direct* control.

The Project Management Institute dedicates an entire chapter of its PMBOK Guide to 'project schedule management', and while we will not delve into this topic in anywhere near the same depth here, the main processes advocated for schedule management provide a useful framework to structure this chapter on time. In particular, the PMBOK Guide refers to **defining** activities, **sequencing** activities, **estimating durations** of activities, **developing** a schedule, and **controlling** a schedule (Project Management Institute, 2017, p. 173). At the risk of stating the obvious, projects are managed using **schedules**, but schedules perform a dual role: they allow a project manager to plan ahead and model the future (ideal) course of a project's processes and component parts in the pre-production phase, and they provide a necessary tool to monitor the progress of a project's execution over time in the production phrase. They also play a retrospective, evaluative function in the post-production phase, in particular in a project post-mortem. This chapter is broken down into a discussion of how schedules are managed and the factors that can affect project schedules.

Schedule Management

Some of the tasks and processes described in the sub-sections below delve into the minutiae of schedule management processes and, as such, might seem to be excessive in scale or scope, or even needless to some readers. The latter claim may well be true for the large numbers of straightforward translation projects, such as a translation of a birth certificate or a simple business email. However, beneath the simplistic façade of a mere birth certificate translation lie precisely the same complex processes; the only difference is that many of these processes will have been fully internalised, automated, and streamlined by an experienced project manager when such a simple project arrives in their inbox. The lessons outlined in this chapter can be scaled from the miniscule to the massive, and the application of these principles by project managers remains the same, whether conscious or unconscious. The aim therefore is to tease out the complexities of these processes, even though they may be the bread and butter of an experienced project manager, for there will always come a time when a sufficiently large or complex project requires more careful planning than others.

Defining Activities

Perhaps the key aspect of schedule management is a clear definition of precisely what tasks need to be carried out for any given project. The most common tool used in project management circles for this purpose is a **work breakdown structure (WBS)** (see Project Management Institute, 2017, p. 156–162); the PRINCE2 method refers to a 'product breakdown structure' (see Office of Government Commerce, 2018, p. 98), which differs only in that it refers to products and deliverables instead of all work activities. The purpose and content of a WBS is closely aligned with the scope and quality constraints, for the very nature of the work that needs to be carried out as part of a project will be determined by precisely which deliverables are required and what quality requirements have been stipulated for them.

For any given translation project – say, for example, the translation of a fairly standard sales agreement between two companies – there is far more work involved than translation alone; moreover, the work involved will take place across the entire project lifecycle, from pre-production through production to post-production. Using this sales agreement as an example:

? What 'work activities' or tasks do you think would be involved in this project?
? How might the work involved change depending on the quality requirements of the project?

With reference to the first question, we could break down the work into lifecycle stages. In the pre-production stage, it might require content analysis (both for word count and for linguistic reasons), the preparation of a quotation for the client, the preparation of CAT tool resources (translation memories, term bases derived from glossaries), the preparation of the project in the chosen CAT tool, the development of a project schedule, and various other smaller tasks. In the production stage, it would require outsourcing to a translator (some might place this within the pre-production stage), the translation itself, and – depending on the level of quality checks required – revision, review, and proofreading. In the post-production stage, the project manager would need to generate the finalised target document from the CAT tool, update translation memories and term bases for future projects, deliver the agreed deliverables to the client, invoice the client, and carry out any closing administration. These are only a handful of the tasks that could feasibly be involved in this project and would form part of a comprehensive WBS. The level of detail that any such WBS goes into would be dictated by the complexity of the project (the number of files, the number of different linguistic and non-linguistic tasks, specialist delivery formats, etc.).

However, identifying these activities in a WBS is only the first half of this process; we now need to *define* them. Take the 'translation' activity, for example. How might the definition for translation in the case of this sales agreement differ from a marketing brochure ('for publication') or a business email ('for reference only')? Each stage of the project needs to have a clear definition in terms of project requirements and scope (see Project Management Institute, 2017, pp. 147–148 and p. 154, respectively). However, that is not to say that these time-consuming definitions are a requirement each and every time a new project is handed to a project manager. One of the obvious advantages of the translation industry is that, while details differ in every case, there is usually a degree of similarity from one translation project to the next. Once a clear definition of the activities has been drawn up for translators on 'translation for publication purposes', for instance, or translations that are for a specific recurring client, even, these definitions (or sets of instructions or procedures) can easily be recycled for future projects, or at least tweaked and adjusted as per the requirements of each individual project. Needless to say, the more specialist the service offered by the LSP (for instance, an LSP specialising in legal translations only), the easier it will be to pre-define and re-use commonly occurring activity definitions.

Try now putting this first step into practice:

?   Prepare a WBS for one of the case studies on the TS Portal.

Sequencing Activities

Identifying all of the activities involved in a project is arguably half the battle, for, if all of the tasks are properly identified and defined, it is far easier to address the matter of scheduling without the risk of suddenly realising, further down the line, that a key activity, or worse pre-requisite activity, has been omitted. The sequencing stage is an important preliminary to the estimation of how long activities will take, as it forms a crucial part of project managers understanding which activities must occur prior to other activities, and which activities could occur simultaneously.

Some of the work activities identified in a WBS will exhibit internal **dependency**: this means that one project activity is dependent on another (Office of Government Commerce, 2018, pp. 109–110). To provide a basic example, the *check* stage of the translation process is dependent on the *translation* stage having already been completed, at least in part; the translator cannot start to check his or her work before he or she has actually translated some of the text. Similarly, in the pre-production stage, a project manager cannot conduct a content analysis and generate a word count, among other things, until the client has supplied the source text. These are just two of the four types of logical dependencies that can exist between project activities (see Box 5.1).

Project dependencies are closely related to project **milestones** (Office of Government Commerce, 2018, p. 113): 'an event on a schedule which marks the completion of key activities' (see also Project Management Institute, 2017, p. 186). In a translation project, it might be the point at which a client signs off on the client–LSP agreement (or purchase order), giving the green light for the project to proceed; it might be the completion of the translation stage; or it might be the completion of the typesetting, meaning

> **Box 5.1 Types of logical relationships and dependencies**
>
> Viewing project dependencies in terms of Activity B being dependent on Activity A oversimplifies the situation somewhat. The examples already given show that two variants on this exist: the translator cannot start to check his or her work until at least *some* text has already been translated, and, in the other example, the project manager cannot conduct a content analysis until the files have been received. These reflect just two of the four types of dependencies or logical relationships identified by the Project Management Institute (2017, p. 190):
>
> (1) **Finish-to-Start (FS)**: where Activity B cannot *start* until Activity A has *finished*;
> (2) **Finish-to-Finish (FF)**: where Activity B cannot *finish* until Activity A has *finished*;
> (3) **Start-to-Start (SS)**: where Activity B cannot *start* until Activity A has *started*; and
> (4) **Start-to-Finish (SF)**: where Activity B cannot *finish* until Activity A has *started*.
>
> > ? Can you think of examples of activities for each of these types of logical relationships in the translation project lifecycle?
> > ? What examples can you identify for each of these logical relationships among the case studies provided on the TS Portal?

that the finished product is ready to be sent to the printers. Identifying key milestones is a useful tool for monitoring schedule compliance, but they start to lose their value if too many milestones are defined in a project, especially in smaller, short-term projects. Another related term that is important in the sequencing of activities is a project's **critical path**. A critical path is 'the sequence of activities that represents the longest path through a project, which determines the shortest possible project duration' (Project Management Institute, 2017, p. 210); in simple terms, it refers to the minimum critical activities that must take place throughout a project before it can be considered complete. The simple milestone example above provides a basic localised illustration of this concept: 'revision' can only take place once 'translation' and 'checking' have taken place before it. However, other simultaneous tasks could be carried out at the same time, perhaps by the project manager. Communicating updated glossaries to multiple translators throughout a project may be a desirable activity to promote quality, but it is by no means a *sine qua non* of a project's successful completion. In more complex projects, there may be multiple critical paths, perhaps following

118   *Evaluating Translation Project Constraints*

different files making up a project or different 'batches' of files, both of which may be distributed among multiple translators.

Again, let us put into practice this activity sequencing stage:

? Using the WBS that you prepared above, sequence the activities from start to finish.
? How would the complexity of sequencing change for one of the other case studies on the TS Portal?

Estimating Durations of Activities

As discussed in Chapter 2, different types of linguistic and non-linguistic tasks are not only costed using different units or metrics (words, hours, pages) but are also scheduled using different performance metrics. For each of the main work activities identified in the WBS, the project manager will need to estimate the amount of time to allocate. In most cases, these estimates will be based on 'throughput' metrics supplied by the vendors themselves (some experienced translators might be able to translate 2,500 words per day, whereas others can manage 4,000 words per day when working in their specialised domain with the benefit of technological support). For each task type, different throughput metrics will need to be used: a reviewer can review more words in a day than a translator can translate, for example; the throughput of a DTP specialist is measured in pages; the time that an interpreter is available for might be measured in hours, half-days, or days; an audiovisual translator might measure his or her workload in minutes. But beyond these simple mathematical calculations alone, which are dependent on the nature of the task itself, there is one element of estimating activity durations that is fundamental to the success of a project schedule: **leeway**. In critical path approaches, this is also referred to as **float**. Both of these terms refer to the amount of time by which an activity could be extended without it affecting the overall time involved in a project process (or the project as a whole). We will explore this estimation stage in two contexts: (1) when a client approaches an LSP with a new project *without* a specified deadline (the easier situation); and (2) when a client approaches an LSP with a new project *with* a specified deadline (the more difficult situation).

In case (1), the lack of a specified deadline affords the project manager a considerable degree of freedom because – provided that the WBS defines the activities appropriately – the calculations involved in ascertaining the required amount of time are very straightforward and will usually be based on metrics specified by the vendors themselves (as noted above). Moreover, if no deadline exists *per se*, the simplest organisational approach to the project will be to outsource the translation to a single translator (irrespective of length), a single reviser, etc. (depending on the level of quality checks required). In case (2), however, these same calculations, based around a translator's daily throughput metrics, may very well dictate that more than one vendor needs to be assigned to each stage. This occurrence, in turn, raises a whole new set of questions: do I, as a project manager, split the translation stage across a large number of translators to complete this stage as quickly as possible, allowing more time for a *single* reviser to work on the translation (thereby improving consistency, quality, etc.)? Or do I split the translation among a lower number of vendors (requiring more time for the translation stage), in turn requiring a larger number of revisers (due to the shorter remaining timeframe for revision)? There is no right or wrong answer to this question (and, indeed, throwing more resources at a project can actually have a detrimental effect on its outcome; see 'Factors Affecting Project Schedules' below). In essence, the answer will come from a combination of the project's agreed scope and quality (and client expectations) and the time available, which will dictate whether the project is 'front-end heavy' or not.

Those quandaries aside, the main factor that must be built into a project's time estimates, without fail, is leeway. In case (1) above, where a deadline is not specified by the client, the project manager will need to pay particular heed to the Goldilocks principle (see Box 5.2) so as not to deter a potential client. But even in case (2), where flexibility might seem to be much more constrained, leeway still needs to be an essential aspect of time estimation. The PRINCE2 handbook offers a number of helpful tips for project managers calculating time estimates for a project schedule (Office of Government Commerce, 2018, p. 110), which I have adapted to the specifics of translation project management:

- work on the assumption that vendors are only productive for 80% of the time. For a translator who claims to translate 3,000 words per day, it may be wise to assume, in the interests of caution, that they can only translate 2,400 words per day;
- assume that vendors working on multiple projects simultaneously (as is often the case in the translation industry) will take longer to complete their tasks due to the complexities of switching back and forth between different tasks, each with their own requirements;
- vendors tend to be overly optimistic and *under*estimate how long a particular task will take (for similar findings in a software development context, see Hill et al., 2000), even if they are aware that previous tasks have generally taken longer than planned. This phenomenon is referred to as the 'planning fallacy' (Buehler et al., 1994). When the tasks involved are particularly complex, this phenomenon is also referred to as Hofstadter's Law (Hofstadter, 1979);
- rely on the throughput estimates provided by the vendors themselves (i.e. translators, reviewers, proofreaders) instead of 'industry-standard' metrics, such as 3,000 words per day for translation;
- always make provisions for unexpected events ('leeway' or 'float'); and

- make sure that any assumptions made by the project manager (e.g. the assumption that the translator can translate 3,000 words per day) are communicated effectively to the relevant parties so that, in this example, the translator can correct the project manager if the assumption is unrealistic.

One of the key findings that starts to become apparent in project management literature, however, is the reliance on experience and prior knowledge of similar projects in the past. Henry et al. (2007), for example, provide a stimulating empirical analysis of the ways in which organisational knowledge or 'memory' influences the ability to generate effective (and accurate) predictions of costs and schedules. Their meta-analyses show that, while various project management estimating practices hold considerable value, there is still a substantial role played by experience and prior knowledge.

Box 5.2 The Goldilocks principle

For those unfamiliar with the British storytelling tradition, the Goldilocks principle is a commonly used analogy to the children's story *Goldilocks and the Three Bears*, in which a young girl – named Goldilocks – happens upon a house in the middle of a forest, belonging to three bears (a father bear, mother bear, and baby bear). Finding some porridge on the dining table, she tastes some from each bowl, finding one to be too hot, another too cold, and the final bowl 'just right'. She then makes similar comments about the comfort of three chairs and three beds before the bears return home to find her asleep in one of the beds. The tale typically ends at this point with little mention of Goldilocks's fate...

While this principle has similar applications across a variety of fields (including cognitive psychology, astrobiology, economics, and statistics), in the context of time management it refers to a timescale that is 'just right': not too long and not too short. When shopping around for quotations from different suppliers, clients will typically opt for the shortest delivery timeframe. However, if the LSP proposes a date that seems too short, it might seem unrealistic and cause the client to consider whether the quality of the product or service is likely to be compromised. Equally, if the LSP errs too much on the side of caution and proposes an excessively long timeframe, the client may be unwilling to wait without good reason. Hence, the Goldilocks principle, when applied to project schedules, refers to the 'sweet spot' between too short and too long, playing off client perceptions and trust.

While these findings are not especially encouraging for the novice project manager, they do nonetheless show the importance of supportive hierarchical structures at LSPs based around prior translation project know-how. Some LSPs may also keep records of individual vendors' performance metrics, or indeed more generalised averages for all projects (perhaps broken down into different language pairs); this is referred to as 'comparative' or 'reference class' estimating (Office of Government Commerce, 2018, p. 117).

Developing and Monitoring Schedules

We finally arrive at the point where our schedule is ready to be developed in full, having first broken down the specific work activities making up the project (together with definitions of those activities), organised the activities into a logical sequence from start to finish, and, lastly, estimated the time required for each activity. The scheduling technique itself can take a variety of forms, and its complexity (or simplicity) will in many respects be determined by the number of activities identified in the WBS.

Gantt Charts, named after their inventor Henry Gantt, are one of the most popular forms of presenting project schedules. They are a type of bar chart, with activities listed vertically from top to bottom along the vertical axis and time represented along the horizontal axis (broken down into days, most frequently, but possibly hours, if the project is short and/or urgent). The width of the horizontal bars reflects the duration of each activity; dependencies, leeway (float), and critical paths can also be shown through a variety of different arrows, lines, and colour-coding. Most pieces of project management software provide Gantt Chart functionalities, and, given their ease of understanding, these charts are the most likely to be used at many LSPs. Some CAT tools, such as Trados Studio, make use of Gantt Charts to visualise project schedules. Such charts make it very easy to monitor project schedules, allowing project managers to mark each activity as complete as the project progresses, but they also allow schedules to be adjusted (in particular, pushed back in time) when the unexpected occurs.

On a more basic level (for smaller or newly founded LSPs looking to adopt a cheaper approach), **spreadsheets** can be used in a similar way to Gantt Charts, listing activities in one column and different time intervals horizontally in the top row, and colour-coding or annotating different cells to organise and plan project schedules as required. **Flowcharts** can also be used to create critical path diagrams in various software packages, and, in the most primitive form, even **activity checklists** with clear annotations on start and end times, and resources assigned to each task, will serve the same purpose of allowing the schedule to be visualised, first, and monitored, second.

The main role of monitoring a project's schedule is to allow the project manager to identify problems as early as possible. However, the project manager needs to be aware of the limitations of planning ahead. The PRINCE2 project management method argues that 'there will be a time period of which it is possible to plan with reasonable accuracy; this is called the *"planning horizon"* [emphasis added]. It is seldom possible to plan with any degree of accuracy beyond the planning horizon' (Office of Government Commerce, 2018, pp. 95; see also 'rolling wave planning', Project Management Institute, 2017, p. 721). In large infrastructure projects, which take place over periods of years or even decades, it is easy to see how intricately detailed schedules could become inaccurate after only a short spell. In the translation industry, such long-term projects are rare. The notion of a planning horizon is of little relevance to short-term projects over periods measured in days alone. However, when the project duration extends into a month or beyond, it would be wise to consider a more detailed approach for the earlier stages (the 'planning horizon') and a higher-level schedule for the later stages, which can be refined and adapted as time progresses. In any case, the success of monitoring a project schedule will in part be dictated not only by how well activities have been identified and defined in the WBS but also by how well project milestones have been defined and managed.

? Using the WBS that you prepared earlier, calculate time estimates for each activity and devise a project schedule.
? Looking at another case study on the TS Portal, what stages might you identify as milestones?

Factors Affecting Project Schedules

Before we move on from the topic of timescales to costs, we will address in this final sub-section some of the factors that affect the ways in which projects are scheduled, both in positive and negative lights; that is, some of the factors that can complicate project scheduling, as well as others that can aid scheduling or that can be manipulated to release pressure on a project schedule. For ease of discussion, this sub-section is divided into cultural, geographical, human, and technological factors.

Cultural Factors

In such a multicultural industry as translation, project managers must always bear in mind what might be happening in other parts of the world where their freelance vendors live. **Public holidays** and **religious festivals** differ from country to country given that most such days are based around days of historical significance (e.g. Victory Day in Russia, Independence Day in the USA, Bastille Day in France) or days or periods of cultural or religious significance (e.g. Christmas around large parts of the world, Chinese New Year, and Eid al-Fitr and Eid al-Adha in many predominantly Muslim countries). Failure to remember that your German translator will be observing German Unity Day on 3 October or that your Spanish translator in Argentina is celebrating Carnaval for two days in February could cause a considerable shock to an otherwise immaculately planned project schedule (another reason to ensure that scheduling assumptions are shared with everybody involved in a project to avoid such shocks). An organised LSP would do well to ensure that as many national holidays as possible are listed in project managers' shared calendars to avoid occurrences such as these. As always, good communication with vendors is crucial too; it is important not to make assumptions about availability, but rather to check if unsure.

Geographical Factors

The invention of **time zones** to standardise time, not just in Britain (where the notion was first conceived in the 1870s) but globally, has revolutionised people's lives and the corporate sphere since the Industrial Revolution, and so many aspects of our day-to-day lives would now be inconceivable without standardised notions of time. For the project manager, time zones can be both a boon and a curse.

To start with the negatives, working on a large multilingual project with translators based in Colorado, USA (UTC-07:00); Brasilia, Brazil (UTC-03:00); Cape Town, South Africa (UTC+02:00); New Delhi, India (UTC+05:30); Seoul, South Korea (UTC+09:00); and Apia, Samoa (UTC+13:00) is enough to give any project manager based in London (UTC+00:00) a headache. But to complicate matters, London, Colorado, and Apia observe daylight savings time (DST) in the summer, pushing the clocks forward by one hour, while Brasilia, Cape Town, New Delhi, and Seoul do not. Fortunately, most digital devices are more than capable of telling you the time in any city in the world at a moment's notice, and calendar software supporting multiple time zones is widely available. Nonetheless, even with this high degree of digital support, project managers need to be careful to check and double check their schedules, especially when the deadline is tight (another reason for sufficient leeway).

However, time zones, when properly harnessed, offer project managers tremendous advantages. It is not uncommon to find large LSPs with offices strategically placed around the world. For example, one of the largest LSPs globally, Lionbridge, has offices in California and Idaho (UTC-08:00), New York and Massachusetts (UTC-05:00), London (UTC-00:00), Paris (UTC+01:00), Tampere (UTC+02:00), Hong Kong, Shanghai, and Beijing (UTC+08:00). As shown in Figure 5.1, the standard 09:00–17:00 working day spread across the San Francisco, London, and Hong Kong offices offers perfect 24-hour project management capabilities. With proper organisation, a project can simply be handed over at 17:00 in Hong Kong to the project management team in London, who can in turn pass it on to the San Francisco office at 17:00 London time, and so on. The New York and Tampere offices can provide backup to pick up the slack in the handover, if required, or offer additional project management support.

124 *Evaluating Translation Project Constraints*

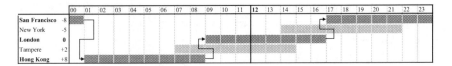

Figure 5.1 Time zones example

This time zone model is equally applicable to linguistic tasks too. Imagine that a 9,000-word Traditional Chinese–English translation is required within 24 hours. You, the project manager based in London, cannot find three translators to work on it in the UK between 09:00 and 17:00 today. However, you see from your vendor database that a translator is marked as available in San Francisco and another in Hong Kong. Starting at 09:00 in London, the first translator completes the first 3,000 words; the linguistic resources and initial 3,000 words are passed on to the second translator in San Francisco, who completes the next 3,000 words; at 17:00 San Francisco time, the project is handed over to the Hong Kong-based translator, who completes the final 3,000 words.

In short, time zones grant project managers access to the *entire* global market of translators, allowing for round-the-clock working on a project (for a discussion of this topic in a software development context, see Taweel & Brereton, 2006). As the idiom goes, 'Make hay while the sun shines'; fortunately, the sun is always shining somewhere in the world. In software engineering, in particular, this notion is often referred to as a 'follow-the-sun workflow'.

? Using the schedule that you devised in response to the questions above, re-model the schedule for working with linguists based in San Francisco, London, and Hong Kong. How much sooner can you complete the project?
? What new challenges would this schedule bring about?

Human Factors

We will not dwell excessively on human factors here, but we will address a few aspects relevant to timescales and scheduling. One might assume that, by adding additional human resources to a project, this will automatically reduce the project timescale (i.e. doubling the human resources reduces the project time by half). While this may be true in some cases, there are a number of principles in project management circles that suggest otherwise. From a resource perspective alone, the **law of diminishing returns** holds that adding more of a particular factor of production (in this case, linguists) will, after a certain point, hinder rather than help production.

In a traditional manufacturing environment, adding too many factory workers could result in workers getting in each other's way, for example. In a translation context, the law of diminishing returns means that, up to a point, adding additional translators to a large project will shorten the time required to complete the translation, but beyond a certain point the benefits will disappear, perhaps because the higher number of translators involved causes consistency issues, requiring more time for quality assurance to correct and harmonise the translations. Extra translators also mean additional barriers to knowledge transfer. Informing new translators of style requirements or preferred terminology and allowing them time to digest the information takes time, complicates the translation process, and generates additional quality risks.

Furthermore, there are parallels between the law of diminishing returns and **Brooks's Law**. Brooks's Law (Brooks Jr., 1995) observes that throwing additional human resources at a project already behind schedule will make the project take more, not less, time. In a similar way to the law of diminishing returns, Brooks argued that it takes people time to reach their optimal productivity (which he referred to as 'ramp up' time), and communication issues are complicated due to the so-called 'combinatorial explosion' (i.e. the number of different directions in which messages need to be communicated). While Brooks based these principles on the field of software development, it is not hard to see how they can be applied to a translation project in the same way. Linguists need time to prepare for a project – reading source materials and previous translations, digesting lists of preferred terminology, reading the style guidelines, etc., not to mention technical preparations such as setting up the project in CAT software. Hence, whether a project is behind schedule (as in Brooks's Law) or not (as in the law of diminishing returns), sometimes additional linguists are not the answer.

There is also the psychological element of human factors to consider. Everybody will have worked on a project of some description in their lifetime that they considered to be a waste of time or poorly organised to such an extent that they believed it to be doomed to failure. Unfortunately, translation projects are no exception, and, on rare occasions, what may seem like a simple project can quickly escalate into a mammoth 'Mission Impossible' undertaking that quickly demoralises all those involved, including linguists, project managers, and even the end client. In software development (again), this phenomenon is rather morbidly referred to as the **death march** (Yourdon, 2015). A death march project is 'not one that just has issues with scope, staffing, and meeting tight deadlines; [it] is one where the normal parameters for a project are out of line by at least 50%. [That is,] the staffing, schedule, and/or budget is at least half of what a normal person would expect' (Smith, 2016). Such projects have a huge impact on the well-being of those involved, especially if they know that the circumstances were in fact avoidable through better planning. However, being 'forced' to push on with such a project, including through excessive working hours to make up the lost time, can give rise to **burnout**. A delicate balance needs to be struck between maintaining high levels of productivity and not demanding too much of vendors.

Vendors themselves are not without blame, however; not all time-related problems arise due to poor project management. Vendors are often prone to the aptly named **student syndrome** (Goldratt, 1997), also known as planned procrastination, when a person leaves a task until the last possible moment before the deadline to start work. There is also **Parkinson's Law**, which describes the frequently encountered situation where work 'expands so as to fill the time available for its completion' (Parkinson, 1955). Both of these can be managed, to an extent, by project managers maintaining regular contact with vendors and requesting that they provide regular progress updates. Furthermore, if a vendor has in the past been guilty of starting a project late, other more direct means of 'coercion' can be used, such as staggered deliveries (i.e. delivery of a certain volume every day, or every few days).

Technological Factors

Finally, a brief note on technological factors. The use of CAT tools (especially when post-editing machine translations) can provide considerable benefits to speed up the translation process by harnessing translation memory matches, propagating repeated segments, and automatically translating or converting figures. However, not all LSPs use the same CAT tools. One might prefer Trados Studio, while another likes to use memoQ, and another Memsource. If a translator is only familiar with one of these tools, it is inevitable that, despite their similarity in core features, they will work slower in a new tool than one with which they are familiar.

* * *

In summary, this discussion of the factors affecting timescales might sound as if a project manager's scheduling will be doomed to failure. However, these are, in most cases, worst case scenarios. To use yet another well-known adage: 'Plan for the worst, hope for the best'. The project manager needs to balance the potential risks (more on this in Chapter 10) of these eventualities occurring against the ideal project timescale. As the Goldilocks principle suggests, a careful balance needs to be struck between allowing *some* leeway in the project schedule and not overloading the schedule with too much spare time. While clients will always be pleasantly surprised to receive a project ahead of schedule, there is little to praise if the schedule is relaxed to the point that the client decides to take their business elsewhere.

* * *

Topics for Discussion and Assignments

1. Based on this chapter, your own knowledge, and drawing on the case studies on the TS Portal, explain, with examples and your own experience if applicable, the extent to which timescales are a key constraint on translation projects.
2. Who holds the key role in managing timescales in a translation project: the project manager, the vendor(s), or the end client?
3. Based on your classes or own experience of using CAT tools, in what ways does the use of CAT tools (including machine translation and post-editing) decrease the amount of time required to complete a translation project, if at all?

Further Reading

Dunne (2011) is a leading source on 'managing the fourth dimension' in localisation project management. The focus in Dunne's chapter is on localisation projects, and it brings a number of more technical steps into the workflow, while more generally reinforcing and complementing many of the messages conveyed in this chapter.

As a good bridge between this chapter and Chapter 6 on cost, do Carmo (2020) looks at the close relationship between time and money in the translation industry, with a particular focus on different job roles and pressures on time (and on money).

References

Brooks Jr., F. P. (1995). *The mythical man-month: Essays on software engineering.* Addison-Wesley.

Buehler, R., Griffin, D., & Ross, M. (1994). Exploring the 'planning fallacy': Why people underestimate their task completion times. *Journal of Personality and Social Psychology*, 67(3), 366–381.

do Carmo, F. (2020). 'Time is money' and the value of translation. *Translation Spaces*, 9(1), 35–57. https://doi.org/10.1075/ts.00020.car

Dunne, K. J. (2011). Managing the fourth dimension: Time and schedule in translation and localization projects. In K. J. Dunne & E. S. Dunne (Eds.), *Translation and localization project management: The art of the possible* (pp. 119–152). John Benjamins.

Goldratt, E. (1997). *Critical chain.* North River Press.

Henry, R. M., McCray, G. E., Purvis, R. L., & Roberts, T. L. (2007). Exploiting organizational knowledge in developing is project cost and schedule estimates: An empirical study. *Information & Management*, 44(6), 598–612. https://doi.org/10.1016/j.im.2007.06.002

Hill, J., Thomas, L. C., & Allen, D. E. (2000). Experts' estimates of task durations in software development projects. *International Journal of Project Management*, 18(1), 13–21. https://doi.org/10.1016/S0263-7863(98)00062-3

Hofstadter, D. (1979). *Gödel, Escher, Bach: An eternal golden braid.* Basic Books.

Office of Government Commerce. (2018). *Managing successful projects with PRINCE2 2017 edition* (6th ed.). The Stationery Office Ltd.

Parkinson, C. N. (1955, 19 November). Parkinson's law. *The Economist.* Retrieved 7 June 2020 from www.economist.com/news/1955/11/19/parkinsons-law

Project Management Institute. (2017). *A guide to the Project Management Body Of Knowledge (PMBOK® guide)* (6th ed.). Project Management Institute, Inc.

Smith, A. H. (2016). *Death march III: How to manage a deeply troubled project and survive* [Paper presentation]. PMI Global Congress 2007, Atlanta, USA. Retrieved 4 June 2020 from www.pmi.org/learning/library/six-constraints-enhanced-model-project-control-7294

Taweel, A., & Brereton, P. (2006). Modelling software development across time zones. *Information and Software Technology, 48*(1), 1–11. https://doi.org/10.1016/j.infsof.2004.02.006

Yourdon, E. (2015). *Death march* (3rd ed.). Prentice Hall.

6 Costs

> **Learning outcomes:**
> - Develop costings for translation projects based on common approaches and margins
> - Link assessments carried out for project schedules to project costings and quotations
> - Understand how the market forces of supply and demand influence the cost of translation projects
> - Consider the extent to which price elasticity plays a role in the cost of translations
> - Appreciate how and why project managers might need to consider wider economic factors when developing costings for translation projects

As noted in Chapter 2, in order to calculate the cost of a project to quote to the client, most LSPs use fairly simple price grids broken down into different languages (French into English, German into English, Italian into English, etc.), different text domains (law, medicine, marketing, etc.), and different language services (translation, editing, proofreading, etc.), and the project manager's role consists typically of identifying the correct unit price and multiplying by the relevant figure. Smaller LSPs, however, leave a lot more discretion to project managers. And for those looking to set up their own LSP, this may be entirely uncharted territory. The aim of this chapter, therefore, is to explore the economics behind price formation in the context of the translation services industry. For many, this knowledge might seem superfluous, but the economics of the translation industry has been largely ignored. Some exceptions to this statement include Pym et al. (2012), Pym (2017), and the wider (but connected) concerns of 'information economics' covered in various publications by Chan (2005, 2009, 2010, 2013, 2017). This chapter explores some of the deeper-lying mechanisms behind price formation in order to arrive at a better understanding of how costs can be managed.

DOI: 10.4324/9781003132813-8

The cost element of a project is one of the most critical to its overall success, both for the LSP and for the end client. If a project is well costed, it can bring significant financial gains for the LSP; if it is poorly costed, it can cause the LSP to make a loss on the project. Cost has the greatest constraining role in the project lifecycle during the pre-production stage (see Chapter 2) and forms part of the critical 'feasibility study' stage of preparing a project. In this section, we will first look at how translation projects are costed, drawing on a number of practical examples, before considering some of the economic factors that play a role in the cost of translation services.

As discussed in Chapter 2, the quotation forms the first substantial step of a translation project and plays an essential role in whether or not the client chooses to proceed with the translation service or not. In addition to an indication of the likely timescale (see Chapter 5), the quotation needs to set out clearly a full breakdown of the cost of the relevant service. Different translation tasks (translation, editing, DTP, etc.) will be broken down using different metrics (characters, words, lines, pages, hours, etc.), and different rates are used for different quotation metrics. For the translation project manager, the costing of a project, and the resulting quotation submitted to the client, is a delicate balancing act between what the LSP will be required to pay to its vendor(s) and what the client is willing to pay for the service; other factors intrinsic to the LSP also play a role in this calculation.

In basic terms, the quotation sent to a client will be based on the following calculation:

Vendor Costs + LSP Costs + Margin = Total Cost

The outsourcing-based model that reigns supreme in the translation industry means that the LSP is, technically speaking, the *first buyer* of the translation service: the service is first sold by the translator to the LSP. The *second buyer* of the translation service is then the end client. The LSP acts as the intermediary in this transaction and will therefore need to cover additional fixed and variable costs, as well as incorporating an appropriate profit margin. Let us look first at how translation service vendors (i.e. individual translators, interpreters, editors, proofreaders, etc.) set their prices, for this element of the transaction is where the majority of the total cost of a translation project arises.

Vendor Costs

When an LSP approaches a vendor for a quotation to translate a document from language X into language Y, the translation project manager will, in many cases, have already carried out an initial analysis of the document, breaking it down into appropriate metrics or units such as characters, words, pages, or hours. The LSP will also stipulate precisely what type of task is expected of the linguist: does it need to be translated, edited, proofread, etc.? These preliminary questions form the basis for the translator's costing:

- What type of linguistic task is being requested?
- How many 'units' are there?
- Are the units based on the source text or an estimate of the target text?
- What is the subject matter?
- When is the deadline?

These processes and calculations have already been discussed on a basic level in Chapter 2. For most language professionals, the task and number of units alone is sufficient to provide a quotation; most translators will have relatively fixed charges per word, for example, or at least a range of charges dependent on the subject matter and on the deadline (is the project urgent or not?). However, it is important to examine and reach an understanding of how these prices are formed by translators and the types of factors that influence what language professionals charge for their services.

? Which factors influence the prices that translators charge for their services?
? What types of translation projects do you expect a translator to charge the most for? Why?
? Beyond language-related services alone, what other costs might a translator 'build in' to their rates?
? In what ways might a translator 'add value' to their service?

The rates charged by a translation professional will vary considerably from one vendor to the next, governed by a whole host of factors specific to the vendor and by the economy as a whole. One of the most obvious factors governing the price of translation services is the **language pair**. This factor is highly susceptible to the market forces of supply and demand (see Box 6.1). There will be far greater demand for some language pairs than others, due primarily to economic factors such as international trade and cooperation. Demand for translations of automotive documentation from German into English, for example, will be high, as Germany sells many of its cars in the UK. Similarly, there will also be a far greater supply of some language pairs than others, governed by the same economic factors, as well as geographic and educational factors. The supply of translations from Xhosa into Maori, for example, will likely be low (perhaps non-existent), firstly because demand for such translations will be equally low, but also because educational establishments in Polynesia do not offer courses on Xhosa into Maori translation, to the best of my knowledge. Hence, any translator able to translate in this pair would have had to have learnt it by some other means with considerable individual effort.

Box 6.1 Supply and demand

Like any other economic sector, the translation industry is subject to the laws of supply and demand, which hold that when the price of a product or service increases, the quantity purchased will decrease, and when the supply of a product or service decreases, the price will increase. The **market forces** of supply and demand operate on both sides of the translation project manager. On the vendor side, they affect the prices at which translation services are sold to the LSP by language professionals; on the client side, they affect the prices at which translation services are sold to the client by the LSP.

On a basic level, since the translation industry is based around intangible products, when a buyer (either the LSP or end client) pays for a translation, the payment is made for the *time* that it takes for a translator to supply a finished translation of a text, in addition to the intrinsic added value of the service provided by the translator and other factors of production such as capital (skills, abilities, and education). How valuable that time is, in monetary terms, will depend on a balance between demand – the amount of a particular translation service that a buyer is willing (and able) to buy at a particular price – and supply – the abundance or scarcity of that particular translation service. *Ceteris paribus* (a phrase commonly used in economics, meaning 'all things being equal'), the price of the service will settle at a point where the quantity demanded is equal to the quantity supplied, referred to as **price equilibrium**.

The effects of changes in supply and demand on price and quantity can be mapped on **supply and demand curves**. Figure 6.1a shows an example of a supply curve (S) and demand curve (D) intersecting at the equilibrium, or market-clearing, price and quantity. In this graph, the quantity supplied is equal to the quantity demanded: because there is no excess supply or demand, there is no pressure for prices to change. If prices were set higher by suppliers, demand would fall, resulting in surplus supply ($Q_S > Q_D$); if prices were lower, demand would rise, resulting in a shortage of supply ($Q_D > Q_S$). In the former situation, this would put pressure on suppliers to reduce prices to shift their surplus; in the latter, the pressure would be on buyers to pay more for the supply and outbid other buyers. Eventually, the market would return to equilibrium once again.

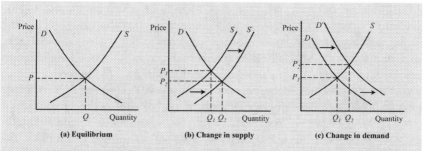

Figure 6.1 Supply and demand curves

In other cases, however, a change in supply or in demand can bring about a shift in prices. As Figure 6.1b shows, an increase in supply (S to S´) – due to an increase in output or more efficient operations, for example – results in downward pressure on prices due to surplus supply, assuming demand remains the same. If, however, as Figure 6.1c shows, demand were to increase (D to D´) – due to an increase in businesses' purchasing power, for example – and supply were to remain the same, this forces prices up.

Bearing this in mind, in the case of a common language pair, such as French into English, the cost of a translation service will be average, as the translator market in Europe is not only relatively well supplied with French into English translators but, equally, demand is relatively high for French into English translations. An unusual language combination, such as Swedish into Swahili, would likely command a similar, if not *lower*, price under ordinary conditions, as the demand for such translations is likely to be extremely low. However, if we consider a case where Swedish businesses suddenly announce a raft of contracts with enterprises in Kenya (demand increases), but the global translation industry is endowed with only a single Swedish into Swahili translator (supply remains low), the price of the service will rise dramatically (see Figure 6.1c in Box 6.1). In a parallel hypothetical case where France bans all foreign trade with the United Kingdom (demand for French into English translations decreases substantially in the UK), French into English translators in the UK will have excess supply, forcing prices down (see Figure 6.1b in Box 6.1).

Project domain or **technicality** is another major factor affecting the cost of translation services and further plays into the effects of supply and demand in the market. Translators specialising in relatively broad, well-supplied domains such as retail, travel and tourism, and market research will be unlikely to command prices as high as those specialising in highly niche fields, such as paediatric cardiology or gas-cooled nuclear reactor maintenance, for instance, especially if such expertise can be backed up by industry experience in the relevant domain. Some translation projects might require **specialist services** and **software**, such as Adobe InDesign for DTP work or Passolo for software localisation, for which freelance translators may have to pay a hefty price tag up front. Such a substantial outlay on fixed capital, on the part of the translator, will in many cases be incorporated into price formation, not solely to recover some of the initial investment but also to make a *return* on that investment. Another common cause of increased charges is the **urgency** of the project: shorter timescales tend to result in higher costs (see 'Timescales' at the start of this chapter) if additional resources cannot be added to the project. We should also not forget about how CAT tools and alternative workflows such as post-editing machine translated output can *reduce* the cost of translation projects.

This discussion might beg the question of why, exactly, a project manager might need to know how individual language professionals price their services. After all, if a translator reports that he or she will charge £80 per 1000 words for a particular text, why does it matter *how* that translator arrived at that price? The reason is **substitution**. If a translation project manager is trying to outsource a project to his or her favoured translator, but the translator's price is too high for the project's budget, the project manager needs to understand how best to find a translator whose prices will be within the project's budget. Hence, there will always be substitute solutions for a project that could prove cheaper; it's simply a case of finding them, and understanding which factors affect cost will make that search easier. We should also remember that substitution for vendors exists in other forms such as machine translation with or without post-editing, both of which come with certain pros and cons. For more on substitution in the translation industry, see Beninatto and Johnson (2017).

To return to our Swedish into Swahili example above, let us assume that only one such translator exists. He or she could essentially charge as much as they wished for the privilege of translating the business documents into Swahili; the demand exists, and one way or another the Swedish businesses need their documents to be translated. There is no **perfect substitute** available to the project manager: no other Swedish–Swahili translator exists. However, as is common practice when unusual language pairings are concerned, one or more 'pivot languages' could be employed (often referred to as 'indirect translation'), which may well prove cheaper than the exorbitant fees that our Swedish–Swahili translator wishes to charge. Comparatively speaking, there are plenty of Swedish–English translators, and, while the supply is hardly abundant compared to other language pairs, there are still numerous English–Swahili translators. In economics, this is an example of an **imperfect substitute**. To provide another example, suppose we needed to translate a maintenance manual for a gas-cooled nuclear reactor from French into English, but the one French–English translator with real expertise in this field wants to charge double that of the next best option, who does not have direct expertise in the domain. An imperfect substitute, therefore, might be to have the document translated by the 'next best option' at half the price, then pay for the translation to be reviewed by a monolingual domain specialist in gas-cooled nuclear reactors.

LSP Costs and Margin

We now have a basic understanding of how language professionals determine their own prices, based on factors such as language pair, domain, specialist services and software, and urgency. These elements contribute to the *Vendor Cost* component of the *Total Cost*. Next, we need to consider how the LSP in turn calculates its own costs and margin before the quotation is ready to submit to the client.

As noted in Chapter 2, in many cases, an LSP will adopt a practice of applying a certain percentage on top of the vendor cost. For example, an LSP may add 40% to the vendor cost of each project. Hence, if a translator charges £100 for his or her services, the LSP would charge an additional £40 on top (a total of £140). What this percentage comprises will be specific to each LSP and will likely have been calculated by members of the senior management team to make a contribution to overheads (utility costs, employee salaries, office consumables, etc.) as well as to generate a small profit margin (in the example above, the gross margin of £40 may, for instance, be split 75:25 between overheads and profit). The alternative approach adopted by some LSPs is to use a fixed 'management fee' in addition to the vendor cost. This management fee would likely be calculated in a similar way to cover overheads and generate profit, but, unlike the percentage margin approach, which is variable, a management fee is fixed, or it might be 'banded' (for example, projects with a vendor cost of £1–£100 have a management fee of £20; £101–£250, £50; and so on). This situation is the most straightforward: a client approaches an LSP with a project, asks for a quotation, the LSP calculates the vendor cost, adds the LSP costs and margin, and submits the quotation to the client.

In other more complex cases, the approach to costing is constrained from the outset: a client approaches an LSP with a project and a strict budget (£100, for example). In this case, the costing method is reversed: the project manager would first calculate the LSP costs and margin (say, 20% of the total cost: £20), then attempt to find a translator who will carry out the work for the remaining sum or less (<£80). It is at this point that effective vendor management truly comes into play. Having a well-organised and up-to-date database of vendors and their fees makes this task immeasurably easier – if not to find the ideal linguist for the job, then at least to identify those linguists who could be approached to negotiate their costs.

136 *Evaluating Translation Project Constraints*

? Imagine that you wanted to have your birth certificate translated into English (or Chinese, if already in English). How much do you, as a client, believe the translation should cost? How much of this amount do you believe is passed on to the translator, and how much is kept by the LSP?
? Is it fair and ethical that some LSPs charge the same as the translator on top of the latter's cost (i.e. a 100% margin)?
? What strategies might you employ as a project manager to negotiate a vendor's cost down? How might you appeal to the translator to reduce his or her charge for one project, for example?

Sometimes, however, macroeconomic conditions can complicate matters further for a project manager. If a client approaches an LSP from another country where goods and services are cheaper, the budget will likely be significantly more constrained than usual. Fortunately, the same macroeconomic factors can work in the project manager's favour: another factor influencing the price that translators charge is therefore **cost of living**. Translators working in a country with a high cost of living index, such as Switzerland, are likely to charge more than those working in one with a low cost of living index, such as Afghanistan. This is an example of **purchasing power**: $1,000, for instance, can buy far more in the way of translation services in Afghanistan than it can in the USA.

This example brings us to another important economic factor: **exchange rates**. Day-to-day fluctuations in global exchange rates can cause problems with the fixed management fee approach, especially when large-scale macroeconomic shocks occur. Take, for example, the effect on exchange rates of the UK's Brexit referendum in 2016. The day before the result of the referendum was announced, the GBP/USD exchange rate was $1.50. Once the result was announced, it fell to $1.32 (–$0.18, its largest drop in 30 years), dropping even further to $1.18 in October when plans for triggering the UK's exit from the EU were announced. The financial implications of these changes for LSPs are explored in Box 6.2.

As a result of these myriad factors influencing the cost of a translation and how much to charge the end client, the appropriate percentage to add to the vendor cost needs to be carefully managed. In larger LSPs this will fall within the remit of senior management, but in smaller LSPs, this margin may be managed on a project-by-project basis, at the discretion of the project manager. Hence, as with timescales, sufficient **leeway** needs to be built not only into the expected vendor costs but also the amount to be quoted to the client, not to mention any risks that might arise during the course of the project that could add to these costs (see Chapter 10). Here again the Goldilocks principle applies (see Chapter 5): the leeway built into the cost needs to be 'just right' – not so much that it puts off the client, but not too little that the final margin is too small.

Box 6.2 The effects of exchange rate fluctuations

On Monday 20 June 2016, the French company Amitié approaches the LSP Best of British Translations and requests the translation of a 40,000-word legal document from French into US English. For this purpose, the LSP decides to commission a US-based legal translator, Samuel Wilson, to provide the translation at a cost of $0.10 USD per word. The project manager calculates the GBP value of the vendor cost ($4,000) at the time of commissioning based on the current exchange rate (£1.00 = $1.47), yielding a GBP vendor cost of £2,721.09, then adds the LSP's standard 40% margin to this cost (£1,088.45), arriving at a total cost of £3,809.54 to quote to Amitié.

On Friday 24 June 2016, the result of the Brexit referendum is formally announced, causing an already anxious GBP foreign exchange market to plummet. Despite the external political and economic upheaval, the translation project progresses without a hitch and is delivered to Amitié four weeks later on Monday 18 July 2016. Mr Wilson raises his invoice on the same day for the $4,000.00 he quoted for the translation, payable within one month. In turn, Best of British Translations raises its own invoice for Amitié for £3,809.54, which Amitié pays the next day.

Four weeks later, on Monday 15 August 2016, the accounts team at Best of British Translations pick up Mr Wilson's invoice for payment as per their standard payment term. By this date, the GBP/USD exchange rate has dropped to £1.00 = $1.28. When the payment is made, instead of the initially expected outlay of approximately £2,721.09 (based on the exchange rate at the time of commissioning), the actual cost of the translation to the LSP has risen by £403.91 to £3,125.00. The initial budgeted margin of £1,088.45 has reduced to £684.54 (approximately 40% less) before the bank's foreign exchange commission and other charges have been added. From a financial perspective, this is considered a failure of the project, as it has failed to meet the LSP's minimum internal project margin of 30%, given that the project's actual profit margin was approximately only 18%.

Evidently, such economic shocks are neither predictable nor capable of being directly influenced by LSPs (or other economic agents individually), and the example presented in this box is an extreme case. Nonetheless, this example shows the importance of building sufficient leeway into the cost, as well as into the project schedule.

Price Elasticity

Despite these difficulties associated with costing a project, it can be argued that economics is largely on the side of the translation industry, for a variety of reasons, even if the industry reality does not reflect this observation. To explore this further, let us turn to an economic concept known as **price elasticity**, and more specifically **price elasticity of demand** and **price elasticity of supply** (see Box 6.3). Elasticity is an important concept in the economics of LSPs because of both the nature and the supply and demand of translation services. In general terms, substitution – the replacement of one service with an alternative service – is not a viable option in the translation industry; one

---

Box 6.3 Price elasticity

Price elasticity is a term used in economics to refer to the responsiveness of either supply or demand to changes in price. The price elasticity of demand refers to the responsiveness of demand to changes in prices. If demand is highly responsive to changes in prices, it would be described as **elastic**; if it were not very responsive at all, it would be described as **inelastic**. The price elasticity of supply is the same: elastic supply means that supply is highly responsive to changes in prices; inelastic means that it is not responsive to changes in prices.

Various factors affect the **price elasticity of demand** and whether or not demand for a good or service is described as elastic or inelastic. Figure 6.2a shows two demand curves: D_1, which reflects inelastic demand, and D_2, which reflects elastic demand. When the price increases (from P_1 to P_2), the inelastic demand curve D_1 shows only a *small downward* shift in quantity demanded (Q_1 to Q_2); D_2, in contrast, shows a *significant downward* shift in demand.

The main factor influencing the price elasticity of demand is **substitution** and the related concept of **competition**: are substitute or competing goods or services available? If one brand of toothpaste increases in price, demand for that brand would likely fall and demand for another (cheaper) competing brand would increase. Toothpaste therefore provides an example of elastic demand. Petrol, however, is an example of inelastic demand. If petrol prices increase (as they frequently do), clients will still buy petrol, as, for petrol car owners, there is no other alternative when you need to drive to work. Another factor is **income**, or the percentage of income represented by the good or service. Hence, if the good or service accounts for a large proportion of a household's income and prices increase, then demand will likely fall. **Necessity** is also important: if the good or service is necessary (such as petrol, above), demand will likely be nearer the inelastic end of the scale. The final main factor affecting the price elasticity of demand is **time**. If the good or service is not purchased frequently, clients are less likely to be sensitive to price. Another situation involving time concerns the duration of the change in price: a short-term change in price is unlikely to result in a significant change in habits; a longer-term change in price will allow clients more time to shop around for alternatives.

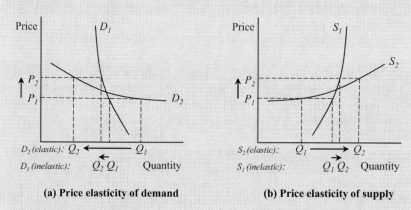

(a) Price elasticity of demand (b) Price elasticity of supply

Figure 6.2 Price elasticity

The **price elasticity of supply** is affected by an array of factors relating largely to the **production process**, including the availability of raw materials or resources, the length and complexity of the production process, the mobility of factors of production (how readily can capital be 'repurposed' for another good or service?), and whether spare or excess production capacity is available. Figure 6.2b shows two supply curves: S_1, which reflects inelastic supply, and S_2, which reflects elastic supply. When the price increases (from P_1 to P_2), the inelastic supply curve S_1 shows only a *small upward* shift in quantity supplied (Q_1 to Q_2); S_2, in contrast, shows a *significant upward* shift in supply. The supply of new houses is an example of inelastic supply: it takes years for large-scale housing projects to be completed, and it can be difficult to mobilise resources quickly to capitalise on a potentially short-term increase in house prices. The supply of manufactured goods tends to be more price elastic, as it is easier to store excess production, it might be possible to switch from manufacturing one good to another substitute good, and production facilities often have a certain amount of spare production capacity that can be activated to take advantage of an increase in prices.

140 *Evaluating Translation Project Constraints*

cannot 'make do' with accounting services *instead of* translation services, for example. First, read Box 6.3 and consider the discussion points below. We will then look at price elasticity in more detail in relation to the translation industry.

- ? How would you categorise the price elasticity of supply and demand in the translation industry?
- ? Why could it be argued that *demand* in the translation industry is price inelastic?
- ? Why could it be argued that *supply* is also inelastic?
- ? How might price elasticity differ between the client and the LSP and between the LSP and the vendor?

Let us look first at the **price elasticity of demand in the translation industry**. In basic terms, the question that we are considering is this: will clients rush out to purchase more translations if the cost of translations drops? Patently this is not the case. Consider the factors affecting the price elasticity of demand, as noted in Box 6.3. Are substitute services available to a client (or an LSP) wanting to procure translation services? No. As noted above, we cannot replace a translation with accounting, legal, or any other professional service. How much of the client's (or LSP's) income does the cost represent? For a private individual, the cost of a translation may be a factor governing *which* LSP the client decides to commission, but, in most cases, the client will still proceed with the translation one way or another; it may just be that a higher quotation causes the client to seek out alternative prices from other LSPs (price inelasticity does not mean that buyers are not sensitive to high prices on a smaller scale). For a large corporate entity, however, such as a law firm, the cost of a translation will often pale into insignificance alongside the legal fees themselves in a complex legal wrangle. Besides, in litigation, these costs will often be passed on to the losing party. Finally, is the translation necessary (and can it wait)? A pressing need for a translation will likely make demand extremely price inelastic. A student seeking a translation of his or her diploma for enrolment at a foreign university *needs* the translation one way or another, otherwise enrolment is impossible. Bearing all of these considerations in mind, demand in the translation industry is price inelastic: demand does not increase when prices fall, and nor, importantly, does it decrease when prices increase.

Now let us turn to the **price elasticity of supply in the translation industry**, i.e. the extent to which supply increases in response to an increase in price. First, consider the main factor of production: the translators themselves and the intellectual capital that they embody. If, say, the price of Chinese into Japanese translations was miraculously to skyrocket, we would not see droves of Norwegian into Swedish translators flocking to pick up the slack in supply. Learning a new language, or even a new area of expertise, takes time. In the long term, therefore, with sufficient motivation in the form of sufficient market demand and a sufficiently large increase in prices, we might see some negligible level of retraining, or new training in the form of new graduates leaving university, but only on a very low level, as the vast majority of translators are constrained to working into their native language, which, by definition, does not change. Many translators, of course, work with more than one language pair, so some degree of 'redeployment' is possible, but on a larger economic level, such a shift is unlikely to occur, or would at least require considerable time. Next, how long and complex is the production process? No amount of money can make a translator translate faster (ignoring technological factors, of course), so on a simple level, an increase in the price willing to be paid for a translation will not result in an increase in supply. The only way in which this might manifest itself is through additional surcharges: if translators were willing to work longer hours (in return for increased pay), some additional supply is possible. Nonetheless, such an increase in production will be highly localised; the price increase will not cause large-scale market-level shifts in supply. This factor is also related to spare or excess production capacity. Admittedly, not all translators work to capacity one hundred percent of the time, but again, any 'freeing up' of excess capacity will be localised, not industry-wide. It is therefore becoming increasingly clear that supply in the translation industry is highly price inelastic: it does not respond to price increases with increased production.

Why does this matter to our project manager? Recall we mentioned above that the translation industry is in a fortunate economic position – technically speaking, at least. For one, prices in the translation industry should be relatively stable, from an economic perspective, on both the supply and demand sides, even if we are seeing downward pressure on rates due to other factors. But more importantly for the LSP, translations are a **necessity good**: they are relatively insensitive to changes in income. Admittedly, there will be occasions where a corporate client delays the procurement of translations until a later point in time when cash flow has improved, but, in most cases, clients enquiring about translations (and related services) are in the market to buy. On the vendor side, because of the rapid growth of the language industry – and its continued growth (see the various statistics and sources referenced in Moorkens, 2020) – the supply – estimated to be 330,000 professional translators in 2012 (Pym et al., 2012) – often struggles to keep up with demand. So vendors, while busy, are equally very much in the market to sell. *Ceteris paribus*, a shortage of supply causes prices to rise, but, because demand for translation services is highly price inelastic, these increased prices can *in theory* be passed on to end clients with little impact on demand overall.

On a practical level, clients find it difficult to compare translation services between different LSPs. The main reason for this is that LSPs only rarely publish their fees online: to receive a quotation, the client must first make contact and the quotation must be carefully tailored to the specifics of the project in question. Comparing quotations between multiple LSPs, therefore, is a highly time-consuming venture for clients. The initial contact and request for a quotation from a client is often half the battle for an LSP; once the client has taken the carrot, economics is on the side of the LSP in most cases.

* * *

While the basics of pricing a project were addressed in Chapter 2, in this chapter we looked to move beyond basic mathematical calculations to consider how supply and demand influence the prices that linguists charge to LSPs and the prices that LSPs can charge to end clients. In turn, we applied the notion of price elasticity to supply and demand in the translation industry to consider the sensitivity of end clients and linguists to changes in prices, with a view to reaching an understanding of the wider economic mechanics shaping price formation in the industry. As we shall see, besides timescales and costs, quality and scope provide yet more factors for project managers to weigh up, balance, and offset throughout the project lifecycle. This is the focus of Chapters 7 and 8, in which we will look at the relationship between scope and quality, quality and time, and quality and cost.

* * *

Topics for Discussion and Assignments

1. Perform a rudimentary economic analysis of supply and demand for your language pair(s) and domain(s) of interest based on your personal impressions and, if possible, a wider review of market data, if available. Consider looking at local translator associations and industry research bodies such as Nimdzi, Slator, and CSA Research to help with this task.
2. In light of what you have learned about price elasticity in the translation industry, is there any merit to LSPs offering discounts or 'money-off vouchers'? In which cases might there be a benefit to doing so?
3. Reflecting back on Chapters 5 and 6, and using examples from case studies on the TS Portal, discuss the relationship between the 'timescale' and 'cost' constraints in the translation industry.

Further Reading

Although lacking in further reading and references, given the nature of the book, Beninatto and Johnson's *The General Theory of the Translation Company* (2017) brings in a number of interesting perspectives from economics in an accessible and engaging style. Part II (pp. 17–108) is one of the more relevant sections of the book and covers topics such as supply and demand, and substitution.

For a more rudimentary introduction to (micro)economics and market forces, Dixit (2014) is an excellent source. In particular, Chapters 2, 3, and 4 cover the economics of supply and demand, and markets more generally, and therefore provide a good introductory grounding that can be applied to the translation industry.

References

Beninatto, R., & Johnson, T. (2017). *The general theory of the translation company*. Nimdzi.

Chan, A. L. J. (2005). Why are most translators underpaid? *Translation Journal*, 9(2). Retrieved 16 July 2021 from www.translationjournal.net/journal/32asymmetric.htm

Chan, A. L. J. (2009). Effectiveness of translator certification as a signaling device: Views from the translator recruiters. *Translation and Interpreting Studies*, 4(2), 155–171.

Chan, A. L. J. (2010). Perceived benefits of translator certification to stakeholders in the translation profession: A survey of vendor managers. *Across Languages and Cultures*, 11(1), 93–113. https://doi.org/10.1556/Acr.11.2010.1.6

Chan, A. L. J. (2013). Signal jamming in the translation market and the complementary roles of certification and diplomas in developing multilateral signaling mechanisms. *The International Journal for Translation and Interpreting Research*, 5(1), 211–221. https://doi.org/10.12807/ti.105201.2013.a11

Chan, A. L. J. (2017). An economist's proposal for the study of the translation profession in southeast asia. *MANUSYA: Journal of Humanities (Special Issue: The Asian Translatorship: Translator, Agency, Approaches)*, 23, 85–97.

Dixit, A. (2014). *Microeconomics: A very short introduction*. Oxford University Press.

Moorkens, J. (2020). Translation in the neoliberal era. In E. Bielsa & D. Kapsaskis (Eds.), *The Routledge handbook of translation and globalization* (pp. 323–336). Routledge.

Pym, A. (2017). Translation and economics: Inclusive communication or language diversity? *Perspectives: Studies in Translation Theory and Practice*, 25(3), 362–377. https://doi.org/10.1080/0907676X.2017.1287208

Pym, A., Grin, F., Sfreddo, C., & Chan, A. L. J. (2012). *The status of the translation profession in the European Union*. Publications Office of the European Union.

7 Scope

> **Learning outcomes:**
> - Understand that a clearly defined scope is important to the success of a project
> - Be aware of the pitfalls of scope creep and what it means in practice
> - Appreciate the importance of knowing your client and the critical educational role of project managers
> - Develop an awareness of the knowledge that project managers should possess about translation and about procuring translation
> - Use prioritisation techniques to delineate the scope of a translation project

In the 1764 publication *Dictionnaire philosophique*, Voltaire wrote: 'Le mieux est l'ennemi du bien, mais le pire est l'ami de l'excès', or 'Best is the enemy of good, but worst is the friend of excess'. While the very notion of project management as we know it today was but a distant fantasy in the 1700s, this simple aphorism bears a great deal of relevance to scope management. In simple terms, perfection is not only nigh impossible but also unnecessary; a simpler plan of action will often achieve the required goals with less effort and less complexity than a convoluted and hugely resource-intensive project. Indeed, greater complexity and greater scope in a project will often simply result in diminishing returns, a point already mentioned in Chapter 5. There are also clear links here with the so-called Pareto Principle (see Chapter 8, Box 8.3, for more details), according to which it would take only 20% of the project's duration to achieve 80% of the performance targets, while it would take the remaining 80% of the project's duration to push for completion of the remaining 20% and achieve 100% 'perfection', if we assume that such a thing is even possible.

There is an entire meta-language relating to scope and scope management, some of which will be addressed in this chapter, including the MoSCoW method and Kano model, which are introduced in the second half

DOI: 10.4324/9781003132813-9

of the chapter. One of the first terms we will address, though, comes from renowned political scientist and economist Herbert Simon, who proposed a novel portmanteau word that encapsulates the underlying objective of scope management: **satisficing**, a portmanteau of the verbs 'satisfy' and 'suffice'. In his acceptance speech for the Nobel Prize in Economics in 1978, he said:

> Decision makers can satisfice either by finding optimum solutions for a simplified world, or by finding satisfactory solutions for a more realistic world. Neither approach, in general, dominates the other, and both have continued to co-exist in the world of management science.
>
> [Simon, 1978]

The concept of satisficing involves exploring a number of different paths of action that can bring about one or more end goals and objectives. Echoing Voltaire, Simon argued, in essence, that perfection is not possible, and it is more realistic to aim for a satisfactory and sufficient (ergo, 'satisficing') solution, given that the world itself is complex. Therefore, the first course of action in a given scenario that meets the need – or the option that seems to satisfy the most needs – would be selected, as opposed to the solution that fulfils *all* of the needs.

In the realm of translation studies, one notion that has started to come to the fore in recent years is that of 'fit-for-purpose translation' (Bowker, 2019). As Bowker notes, this concept emerged with the advent of CAT tools, when the translation marketplace started to be divided into what might be referred to as 'bulk' and 'premium' markets. Demand on the premium market was satisfied by skilled human translators, in the main, while the bulk market was catered for by incorporating the ever-greater use of technology, 'offer[ing] a low-cost, quick-and-dirty solution that encouraged these technology-dependent translators to focus on processing large volumes of text in order to earn a living' (Bowker, 2019, p. 453). Bédard (2000) delineated three levels of service quality: 'prestige' (referring to a small number of documents, such as high-level correspondence and prestigious publications), 'artisanal' (carried out by so-called 'good' translators), and 'industrial' (referring to high volumes of text).

As you can see, this line of thinking starts to drift unerringly close to questions of 'quality' (addressed in Chapter 8). Indeed, scope and quality cannot be fully disentangled, as they are more closely related to one another than, say, timescales and cost. As will become clear in this chapter, scope refers more to deciding *what* needs to be done and *how*, while quality refers more to how to evaluate the output (and, indirectly, the process undertaken to achieve the defined quality standard). **Scope management**, therefore, concerns developing an understanding of the items that need to be produced and the tasks to be carried out, the quantity and varieties needed of a particular product or service (which are also bound up with notions of quality, of course), and how all of these considerations are linked to questions of time and resources. Evidently, as noted in Chapters 2 and 3, these questions are all closely linked to the translation brief and project specifications (see Nord, 2018, inter alia), so it is important to keep in mind these underlying theoretical connections within translation studies.

A Buyer's Guide

Project managers play an invaluable role in defining the scope of a project, not just in terms of delineating the technical steps that a project will require via a work breakdown structure (see Chapter 2) but, more importantly, through their know-how and understanding of what translators do and how they work. As noted at various points throughout this textbook, many clients tend to know very little about translation in the main. It is for this reason that some translator associations have started to develop so-called 'buyers' guides' to try and educate clients more in this regard (see Box 7.1). Sadly, they tend to have limited reach and are often difficult to find, in part because many translator associations are not even widely known among linguists (see Chan, 2013, p. 214), let alone the wider public. The project manager therefore needs to act as a walking, talking buyers' guide and help the client to understand what they need and what they might want to consider including in a project's scope.

Of course, commercial pressures do bleed into this area. It would be naïve to think that LSPs do not face the same pressures as other businesses, i.e. to sell their products and services and to generate revenue and profit. From a scope perspective, this would often take the form of **upselling**, where, after a client has already committed to certain products or services, a company employee will try to encourage them to purchase additional products or services to 'enhance' the offering. For now, however, let's leave upselling to one side and focus more on PMs offering only what is necessary to achieve a project's objectives. The PM's role lies, on the one hand, in understanding what the client needs, wants, and expects, and, on the other – and perhaps more importantly – in advising on what is actually possible and realistic and guiding their expectations as to what is delivered.

The PMBOK distinguishes between two concepts, both of which are important in translation, given the blurred line between whether we are delivering products or services (or both):

- **Project Scope**: 'the features and functions that characterize a product, service, or result'; and
- **Product Scope**: 'the work performed to deliver a product, service, or result with the specified features and functions' (Project Management Institute, 2017, p. 131).

Naturally, project scope *includes* product scope to an extent, but viewing these two concepts as distinct entities can be helpful. The product scope,

Box 7.1 Buyers' guides

Because so many clients have very little experience or understanding of what translation involves, a number of industry associations have resorted to the creation of so-called 'buyers' guides' to shed some light on the various factors that need to be borne in mind when procuring translations.

Experienced translator Chris Durban collaborated with the Institute of Translation and Interpreting (ITI) and the American Translators Association (ATA) to publish *Translation: Getting It Right* (Durban & ITI, 2014), which has now been translated into ten languages in addition to the original English (both UK and US variants). The preface explicitly states: 'If you're not a linguist yourself, buying translations can be frustrating. The suggestions in this guide are aimed at reducing stress and helping you get the most out of your translation budget'.

The guide addresses a number of very poignant sub-sections:

- Does it really need to be translated?
- How much will it cost?
- Resist the temptation to do it yourself
- Tell the translator what it's for
- An inquisitive translator is good news
- Translators and bilinguals: take a closer look
- Choosing a translation provider

The Japan Association of Translators (JAT) has a similar guide on *Working with Translators* (JAT, n.d.), which also covers aspects such as cost, time, quality, how to select providers, and working with translation companies.

Project managers need to have this knowledge at their fingertips. They need to understand the pros and cons of having certain documents translated (or not), how much translations cost, how long they take to produce, what the different levels of quality are and how they differ, and – particularly important for project managers – how to select good vendors to carry out the work.

Read *Translation: Getting It Right* and answer the questions below:

? Do you notice any areas not covered in this guide?
? Are there any aspects that are over-simplified, inaccurate, or unclear in your opinion?
? What are your impressions regarding the format in which this guide is presented (length, layout, design, etc.)?
? How easy is it to find and access this guide?

for example, is guided by the client's needs: namely, what are the functional requirements of the product or service that is being provided? In contrast, the project scope is very much process-oriented: how will the PM deliver on the product scope? And what work is required and what methods will be used to achieve these targets?

Much of the planning of project (and therefore product) scope is predictive in nature – deliverables and processes are defined at the start of the project and any changes to the scope are managed as and when they arise – but scope plans also have to be responsive and flexible. The PM adds considerable value here, not only by helping the client to understand what they want and need, but also in using their experience (or the experience of other PMs, for those new to project management) to predict project processes and risks, and to adapt to any unexpected or planned changes in project scope.

Scope Planning

In the field of software development – which, readers will by now have recognised, seems to inform a great deal of project management principles and approaches – there is a common adage that 'worse is better'. This should not be construed as meaning that we want poor quality solutions(!), but rather that *simplicity* is often what we should be aiming for (as alluded to at the start of this chapter). In short, there is no need to add complexity to project management where complexity is not needed.

Direct and regular communication with and understanding of clients is fundamental to assessing fully the potential scope of a project during the pre-production stage. In essence, we are referring to managing *relationships* here: getting to know your client. Not to see them as dollar signs, metaphorically speaking, but as an individual or as a corporate identity. Unlike many automated translation platforms and other emerging developments in the platform economy (see Fırat, 2021; Moorkens, 2020), project managers offer the important human touch in understanding what the client does, how they work, and how translation fits into what they do. This can be construed in general terms – what role does translation play? – and in more specific terms – why this particular translation project? This is the first step in what the PMBOK refers to as 'collect[ing] requirements': 'determining, documenting and managing stakeholder needs and requirements to meet objectives' with a view to 'defining the product scope and project scope' (Project Management Institute, 2017, p. 138).

We have already covered, in Chapter 5 on timescales, the **work breakdown structure (WBS)**, which is a tool to identify the tasks that need to be carried out as part of a project. Of course, the WBS is inextricably linked with scope, as it provides a direct list of all the tasks that need to be carried out. But the WBS can also be very high level and offer little detail on the specifics of what needs to be done. There are two useful concepts in project management that we can borrow from the PMBOK and PRINCE2 frameworks to tie together the conflict over whether translation (broadly defined) is a process or a product, or indeed both (for a stimulating philosophical angle on this question, see Blumczynski, 2021).

? What is your opinion on this question? Translation: process or product?

Looking at scope from a **product** perspective firstly, the PRINCE2 framework defines a product as an 'input or output, whether tangible or intangible, that can be described in advance, created and tested' (Office of Government Commerce, 2018, p. 25). Translation projects are likely to be so-called 'output-oriented projects', as the project manager 'agrees and defines the project's products prior to undertaking the activities required to produce them' (Office of Government Commerce, 2018, p. 26). In this framework, the focus on products tries to ensure that all work carried out as part of a project is done with the end product-oriented goal in mind and, therefore, helps to mitigate scope creep (see below), in addition to ensuring that the product requirements are fully satisfied. Hence, a **product description** (Office of Government Commerce, 2018, p. 26) defines 'each product's purpose, composition, derivation, format, quality criteria and quality method', according to the PRINCE2 framework.

If we view scope from the **process** perspective, the PMBOK (which is more process oriented than PRINCE2) refers to a **project scope description** that covers both project and product scope through a description of progressive stages to achieve the defined characteristics of the desired product, service, or result. The WBS plays an important role here in subdividing 'project work' into smaller, more manageable components, referred to as 'decomposition' (Project Management Institute, 2017, p. 158).

Combining these two perspectives with the notion of a 'translation brief' or 'commission' widely referenced in translation studies literature, we can start to think about how the product and process perspectives in fact work in tandem to assist project managers (and, in turn, vendors) in determining what specifically needs to be done. The translation brief – which should be elaborated by the project manager, with input from the client based on their needs and expectations (often with guidance from the project manager as to what is possible) – is evidently product focused, as it states specific objectives or characteristics that are required of the deliverables. The project manager will need to extrapolate from the brief the specific project stages and elaborate a WBS ('decomposition') to understand the scope of the processes required to complete the project. Hence, the WBS (process oriented) is what helps the project manager to achieve the brief (product oriented), and therefore to accomplish the designated project objectives and complete the required deliverables to specification; but the WBS is derived from the brief itself. An important cyclical relationship therefore exists between the two, tying together neatly the ambiguity of translation as a process and a product.

However the WBS and/or the translation brief are defined, the project manager has several simultaneous roles with regard to scope management:

- to set up the project in such a way that vendors can focus on their delegated task(s);
- to deliver the project such that it is economically, temporally, and qualitatively acceptable to the client; and
- to complete the project such that it is economically, temporally, and qualitatively feasible and practicable for the LSP from a business case perspective.

The three points can, in a sense, be linked to the two main roles of satisfying the client's needs and managing the client's expectations. If the translation brief is properly defined and does not create unrealistic expectations on the part of the client in terms of quality, delivery deadline, or any other variable, but still satisfies the client's needs, then it follows, generally, that the project will have been well designed so that vendors can do what they do best (namely, the very act of translation and related services), and the project has been delivered in such a way that it is acceptable to the client. The final bullet point is more complex: sometimes sacrifices have to be made by project managers in order to satisfy the client. Where mistakes are made by vendors, or delays occur in the production process, sometimes this can have an impact on the financial success of the project from the perspective of the LSP.

Scope Creep

Because project management is in many respects about finding appropriate ways to satisfy clients, it is all too easy to fall into the trap of doing everything in your power to deliver what the client wants and more besides. There are three terms used to describe this phenomenon: scope creep, gold plating, and, more colloquially, kitchen sink syndrome. **Scope creep** refers to 'the uncontrolled expansion to product or project scope without adjustments to time, cost and resources' (Project Management Institute, 2017, p. 168). **Gold plating** is an extreme form of scope creep, whereby the project manager chooses to continue working on a project in the (hopeless) pursuit of perfection when 'good enough' has already been achieved. The rationale behind gold plating is that a client will be delighted to see a product that is even better than they had originally hoped for (let alone asked for or required). Not only does this introduce new risks into the project, but it could also result in (a) the client being less satisfied in the delivered product(s) and (b) the project costing more money and taking more time to complete. **Kitchen sink syndrome** – derived from the English expression 'to throw everything but the kitchen sink at something' – is a form of uncontrolled growth in the project's scope, usually due to it not being properly defined or monitored.

Sometimes this can occur as a result of a misunderstanding between the client and the project manager, but it can often be due to the project manager throwing additional resources or imposing additional 'features' on the product(s) that are simply not needed.

Scope creep is therefore when something is added to the project that is not explicitly included in the original project scope and is likely not factored into the costing or timescale. It is therefore a case of doing more without charging extra for it and without (necessarily) adding time to the project schedule. As noted above, this tends to occur when the scope is poorly defined and the project manager feels that an additional step will make the project better in some way, but fails to fully take this into account. Poor project planning can also result from poor communication with the client and poor management of client expectations.

To offer one common example: what level of quality is needed in a project? A client might make no specific comments about quality, but an inexperienced project manager might believe that publishable quality is required, resulting in the project manager planning not only for translation but also revision and more, which was not needed in this case. However, the client has quite a strict budget and has placed a lot of pressure on the project manager to keep costs down. Yet since the project manager has *assumed* (and not checked) that quality is important, this causes a problem from a financial perspective. An experienced project manager would at this stage likely point out to the client that higher quality costs more money, at which point the client would normally explain that publishable quality is not required, thereby solving the problem. The inexperienced project manager did not do this, however, requiring the project to be carried out by cheaper (and potentially worse) vendors or significantly reducing the LSP's margin. This in turn affects the LSP's ability to cover its costs and generate a profit. The quality delivered to the client was higher than required, has cost the LSP more money, and has taken more time to complete. The client was happy with the end project but unhappy with how long it took to deliver the translation because of the unnecessary steps added to the process.

Another example relates to post-editing. As noted in Chapter 3, light post-editing focuses on achieving a 'merely comprehensible text' without trying to produce a product equivalent to a human translation (International Organization for Standardization, 2017, 3.1.6). Clients will likely have little understanding of post-editing. Indeed, the first time that many will hear of post-editing is from a project manager who might suggest that post-editing is a faster and cheaper way to produce a translation in certain contexts, depending on what the translation will be used for. To then speak to the client about 'light' and 'full' post-editing, even if explained in terms of 'comprehensible' versus 'human quality', may still not help the client to understand the likely quality of what will be delivered at the end of the project. This is where a series of samples can help. If the project manager has a ready-made set of four authentic target-language versions of a short

Box 7.2 Samples of different translation services

Below are four different translations of a short source text on the development of a flying car (www.futura-sciences.com/tech/actualites/taxi-volant-leo-coupe-hypercar-volante-file-400-km-h-92898/). As you read the English translations (machine translation, light PE, full PE, and human), write some notes on the following:

? How would you describe the different translations to a client?
? How would you signal the differences between each version?
? Why do certain infelicities still remain in the light and full post-edited versions of the texts?

Source text (French)

Urban eVTOL prévoit de construire un prototype à taille réduite et de le tester en 2022. Il lui faudra trouver des investisseurs pour poursuivre l'aventure et financer la fabrication de prototypes opérationnels à taille réelle. Viendra aussi l'épineuse étape de la certification qui peut prendre plusieurs années. L'entreprise dit vouloir viser les marchés les moins exigeants dans ce domaine et pense pouvoir viser un prix de vente de 290 000 dollars (environ 246 500 euros au cours actuel). Affaire à suivre.

Raw machine translation output (English)

Urban eVTOL plans to build a reduced-size prototype and test it in 2022. It will need to find investors to continue the adventure and finance the manufacture of full-size operational prototypes. The thorny step of certification will also come, which can take several years. The company says it wants to target the least demanding markets in this area and thinks it can aim for a sale price of 290,000 dollars (about 246,500 euros at the current price). Case to follow.

Light post-edited output (English)

Urban eVTOL plans to build a reduced-size prototype and test it in 2022. It will need to find investors to continue the venture and finance the manufacture of full-size operational prototypes. The thorny step of certification will also come, which can take several years. The company says it wants to target the least demanding markets in this area and thinks it can aim for a sale price of 290,000 dollars (about 246,500 euros at the current price). More to follow.

Full post-edited output (English)

Urban eVTOL plans to build a reduced-size prototype and test it in 2022. It will need to find investors to continue the venture and finance the manufacture of full-size operational prototypes. The thorny step of certification will also come, which can take several years. The company says it wants to target the least demanding markets in this regard and thinks it can aim for a sale price of 290,000 dollars (about 246,500 euros at current prices). More to follow.

Human translation (English)

Urban eVTOL is planning to build a small-scale prototype to test in 2022. It needs to find investors to back the venture and fund the manufacture of full-size operational prototypes. Next will come the tricky stage of certification, which can take several years. The company is looking to target markets where certification requirements are less stringent and is aiming for a sale price of $290,000 (about £220,000 at current prices). Watch this space.

---

source-text paragraph – raw machine translation, light post-editing, full post-editing, and human translation – this will make it much clearer to the client what the potential differences are. There may be a very small investment by the LSP here to pay three independent vendors to produce the light, full, and human versions of the translation, but if the paragraph is short (e.g. less than 150 words) and carefully selected, it could have a significant educational effect, helping to manage client expectations and facilitate the client's understanding of which level of service is required, and avoiding any assumptions on the part of the project manager. A short example of a sample document is provided in Box 7.2. Ultimately, the client needs to be primed that the quality of post-edited output will not be as high as they might expect compared to human-only services that they might have procured in the past.

It is worth noting that **upselling**, mentioned briefly earlier in this chapter, is not an example of scope creep. Admittedly, the project manager is trying to introduce additional processes or services into the project, but these are *proposals* to the client, which are then either accepted or rejected. If they are accepted, the cost, time, and quality implications of these changes are fully integrated into the project scope (and corresponding cost, schedule, etc.). There is, of course, a very good business case for upselling (as opposed to uncontrolled scope creep), but project managers still need to be cautious of ensuring that all of the implications are fully taken into account. There is also the ethical question of whether project managers should be offering services to clients that they do not really need and capitalising on their ignorance of what translation is and what it involves. Such practices are rare, but ethical and responsible practices should always reign supreme in a field such as translation where business profits are desirable but ultimately secondary to facilitating intercultural communication.

Having mentioned on many occasions now that effective project management and planning is the best way to avoid scope creep, approaches such as work breakdown structures and translation briefs go some way towards obviating this risk. However, another approach advocated by the Project Management Institute is what is referred to as **timeboxing**. In many respects, timeboxing occurs quite naturally in translation projects, provided that workflow stages are clearly defined and assigned to relevant vendors. Timeboxing, as the name suggests, involves stipulating a maximum timeframe for a particular task within a project in order to prevent task overrun that would then have a knock-on effect on subsequent tasks. Recalling the famous project management triangle and triple-constraints model, without timeboxing, if certain tasks cannot be delivered within the planned schedule, the deadline has to be extended or more resources have to be added in order to fulfil the predefined scope (increasing cost). With timeboxing, however, the deadline for that task is fixed, resulting in the scope having to be reduced and in the project managers having to prioritise the most important elements first. This is often a principle that rears its head when a project is not progressing well, but it can also inform project planning from the outset if the project manager regards the project as a series of sequential timeboxes that cannot be extended. Viewing a project in this way results in less ambitious schedules and more leeway in the planning, and therefore in less chance of delays and having to reduce scope. As the PMBOK notes, 'Time-boxing helps to minimize scope creep as it forces the teams to process essential features first, then other features when time permits' (Project Management Institute, 2017, p. 182). Equally, as noted in Chapter 5, ensuring that there is not too much leeway in the definition of the timeboxes will ensure that there is less opportunity for scope creep beyond the point of diminishing returns.

In short, effective scope management is about avoiding undertaking any task that was not explicitly asked for or included in the project brief by the client. If, however, a specific task later becomes necessary – for instance, an additional quality assurance stage due to concerns over a poor-quality translation – then this is a very different matter, as it would have implications for the LSP's relationship with the client, and any potential costs and increase in timescales that may be incurred will simply have to be borne by the LSP, if the LSP itself is at fault. It is therefore a delicate balance between assuming that a finished translation is 'fit-for-purpose' (even if one or two doubts might still remain – after all, it is impossible to eliminate doubt entirely) and instantly rushing to find another pair of eyes to double check a translation every time a doubt arises. It is here that persistent scope creep from one project to the next can rear its head – which needs to be avoided at all costs.

Prioritisation Methods

Good project management often involves balancing competing priorities and making (sometimes difficult) decisions as to whether to include or exclude a particular task from a project based on various project constraints, but most frequently cost and timescales. In most cases, intuition and experience are good to rely on for more senior project managers, but sometimes even the most experienced project manager will need additional tools to help decide the best approach to what should be included in a translation project. The two sub-sections below – on the MoSCoW method and the Kano model – offer two useful tools to break down and prioritise project elements from various perspectives.

The MoSCoW Method

One of the most widespread methods used in project management to aid scope management is the so-called MoSCoW method. Specifically, this is the technique advocated in the PRINCE2 project management framework to aid prioritisation. MoSCoW stands for **'Must have'** (M), **'Should have'** (S), **'Could have'** (C), and **'Won't have'** (W). (The letter 'o' is added twice to aid pronunciation and make the abbreviation resemble a recognised word.) Occasionally, the W is used to refer to 'Won't have *this time*' (i.e. it might be included in a future project) or even 'Wish'. The rationale behind this system is that complex projects often involve far more work than the time and budget strictly allow, so certain items need to be prioritised over others. The fact that the categories use English modal verbs that are relatively easy to understand also makes this approach preferable compared to fairly arbitrary (and subjective) categories such as 'Low', 'Medium', and 'High' priorities.

In the PRINCE2 framework, all of the definitions relating to the MoSCoW method draw on something called the **business justification**. We will explore this in more detail in Chapter 9, but, in short, the business justification relates to there being a justifiable reason to start the project (Office of Government Commerce, 2018, p. 20). This justification is then used to drive decision-making in order to ensure that the project continues to be aligned with the benefits sought from the project. In simple terms, therefore, a client requiring a translation will stipulate a certain goal for that translation (e.g. signing a new business contract with a foreign company). The project will need to be designed and managed in such a way that it facilitates the company signing the new contract with the overseas company. If, at any time, the project starts to deviate from this goal (e.g. the translation is not likely to be ready on time for the planned signing of the contract), then it can be said that the project benefits are no longer being fulfilled. A business justification can draw on project-specific circumstances, on laws and regulations, and on the wider corporate context of the business's strategy and project portfolio overall.

Bearing this in mind, we can now look at how the elements of the MoSCoW method are defined (see Office of Government Commerce, 2018, p. 116). For clarity, 'elements' can refer to any aspect of a project, including delivery by certain deadlines, distinct service offerings such as proofreading and desktop publishing, and even specific resource deliverables such as providing translation memory and term base files upon completion.

Must-haves
These refer to elements that are critical to the business justification for the project as a whole or to a specific timebox within the project for it to be a success. This category also covers aspects such as legal and regulatory requirements, including compliance with ISO certification, in the case of ISO 17100:2015-certified projects. The revision stage is therefore a 'must-have' in such ISO-certified projects, otherwise the project would fail to meet the requirements of the certification.

Should-haves
These elements are important, but not critical, to the business justification. As such, if these elements are not present in the project, the project – and the business justification – will not be as strong, but it will not automatically cause the failure of the project. Often, 'should-haves' are not time critical, and there are also alternative ways to satisfy the client's needs, meaning that delays in delivering on the 'should-haves' are more acceptable to the client and the project's specifications.

Could-haves
Elements classed as 'could-haves' are desirable, but not critical, to the business justification of the project. If these elements are left out of a project, it will not have a fundamental impact on the strength of the outcome. Often, these are project elements that would improve the end user's experience or improve customer satisfaction in return for a small increase in cost and time, and they will therefore be contingent on the client's and/or the LSP's schedule and budget for a project.

Won't-haves

This is the lowest level of priority, and these elements will not be delivered as part of the project. It may seem counter-intuitive to list aspects of a project that will not be included, but it can be a useful tool for two reasons. Firstly, it lays down in writing, unambiguously, what will *not* be delivered in the project (to avoid any doubt or misunderstandings). Secondly, it can serve as a prompt after the project for items that were considered but excluded from the project in its initial form. Just because something is classified as a 'won't-have' does not mean that it is not valuable. These tasks or deliverables can later be added in a future project if time and budget allow (hence this part of the MoSCoW acronym sometimes being described as 'Won't have *this time*').

In order to explore these concepts further, we will use the case study developed in Chapter 2 of this book. The initial project enquiry can be found in the second example presented in Box 2.1, the project analysis in Box 2.2, the schedule in Box 2.3, the resource assessment in Box 2.4, and the quotation in Box 2.5. By way of a brief reminder, in this case study, the client was looking to launch a newly branded website (approximately 45,000 words) in Arabic, French, German, and Spanish alongside the source-language English version within approximately one month. In the sub-sections below, we will explore this project from both the client's perspective and the LSP's perspective. Inevitably, opinions can differ as to what constitutes essential and desirable aspects of a project, and which elements should be prioritised over others.

? Before reading further, try to carry out your own MoSCoW analysis of this case study and compare with the notes below.

Client Side

In this particular case study, the client's initial reflection on priorities may only consider their own internal company priorities: the company is looking to launch a newly branded website and *everything* must be perfect by the launch date. This is all very well and good, but it is of little help to the project manager, who will be required to ascertain in much more detail which elements are truly essential and which allow a little more flexibility. This is where the project manager's expertise comes into its own in terms of *asking the right questions*.

- **Are all languages required at the same time? Are all languages even required right now?**

These two questions draw not only on the requirements for the translation project itself but also on the wider details surrounding the client's business operations. The dialogue between the client and the project manager is important here to determine not only what is necessary, but what is realistic. As the case study discussions in Chapter 2 show, it is perfectly possible to deliver all of the translations on time and with a reasonable budget.

However, the client might not have £45,042 to spend on a translation right now. With some prompting from the project manager, the client could be encouraged to look over the company's financial and website traffic data for the last year and last five-year period, for example. Let's assume that the client reveals to the project manager that, ignoring work from English-speaking clients, French clients account for 30% of their work, German for 20%, Spanish for 20%, Arabic for 10%, and a variety of other locales for the remaining 20%. This might suggest that French should be the highest priority. This is arguably a rather simplistic perspective, though: French clients must not have too much difficulty accessing and using the English-language website in its current form, while German-, Spanish-, and Arabic-speaking clients account for a lower individual (but a higher collective) percentage of income. Combine this with web traffic data, for example, and it could change the picture entirely. It might be that traffic from Arabic-speaking countries is very high, but the number of orders placed is comparatively low, implying that there is high demand among Arabic-speaking clients, but the website is not adequately localised to captivate their interest.

Given the growth potential of the Arabic market (and the greater linguistic differences between English and Arabic than between English and other European languages), there is a strong case for prioritising the Arabic-language version of the website over others. Similar conclusions could be reached for Spanish using the web traffic data. It might be that a large percentage of the traffic is actually coming from Spanish-speaking Latin America as opposed to Spain, suggesting either that the Latin American locale should be the target variety for Spanish, or that the website could be translated for both the Latin American *and* the European Spanish locales separately.

There are therefore strong business case arguments for selecting which language(s) to prioritise over others, especially if budgetary constraints mean that not all languages can be pursued simultaneously, or if it becomes apparent that multiple variants of a specific language might be required to cater for different locales.

- **What level of quality is required?**

As noted at various points in this book, many clients simply do not understand a great deal about translation and related services such as revision, let alone newer, more specialist services such as post-editing. Again, the client's initial impression is likely to be that quality is paramount. In fairness, for a very public-facing website that is intended to market the client's services, this is a reasonable assumption to make. Indeed, this was the rationale for including 'revision' and 'harmonisation' when planning the schedule and quotation for this case study in Chapter 2.

The temptation might be to offer the client maximum quality by running the project through revision, review, proofreading, and, if required, harmonisation stages, but these inevitably add cost. The project manager will therefore need to offer a clear explanation of the benefits of each additional workflow stage, as well as the additional time and cost that each stage would add to the project.

Scope 159

However, there is more than one way to achieve high-quality translations. Firstly, the choice of translator can make a big difference. Selecting a highly qualified, extremely experienced translator (who will likely charge more for his or her services) is one way to minimise the risk of poor quality from the outset. Secondly, the choice of reviser can make an equally significant impact. Combining a high-quality, proven translator with a high-quality, proven reviser is likely to be a recipe for success, but it will almost certainly add considerable cost to the project. Thirdly, simply running the project through all possible quality assurance processes will potentially aid quality, but it could also complicate matters by adding more opinions into the mix (and more potential to introduce errors). As the English idiom insightfully notes: 'Too many cooks spoil the broth'. So the added cost of all of these stages will not necessarily translate into higher quality. One aspect that many clients should be offered when materials are public-facing and have a significant impact on the company's image is having the work proofread by a domain expert (in this case in web design). This would help not only with terminology and phraseology (and picking up any errors that crept through earlier quality assurance stages), but also in terms of checking and testing the final layout, design, and usability as a website.

The pros and cons of the different approaches (and the cost and time implications) will need to be clearly explained to the client so that an informed decision can be made.

- Is the budget limited? Or is the timescale particularly tight?

If budget and/or timescale are more limited, there are of course approaches that can harness technology to speed up the project and reduce costs. Machine translation followed by post-editing by an experienced (and, again, *proven*) post-editor to bring the translations up to human-standard quality is likely to be far cheaper (and faster) than human translation from scratch. It will, however, still need to be revised in all likelihood to avoid any simple mistakes creeping through to the final product. The implications of using MT – as well as how MT can be combined with other language resources such as TMs, and even internal LSP-built MT engines – will need to be clearly explained to the client so that he or she can ascertain the costs and benefits of pursuing a heavily technology-driven solution in the interests of saving time and money as opposed to a more 'traditional' human-driven approach.

In practice, therefore, a MoSCoW analysis of this case study (from the client's perspective, at least) might be as presented in Table 7.1.

As can be seen in Table 7.1, it has been decided, based on the client's discussions with the project manager, that the Arabic translation of the website is the main priority due to the significant growth potential in that market (as shown by the already high web traffic to the English-language site from the region) and that the Arabic-language website must be live by

Table 7.1 Client-side MoSCoW analysis

Must-haves	• AR translation to tap into growing market demand and web traffic • AR version must be ready by launch date without fail • Human translation (no use of MT) • Revision ('four-eyes principle') of all translations due to public-facing nature of copy
Should-haves	• FR translation • DE translation • ES translation (European Spanish) • FR, DE, and ES versions ideally ready by launch date
Could-haves	• Proofreading in final format by target-language web design experts
Won't-haves	• ES translation (Latin American Spanish) to be explored (provisional costing, schedule, etc.) • Review not deemed necessary • MT not to be used

the launch date without fail. Other 'must-haves' include the use of human translation only and also revision so that all translations are at least edited by another professional translator. The French-, German-, and Spanish-language versions of the website are important, hence their classification as 'should-haves', and they should ideally be ready by the launch date if possible. Proofreading by a domain expert is listed as a 'could-have', as this would help to improve the end quality and usability of the website, but it is contingent on cost and time. The 'won't-haves' are the Latin American version of the website, which the client has agreed to explore further with the project manager, as well as review (which is not deemed necessary) and the use of MT (which the client wants to avoid at all costs).

Evidently, based on this MoSCoW analysis, the scope (as well as the cost and timescale) of the project as originally envisaged in Chapter 2 would need to be adapted by the project manager to satisfy the client's needs. However, there are elements where the LSP's own needs may need to be borne in mind.

? Having read this section on the client-side MoSCoW analysis, would your MoSCoW analysis change if viewed from the perspective of the LSP and its own business needs and wants?

LSP Side

On the LSP side, it is all too tempting to throw everything but the kitchen sink at a project (especially a high-value project for a new client) in the interests of pleasing the client. There will of course be some overlap with the client-side MoSCoW analysis, as the project manager is ultimately trying to deliver on what the client needs, but sometimes LSP constraints will force certain elements to be included in, or excluded from, a project's scope. Often, these sorts of adjustments to scope result from differing goals between the client and the LSP. On a simple level, for instance, an ISO 17100:2015-certified project will have 'revision' under the 'must-have' category, as this is mandatory for such projects. But some of the considerations involved in prioritising processes for an LSP are more complex. Let us now consider three poignant questions that the project manager might have to grapple with when determining how to progress this project further.

- **Can the client afford to pay more than the £45,042 initially quoted?**

After the preliminary quotation has been provided to the client (see Box 2.5 in Chapter 2), the client's priorities have been clarified somewhat (see Table 7.1). It now transpires that the Arabic version is the highest priority, with an absolute red line on delivering by the stated launch date. The client would still like the French, German, and Spanish versions to be delivered though, although the deadline can be slightly more flexible if delivery by the launch date is not possible. However, the client has also indicated that proofreading is now a 'could-have', after discussing the benefits of this option with the project manager. The use of MT has been completely ruled out for this project.

In order to build in additional leeway and time, it would be advisable for the project manager to use experienced and proven AR vendors for the translation and for the revision stages, and to pay the higher rates that this would likely entail. An urgency surcharge would also likely be needed to bring completion of the initial translation and revision stages forward and free up time for the newly added proofreading service, which would also add additional cost. Based on the client's analysis of financial records and web traffic, the decision to prioritise the Arabic-language version of the website is well justified, and this course of action by the project manager is aimed at delivering the best possible quality for this language, while also respecting the deadline. Naturally, however, this also increases costs.

The knock-on effect of this is that the FR and DE translations may need to be de-prioritised. The ES financial data was not especially remarkable, but the potential demand in the Latin American market might actually point to a good business case for prioritising the Latin American translation over the European translation and sidelining the FR and DE translations to 'could-haves'. The second ES translation (either European or Latin American, depending on the initial choice) could then follow in a separate project when budget allows.

- **Could the client be persuaded to consider MT?**

Some clients are simply averse to the use of MT because they have seen the plethora of internet memes and jokes about so-called 'translation fails', but they do not understand some of the benefits that the responsible use of MT can bring to a project. Firstly, there are multiple forms of MT, ranging from the freely available Google Translate, with which nearly everybody is familiar, through to bespoke, LSP-built MT engines trained on specialist corpora derived from years' worth of human translations. Not only that, but new adaptive MT engines can combine with and complement extensive TM databases (and TBs besides) to deliver draft translations that range, from one sentence to the next, from pure machine translated segments to highly adaptive sub-segment level combinations of MT and TM entries. Most clients – and indeed many professional translators, for that matter(!) – are completely oblivious to the possibilities and capabilities of modern MT engines and CAT tools.

With some careful guidance (and potentially the use of carefully selected examples, as explored in Box 7.2), some clients can be persuaded to trial an MTPE workflow, especially if there are not only satisfactory safety nets in the form of subsequent revision and proofreading stages but also adequate 'customer satisfaction' guarantees supplied by the LSP to reassure the client that if they are not happy with the end product, the LSP will resolve the matter at its own expense. There is of course a degree of risk here for the LSP, but, provided that the client is sufficiently informed of the strengths and weaknesses of MT and MTPE approaches, it can offer certain advantages.

In this case study, for instance, while human translation might be pursued at all costs for the AR version of the website (especially since MT for AR is not especially successful in many instances), MT could be trialled for the FR, DE, and ES versions, given the closer similarities between these European languages and English. Adopting this approach would help to offset the increased cost of the AR website (due to the use of a high-quality translator and reviser, plus urgency surcharges and proofreading), as well as making it more likely that the content would be ready by the launch date (a 'could-have', according to the MoSCoW analysis).

- **Will the quotation cover the LSP's vendor costs and overheads?**

Behind all of the other considerations surrounding different services and levels of quality, we have to remember that an LSP – of any size – is still a business that needs to cover its costs and, ideally, generate profit. There is naturally a delicate ethical balance here, and the size of the LSP will often determine whether the ethical stance is within the project manager's control or not. All businesses have costs to cover. In the case of LSPs, there are vendor costs that are directly tied to the services being provided, but there are also overheads relating to utility bills, rent, staff wages, infrastructure, and various other things besides. Most LSPs will provide clear guidance for project managers on the margin that projects need to achieve (as discussed in

Chapter 6). Sometimes drawing up quotations for clients falls to a dedicated 'sales team' and the project manager plays no part in this, but often (especially at smaller LSPs) the project margin must always remain at the back of the project manager's mind when determining precisely what does and does not fall within a project's scope.

It may be, therefore, that as part of the MoSCoW analysis, an absolute minimum of a 20% margin is a 'must-have' on all projects after vendor costs have been taken into account, as this is the amount that has been determined by more senior members of the LSP management to cover overheads. However, it might be a 'should-have' that the margin should in fact be 40%, which is more desirable, as it not only covers overheads but also generates a certain amount of profit. In some particularly commercially driven LSPs, there may even be performance incentives for project managers to achieve higher margins (which would arguably fall under 'could-haves'). Delving into the ethics of these performance-driven incentives goes beyond the scope of this textbook, but such practices are known to exist and would therefore feature on a project manager's MoSCoW analysis for a project of this nature. For high-value projects for new clients, especially, the MoSCoW analysis may even include an item about ensuring a high level of client satisfaction and, better still, working towards client retention. Needless to say, these sorts of factors on the MoSCoW analysis would not be shared with the client – directly, at least.

Table 7.2 summarises some of these considerations in two columns: one where MT is ruled out entirely, and the other where the project manager has managed to convince the client of the potential benefits of responsible MT use.

The above questions are just some of the issues that a project manager will have to address when trying to prioritise different aspects of a project's scope. Given the interdependent nature of project constraints, scope is closely linked to questions of cost, time, and quality, as well as the benefits of the project and risks involved. The project manager's know-how and expertise play a key role here in advising the client of what is possible, what factors they might need to consider (but have overlooked), and the potential benefits of services such as MT, about which the client might harbour certain myths or misconceptions.

Like with many things in project management, MoSCoW analyses are simply tools that *can* be used in certain contexts. It would be unrealistic and excessively time consuming to undertake such exercises for every single project, but for particularly complex projects and those with a high commercial value they can prove to be a useful tool to understand different client-side and LSP-side priorities and how best these priorities can be reconciled. Even as a mental tool alone – for the project manager to go through various options in his or her head – it can help to separate 'needs' from 'wants' in translation projects.

Table 7.2 LSP-side MoSCoW analysis

	No MT at all	Responsible use of MT permitted
Must-haves	• Cover vendor costs • Achieve a bare minimum of a 20% margin on the project • Proven AR-language translation and reviser (+ urgency surcharge) • Proofreading by AR web design expert • AR translation must be ready by launch date	• Cover vendor costs • Achieve a bare minimum of a 20% margin on the project • Proven AR-language translation and reviser (+ urgency surcharge) • Proofreading by AR web design expert • AR translation must be ready by launch date
Should-haves	• Achieve a 40% margin on the project • ES translation (European OR Latin American)	• Achieve a 40% margin on the project • FR version: MT + post-editing • DE version: MT + post-editing • ES (European or Latin American) version: MT + post-editing
Could-haves	• FR translation • DE translation • FR, DE, and ES versions ideally ready by launch date • Proofreading in final format by FR, DE, and ES web design experts	• FR, DE, and ES versions ideally ready by launch date • Proofreading in final format by FR, DE, and ES web design experts
Won't-haves	• ES translation (European or Latin American, depending on choice above) to be explored (provisional costing, schedule, etc.) • Review not deemed necessary	• ES translation (European or Latin American, depending on choice above) to be explored (provisional costing, schedule, etc.) • Review not deemed necessary

The Kano Model

As noted above, the MoSCoW method is predominantly based on an assessment of project requirements to determine the priority accorded to certain tasks, and indeed whether to include certain tasks in the work breakdown structure at all. The alternative Kano model is based more on client satisfaction with regard to product quality. When we think of how to satisfy our clients, the temptation is – once again – to 'throw everything but the kitchen sink' at the project and to incorporate as many 'bells and whistles' into the service as possible with a view to achieving maximum client satisfaction. The Kano model, however, provides a strong and logical rationale as to why this is not the best course of action, as we will see below.

Scope   165

The Kano model was developed in the 1980s by Noriaki Kano, an expert in quality management. Like MoSCoW, Kano is a prioritisation method, but it is based on how likely certain product (or service) features are to satisfy the client. Kano argued that not all features of a product or service are equal in the eyes of the client, obviating the need to improve all aspects of a company's product or service. By categorising specific features according to a number of priority definitions, the features can then be weighed against implementation costs to determine whether each element of the project's scope is a strategically sound decision or not, based on the project constraints of cost, time, quality, benefits, and risks.

Kano posited five categories of quality needs in relation to features that are fulfilled to a greater or lesser extent when delivering a product or service: 'must-be quality' (当たり前品質), 'one-dimensional quality' (一元的品質), 'attractive quality' (魅力的品質), 'indifferent quality' (無関心品質), and 'reverse quality' (逆品質). Of these five, three are more important and have alternative translations that are arguably more intuitive to readers: **basic** needs ('must-be quality'), **performance** needs ('one-dimensional quality'), and **delighters** ('attractive quality'). Descriptions of all five terms are provided in Table 7.3.

Table 7.3 Summary of Kano model categories

Category (Alternative name)	Description
Must-be *Basic*	Clients expect these features of the products and services. If they are done well, the client's attitude is neutral, but if they are done poorly, clients are deeply dissatisfied. They are not normally specified as part of the brief, as they are usually so basic that they are taken for granted.
One-dimensional *Performance*	Clients are satisfied when these features are present but dissatisfied when they are not. They are often explicitly specified as part of the project brief.
Attractive *Delighter*	Clients are extremely satisfied when these features are present, but they are not dissatisfied when they are not present. Such features are not normally expected of the product or service. They are not necessarily explicitly specified as part of the project brief.
Indifferent	Clients are neither satisfied nor dissatisfied whether these features are present or not. Often, this is because clients are not able to distinguish between different levels of service.
Reverse	This category reflects the potential for client opinions to differ drastically. Some clients may be dissatisfied by certain features even though they may satisfy other clients, and vice versa.

The first place to start in any project is the **basic needs**. For any project to succeed, these basic needs are essential and will result in the failure of the project if they are not properly fulfilled or delivered. On the simplest level, therefore, actually delivering a text in a language different to the source language is probably the most obvious form of basic need in the translation industry. Hypothetically, if the project manager were to simply deliver the source text back to the client and to consider the project complete, this would be a total failure of the project, as the 'translation' (if we can call it that) would neither function nor fulfil its intended purpose of facilitating communication. If any of these basic needs are lacking in the project scope (and in the quality of the end deliverables, of course), it will result in high levels of dissatisfaction for the client.

Performance needs move beyond the bare minimum required for a project and will, if properly fulfilled, increase client satisfaction, but they will also – due to the increased scope – increase cost and time in most cases (as well as having corresponding impacts on quality, benefits, and risks). Adding in additional services such as revision might be considered a performance need in a translation project, as revision will satisfy the client if it is carried out well but will dissatisfy the client if it still results in a poor end translation. Other non-linguistic services such as DTP and consultancy will often fall into this category: they might not be basic needs for all projects – although in some projects where DTP is especially important, it might be a basic need – but it will help to increase the functionality of the products and services delivered and therefore the client's satisfaction. Unlike basic needs (e.g. the overly simplistic example of actually providing a target text in a different language to the source text), performance needs such as DTP and consultancy services will be explicitly stipulated by the client and/or the project manager and explicitly added to the project scope in the form of a translation brief.

Delighters, as the name suggests, are intended to bring about the highest possible levels of client satisfaction, often by doing something unexpected. It can be helpful to think of delighters as bonuses or surprises for the client, or things that add the 'wow' factor. Clients will not miss such product features or services if they are not delivered (provided that they are not stipulated in the project's brief, of course) but may be particularly pleased with the LSP's work if something unexpected comes from such services. One example in a translation context might be a project where the client has said that they only require the text to be translated, telling the project manager 'not to worry about the formatting'. If the project manager not only succeeds in delivering the translation but also in perfectly replicating the original source formatting (especially in a complex Word document with awkward graphics and tables), the client is likely to be unexpectedly delighted with the end product, especially if no promises had been made regarding formatting.

From a project management perspective, delighters are an ideal way to secure client satisfaction. However, they also pose a number of challenges. Firstly, because they are not explicitly stated (or agreed with the client), such an increase in the project's scope will engender a cost (both in monetary and temporal terms) that the LSP will need to cover from the project budget. Secondly – again, because they are not agreed with the client – there is a risk that some delighters could prove to be examples of 'reverse quality', i.e. where the client is actually *dissatisfied* by the presence of a certain feature. Perhaps the client really did not want the complex formatting to be carried over when they said 'don't worry about the formatting'. Thirdly, and perhaps least intuitively, project managers need to be careful with delighters. In the long term, if the project manager consistently delivers projects with little surprises or 'add-ins', clients start to *expect* these services over time. A feature that is exciting today will soon become a known or expected feature if it is included too often. As such, as tempting as it might be to impress clients at every turn, delighters need to be used sparingly lest the 'wow' factor diminishes and subsequently reduces them to 'performance needs' and later simply 'basic needs' (i.e. expectations). The same principle is arguably true of performance needs: over time, these too can begin to drift downwards into the realm of basic needs if the client starts to view them as a basic feature of the translation service provided.

A visualisation of these three main categories and the downward drift across these features over time is provided in Figure 7.1. As the diagram shows, we can conceptualise these categories on two axes, one reflecting the feature's implementation in the product/service (from 'not implemented' to

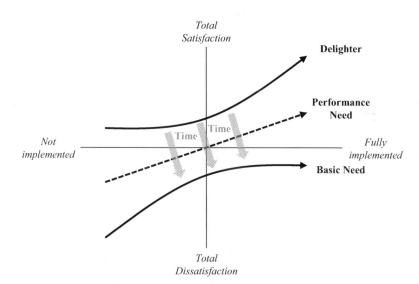

Figure 7.1 Visualisation of the Kano model

'fully implemented') and the other reflecting client satisfaction (from 'total dissatisfaction' to 'total satisfaction'). As we can see, a basic need that is not implemented will result in total dissatisfaction, while a basic need that is fully implemented will still not result in a particularly high level of satisfaction. Conversely, a delighter that is not implemented will have a relatively neutral effect on satisfaction, but one that is fully implemented will achieve near-total satisfaction.

In terms of how to appraise different workflow tasks and their priority, the Kano model, unlike the MoSCoW model (which can arguably take on client-oriented and LSP-oriented guises), is very much driven by client satisfaction. This again is where knowing your client is particularly important, meaning that a strong client–project manager relationship will not require any dedicated effort to prioritise what might be considered 'basic needs', 'performance needs', or 'delighters'. However, for new clients, or for a project different to those previously carried out for a returning client, questionnaires using specially adapted Likert-scales can be employed alongside specific product/service features. Questions can be worded along the lines of: 'How would you feel if we included...?', with responses of 'like', 'expect', 'neutral', 'tolerate', and 'dislike', for example. A meeting with the client is another way to achieve similar results, albeit with a more personal touch that many clients would prefer.

Ultimately, this boils down to learning about your client's needs and expectations so that they can be managed from the very start. While the words of caution about 'delighters' above might imply that we do not want to excite our clients, this could not be further from the truth. But what is important is that project managers do not convey a false impression leading to long-term expectations. For instance, if a particular project has an additional feature or service offered free of charge (perhaps because it was the first project for a new client), it is important to ensure that the client knows this particular feature or service will not always be discounted or free, otherwise this could prove problematic in the future.

* * *

As this chapter has shown, managing project scope in terms of needs and expectations is crucial. The project manager plays an essential role in offering his or her know-how and know-what to inform the client as to what is possible, what is necessary, and what might be desirable in a project, as well as the associated implications for other project constraints (cost, time, quality, etc.). Knowing your client goes a long way towards achieving this. Developing and maintaining strong client relationships are an integral part of good project management practice; if your client trusts you as a project manager, this is often half the battle, as the client will appreciate that you are acting in their best interests and not simply trying to add needless complexity (and cost) to the project, with little or no added value.

When more complex projects come in, project managers sometimes need to undertake a more detailed analysis of what these needs and expectations are. This is where the MoSCoW prioritisation method – geared not only towards product and service features but also workflow stages and processes – and the Kano model – geared towards client satisfaction – can offer useful toolkits to 'decompose' projects and their resulting work breakdown structures into smaller chunks that can be prioritised and either included or discounted depending on the outcome of these analyses.

Inevitably, project scope is very closely related to quality in translation projects. Many elements that are added to a project's scope involve additional quality assurance stages or stages aimed at improving the end usability of a translation product. We can now move on to Chapter 8, where we explicitly address quality, but readers should continue to bear in mind many of the scoping techniques addressed in this chapter in the next chapter and throughout the remainder of this textbook.

* * *

Topics for Discussion and Assignments

1. Using one of the case studies on the TS Portal, carry out a MoSCoW analysis (from the client's and LSP's perspective) and/or a Kano model analysis. If you use both approaches, compare the results between the two.
2. Individually or as a group, design a brochure-type document that explains and demonstrates to clients the differences between machine translation and light and full post-editing (perhaps alongside human translation). Alternatively, prepare this content in the form of a 'sales pitch' presentation to a potential client.
3. Drawing inspiration from existing buyers' guides (see Box 7.1), individually or as a group, design a short 2- to 3-minute educational video or podcast to educate clients on how to buy translation services. You could suggest certain questions that the client should ask when scoping out a good LSP, or suggest specific information that a project manager is likely to need from them. You may also want to touch on questions such as cost and time.

Further Reading

Both Durban and ITI (2014) and JAT (n.d.) are good sources with contrasting approaches to client education. By reflecting on these sources, readers can try to envisage some of the questions that clients are likely to have, as well as some of the questions that project managers are likely to need to ask when preparing a project.

Bowker (2019) is an excellent introductory source on 'fit-for-purpose' translation, which is becoming a widespread term in translation studies and the wider industry.

References

Bédard, C. (2000). Mémoire de traduction cherche traducteur de phrases. *Traduire*, *186*, 41–49.

Blumczynski, P. (2021). Processualizing process in cognitive translation and interpreting studies: A philosophical intervention. In S. L. Halverson & Á. Marín García (Eds.), *Contesting epistemologies in cognitive translation and interpreting studies* (pp. 32–50). Routledge.

Bowker, L. (2019). Fit-for-purpose translation. In M. O'Hagan (Ed.), *The Routledge handbook of translation and technology* (pp. 453–468). Routledge.

Chan, A. L. J. (2013). Signal jamming in the translation market and the complementary roles of certification and diplomas in developing multilateral signaling mechanisms. *The International Journal for Translation and Interpreting Research*, *5*(1), 211–221. https://doi.org/10.12807/ti.105201.2013.a11

Durban, C., & ITI. (2014). Translation: Getting it right. Retrieved 2 August 2021 from www.iti.org.uk/asset/6A607F17%2DACF6%2D4B14%2DA5523B218420B860/

Fırat, G. (2021). Uberization of translation: Impacts on working conditions. *The Journal of Internationalization and Localization*, *8*(1), 48–75.

International Organization for Standardization. (2017). *Translation services – Post-editing of machine translation output – Requirements (ISO 18587:2017)*. International Organization for Standardization.

JAT. (n.d.). Working with translators. Retrieved 5 August 2021 from https://jat.org/about/working_with_translators

Moorkens, J. (2020). 'A tiny cog in a large machine': Digital Taylorism in the translation industry. *Translation Spaces*, *9*(1), 12–34. https://doi.org/10.1075/ts.00019.moo

Nord, C. (2018). *Translating as a purposeful activity: Functionalist approaches explained* (2nd ed.). Routledge.

Office of Government Commerce. (2018). *Managing successful projects with PRINCE2 2017 edition* (6th ed.). The Stationery Office Ltd.

Project Management Institute. (2017). *A guide to the Project Management Body of Knowledge (PMBOK® guide)* (6th ed.). Project Management Institute, Inc.

Simon, H. (1978, 8 December). *Rational decision-making in business organizations* [Nobel Memorial Lecture]. Carnegie-Mellon University, Pittsburgh, Pennsylvania, USA. www.nobelprize.org/uploads/2018/06/simon-lecture.pdf

8 Quality

> **Learning outcomes:**
> - Understand the difficulty in defining quality due to the necessarily relative nature of quality-related concepts
> - Use the six-sigma and DMAIC methodology to manage and measure quality
> - Make use of LQA score cards and error classifications to appraise a translation
> - Conduct short-term and long-term statistical analyses of translation quality using various data
> - Understand the complexity of the cost of quality and how the relationship between cost and quality plays out in the translation industry

Quality is a concept that features very strongly in translation as a practice and as an academic discipline. Look at any translation textbook, university translation programme mark criteria, or corporate description of translation services and the term quality – and related concepts – will undoubtedly be foregrounded. In our everyday lives, as well as in our capacity as linguists, we have an intuitive understanding of what quality is, but generating a conceptual definition can be a tricky exercise. Pym argues that '"quality" … is the relative *excellence* of the thing, usually for a particular purpose' (Pym, 2019, p. 437). The Oxford English Dictionary's definition is very similar: 'the standard of something as measured against other things of a similar kind; the degree of excellence of something'. Paradoxically, the simplicity of these definitions betrays the complexity of the matter, for quality is best appraised in relativistic terms, as stated in both definitions. Quality is not a fixed entity amenable to an easy, all-encompassing definition: it is always relative. A good translation could perhaps be best defined as one that is 'not bad', or 'better' than another translation of the same text. Even this attempt at a definition is not without its flaws. What might be considered 'good quality' in one project may not necessarily be 'good enough' in another. 'Good quality' can mean different things to different people: a translator's opinion may differ from that of an end client.

Philosophical quandaries aside, when managing translation projects, we need to break down this concept of quality into a definition that is amenable to measurement and assessment in light of a specific context of use. The most widespread definition of quality is provided by an international standard – ISO 9000 'Quality management systems: Fundamentals and vocabulary' – which conceptualises quality in terms of its ability to satisfy needs and expectations:

> An organization focused on quality promotes a culture that results in the behaviour, attitudes, activities and processes that deliver value through **fulfilling the needs and expectations** of customers and other relevant interested parties. The quality of an organization's products and services is determined by the ability to **satisfy customers** and the intended and unintended **impact** on relevant interested parties. The quality of products and services includes not only their **intended function** and **performance**, but also their **perceived value** and **benefit** to the customer.
>
> [International Organization for Standardization, 2015, 2.2.1, emphasis added]

Brian Mossop offers a brief, but insightful, analysis of this ISO, once again stressing the relative nature of quality, but also highlighting that various aspects of quality are not even stipulated as a requirement: 'The most important need in translation is accuracy. [Clients] don't ask for an accurate translation; they just assume that it will be accurate' (Mossop, 2014, p. 23). Despite the widespread adoption of ISO 9000:2015, and the certification of many LSPs according to this standard, the guidelines laid down in the standard are arguably too generic to be of great use to the translation industry. The ISO serves a useful signalling purpose to the wider corporate community that an LSP's *processes* are quality-driven (note the reference to 'a culture' of 'deliver[ing] value' in the quotation above), but it does not offer a yardstick specific to the needs of any given industry.

The study of quality in translation requires, first, an elaboration of definitions and measurement criteria, many of which are widely (but inconsistently) used across the industry, and some of which are incorporated into popular CAT tools for use by individual translators and LSPs more generally. Pym describes quality, in the context of translation technologies and technology-supported workflows, as being

> superficially presented as an affair of numbers and rules … Such apparently objective criteria are nevertheless judged and thus ultimately made

meaningful in human terms, incorporating criteria that may include how fast translations are produced, how efficacious they are in the attainment of purposes, how satisfied users are with linguistic products, how happy translators are and hopefully how successful whole communication acts are. Behind the technical numbers, if you know where to look, there are kinds of quality that are ultimately measured in terms of what humans think and do.

[Pym, 2019, p. 437]

A conceptual distinction needs to be made. When an LSP refers to quality, it will typically be referring to the quality of the products that its processes deliver (i.e. translations) or of related services that do not generate a tangible product *per se* (i.e. interpreting). The 'numbers and rules' to which Pym refers tend, in the main, to refer to linguistic criteria: How accurately has the translation conveyed the meaning of the source text? Is term y the appropriate translation of term x in this context? etc. There is also a subsidiary dimension to quality, in terms of the technical usability or functioning of the product: Does the HTML file of the localised website actually work? Is the formatting of the translated product brochure consistent with the original, with text boxes appropriately resized and typefaces suitably localised? The devil, as they say, is very much in the detail in the translation industry:

> Detail explains why there is such a thing as a translation profession, and why students will spend years acquiring the requisite language and other skills to become translators. It is the attention to detail that is seen time and time again to characterize the competent translator. When translators give voice to a characteristic, if not always enabling, modesty about what they do, it is often in the sheer enormity of detail that crowds into the rendition of a text.
>
> [Cronin, 2013, p. 120]

The burden of this attention to detail does not lie exclusively with the vendor; the project manager (and LSP as an organisation) has a responsibility to uphold this detail-driven standard and to consider carefully, with respect to the details of the translation brief and client–LSP agreement, whether the translation itself is 'fit-for-purpose' (for more on this notion, see Bowker, 2019, as well as Chapter 7).

The aim of this chapter on quality, therefore, is to outline a methodology that is widely used across the corporate sphere to monitor and improve the quality of products and services. The underlying objective is to help project managers to achieve the desired and/or necessary level of quality and to monitor quality levels to ensure that they remain where they should, both in the context of individual projects and across the longer-term corporate life of an LSP.

Six Sigma and the DMAIC Methodology

The Six Sigma (6σ) methodology was first developed by Motorola in the late 1980s as a way to improve quality processes and manufacture products with minimal defects. Six Sigma was the brainchild of Motorola engineer William 'Bill' Smith (Smith, 1993) and was based on the statistical variation inherent in production processes, whereby 68% of products fall within 1 standard deviation (±1 sigma) of the mean product quality. Allowing for quality varying by up to ±1.5 standard deviations either side of the mean, Smith argued that, with the right quality control processes (and by asking the right questions to determine the needs and expectations of the client), the product would be virtually defect-free if produced to 'Six Sigma quality' specifications. Statistically, the likelihood of defects would theoretically drop to 3.4 defects per million. In particular, Smith stipulated the need to 'determine the … characteristics of the product necessary to satisfy the customer'; 'identify the key characteristics of the design that control the end-product requirements'; 'identify the process controlling each key characteristic'; and 'determine the target value and the allowable variation for each key characteristic' (Smith, 1993, p. 45). While Smith's context was high-tech telecommunications manufacturing at Motorola, these same questions still bear relevance to the identification of needs and expectations in the context of a translation project.

Although the Six Sigma methodology itself is naturally more geared towards manufacturing processes, it is the quality assessment methodologies it has yielded that are of particular interest in a project management context. Probably the most popular quality measurement and improvement process to derive from the Six Sigma methodology is **DMAIC** (pronounced /dəˈmeɪ.ɪk/ or 'duh-may-ick'), which stands for **Define, Measure, Analyse, Improve,** and **Control.** DMAIC is described as a 'data driven life cycle approach to Six Sigma projects for improving processes' (Basu, 2009, p. 117). It provides a clear and accessible framework for LSPs to measure and monitor translation quality both on a small scale (standalone projects) and on the much wider scale of an LSP's operations across a specified period of time. The methodology can also be applied to a single vendor, a group of vendors, or all vendors working for an LSP. As with many of the techniques described in this book, the suggestion is not that these processes are used continuously for each and every small project undertaken by an LSP. Rather, they should be used strategically for commercially important projects, or to investigate signs of systemic quality failings by one or more vendors or even one or more project managers. Likewise, the DMAIC approach may be employed by project managers, by more senior members of the project management team, or by senior executives at an LSP, depending on the depth and breadth of the proposed analysis. The sub-sections that follow explain the DMAIC process, tailored to the specific nature of translation projects.

Define

Moving away from the conceptual discussion at the start of this sub-section on quality, definitions still prove extremely problematic in the translation industry. ISO 17100:2015 goes some way towards standardising terminology (with regard to commonly confused terms such as revision, review, proofreading, and editing), but concepts such as quality assurance and assessment more generally are almost entirely absent. There is also little consistency across LSPs and the industry as a whole with regard to the use of specific terms to describe certain quality processes. A good example of this terminological confusion is Matis's broad definition of the 'QA phase', which conflates two entirely separate concepts into a single hypernym: 'The QA phase entails checking the linguistic quality of the translation and, in some cases, an evaluation of various technical criteria' (Matis, 2011, p. 147). She then breaks this down into 'linguistic' or 'technical' forms of QA, with the former focusing on the 'linguistic quality of the final document … so that it is easy to read and understand by the target audience' and the latter addressing matters such as layout, readiness-for-market (in localisation), and testing and debugging.

For the purposes of this chapter, we will draw a distinction between two key concepts: **quality assurance (QA)** and **linguistic quality assessment (LQA)**. This largely mirrors Mitchell-Schuitevoerder's distinction between quality *assurance* in the context of CAT tools, which carry out statistical and algorithmic tests on technical features of the product that reflect the process of translation, and quality *assessment*, which she describes as a *human* assessment based on evaluative criteria and 'intuitions to make selective choices as to what is right or wrong' (Mitchell-Schuitevoerder, 2020, p. 94). In summary, her description of the CAT-based QA is that '[QA] checks the quality of the TM and its operator (you) but leaves it to the translator or reviser to perform a quality assessment of the final product according to agreed quality standards' (Mitchell-Schuitevoerder, 2020, p. 94). Note, however, that quality assurance is also often used confusingly as a hypernym to refer to the general post-translation processes of revision, review, and proofreading.

The key distinction between QA and LQA is that QA is an automated process in the main (usually carried out in a CAT tool) and LQA is a human-driven process similar to revision, but with the addition of error categorisation and (sometimes) scoring systems to 'grade' the quality of a translation. Some of the proposed differences are summarised in Table 8.1.

? Using your knowledge of CAT tools, have a detailed look at the QA features of a specific CAT tool (e.g. Trados Studio, memoQ, Memsource).
? What automatic checks do these tools allow you to carry out?
? To what extent are some of these checks useful (or not useful) in a real project?

Table 8.1 Features, principles, and examples of LQA and QA

LQA	QA

• Carried out by a **human** (usually)
• Done by another vendor (e.g. reviser, reviewer)
• May comprise narrative feedback and proposed changes (via Track Changes)
• Focus is on **language**, e.g.:
  o Accuracy (addition, omission)
  o Mistranslation / misunderstanding
  o Style (register, tone, etc.)
  o Grammar (punctuation, syntax, etc.)
  o Terminology
	• **Automated** (e.g. 'Verify' in Trados Studio)
	• Focus is on **technical** (mostly non-linguistic) aspects, e.g.:
	  o Inconsistent translations
	  o Missing or different punctuation
	  o Missing or different numbers
	  o Checks against word lists (e.g. forbidden terms)
	  o Regular expressions
	  o Length checks (e.g. too long/short)
	  o Missing tags or tag order

While terminology for these different forms of appraising distinct dimensions of a translation's quality will differ from one LSP to another, the distinction that one is human-driven, focusing predominantly on linguistic transfer, and the other is machine-driven, focusing on technical features amenable to algorithmic checks within a CAT tool or other software, tends to be widely adopted.

Measure

The second step of the DMAIC methodology is to measure quality in one or more dimensions, part of which entails adopting some means of making QA and LQA amenable to measurement with the benefit of clear and transparent criteria. The aim of measuring quality is to provide a basis for subsequent analysis, identify areas for improvement, and, in the longer term, establish a baseline to control quality and sustain improvements beyond the short-term horizon. It is important to bear in mind that these measurements do not serve to improve quality in and of themselves; they serve only to measure the standard of the underlying quality processes as reflected in the product or service delivery itself and to pinpoint common deficiencies or stages in the workflow where deficiencies tend to occur. As with many elements of project management, the matter of quality can be approached from different perspectives: by focusing on linguistic features on the basis of error scoring methods (**vendor-focused** and, typically, LSP-driven) or by soliciting feedback from clients (**client-focused**, but still LSP-driven for the most part).

One of the more widespread vendor-focused methods used by LSPs is to adopt what could be referred to as **macro LQA scores**. These are score cards distributed to a third party (typically a reviser working on the original translation) and broken down into specific performance categories for which a numerical score (e.g. out of 5) is provided. In many cases, these performance categories also allow narrative comments or a 'global feedback' comment at the end of the score card. The reviser completes his or her revision work and then fills in the score card based on the performance of the translator. An example of such a score card is provided in Box 8.1.

> **Box 8.1 LQA score card**
>
> Score cards (see Table 8.2 for an example) are widely used in the industry to provide a quick and intuitive means to grade the work of a vendor on a very high level with reference to specific aspects of translation performance. Some systems require a numerical score only, whereas others – like the example below – allow comments to provide additional detail on common or recurrent errors. The benefit of these score cards is that they require little (or no) explanation to vendors – a brief definition of the performance categories will usually
>
> *Table 8.2* LQA score card example
>
> | Category | Score | Comments |
> | --- | --- | --- |
> | Accuracy | 5 | |
> | Completeness | 4 | Short paragraph missing on p. 12 |
> | Comprehension | 5 | |
> | Terminology | 5 | |
> | Style | 3 | Register alternates in places between formal and colloquial (marked in text with comments), which is not really appropriate in this text type. |
> | Consistency | 4 | Several terms (e.g. 'contract' vs. 'agreement' and 'lease' vs. 'tenancy') were not translated consistently throughout. |
> | Grammar | 5 | |
> | Spelling and punctuation | 4 | A spellcheck does not seem to have been carried out as some obvious errors were picked up. |
> | Fluency | 5 | |
> | Formatting | 5 | |
> | Overall impression | 4 | For the most part the translation is excellent, but the slight variations in tone, missing paragraph, typos and consistency issues detract slightly. |
> | Other comments? | | The figures in the table on p. 14 do not seem to have been localised (i.e. conversion of 150,00 to 150.00). Some 100% matches have also been edited, against instructions. |
>
> (Scoring Criteria: 1 = Unacceptable; 2 = Unsatisfactory; 3 = Acceptable; 4 = Good; 5 = Excellent)

178 *Evaluating Translation Project Constraints*

suffice, together with descriptors for the numerical scores – and they are very quick to complete while still providing a decent human assessment of a vendor's work. Score cards are frequently completed by revisers when checking a translation against the source and will often accompany a document in which the Track Changes function has been used.

Despite being qualitative grading criteria and requiring subjective input as opposed to a strictly objective or numerical measure, the numerical scores are still amenable to quantification and subsequent analysis. The score card above, for example, has an overall mean score of 4.45, which is between the 'Good' and 'Excellent' descriptors. Some categories could, however, be weighted more prominently (e.g. spelling and punctuation, which one might expect a vendor to be particularly attentive to). The category scores can also be logged in a spreadsheet or database over time (see Table 8.3) and help to identify recurrent problem areas for specific vendors (see basic example below). They can even be accompanied with metadata on domain or language pair (for vendors working with multiple language pairs) to pinpoint whether specific document or language characteristics prove problematic.

Table 8.3 Long-term analysis of LQA score cards

Category	03/01/21	11/01/21	13/01/21	29/01/21	03/02/21	04/02/21	09/02/21	17/02/21	20/02/21	22/02/21	Mean
Accuracy	5	5	5	5	5	4	5	5	5	5	4.45
Completeness	4	5	5	4	5	5	5	5	4	5	4.70
Comprehension	5	5	5	5	5	5	5	5	5	5	5.00
Terminology	5	4	5	5	5	4	4	5	5	5	4.70
Style	3	4	3	4	3	2	3	4	4	3	3.33
Consistency	4	4	5	4	4	4	3	4	4	5	4.10
Grammar	5	5	5	5	5	5	5	5	4	5	4.90
Spelling and punctuation	4	5	5	5	5	5	5	5	5	5	4.90
Fluency	5	5	5	5	5	5	5	5	5	5	5.00
Formatting	5	5	5	5	5	5	5	5	5	5	5.00
Overall impression	4	4	4	5	4	4	4	5	5	4	4.30

? What conclusions would you draw from the summary chart above?
? What advice would you pass on to this vendor?
? What is your view on the relationship between the number or extent of deficiencies in specific performance categories and the 'Overall impression' of a translation?

The shortcoming of these macro LQA scores is that they only offer a very high-level, top-down assessment of a specific translation's quality or the quality of a vendor's work over time; therefore, they make it very difficult (in the 'Analyse' and 'Improve' phases below) to identify tangible and focused defects or targets for improvement if the scorer has not specifically mentioned examples in narrative feedback. This is where **micro LQA scores** – often referred to as **error scores** – can be useful, if used carefully and, importantly, *selectively*. Error scoring approaches rely on various error typologies or **LQA models** not unlike the examples of performance criteria listed in Box 8.1. These typologies (see Box 8.2 for an example) are usually more detailed, but they are also accompanied by specific weightings or categories according to the severity

---

Box 8.2 LISA error typology and implementation

The LISA error typology was designed by the Localization Industry Standards Association as a means to make the quality assurance process as objective as possible by compiling numerical data on errors grouped under certain categories, which can then be analysed statistically. As can be seen in Table 8.4, there are a number of major categories and, within most of these, a number of sub-categories of errors (e.g. Accuracy > Addition). For each error type, depending on the nature of the error, the error can be categorised as 'Minor' (with a penalty of 1 point), 'Major' (with a penalty of 5 points), or 'Critical' (with a penalty of 10 points).

Table 8.4 LISA error typology model

Category	Subcategory	Minor	Major	Critical
Accuracy	Addition	1	5	10
	Omission	1	5	10
	Cross-references	1	5	10
Consistency	-	1	5	10
Country	Country standards	1	5	10
	Local suitability	1	5	10
	Company standards	1	5	10
Language	Spelling	1	5	10
	Punctuation	1	5	10
	Grammar	1	5	10
	Semantics	1	5	10
Mistranslation	-	1	5	10
Style	Language variants/slang	1	5	10
	General style	1	5	10
	Register/tone	1	5	10
Terminology	Context	1	5	10
	Glossary adherence	1	5	10

180   *Evaluating Translation Project Constraints*

Many CAT tools now allow project managers to set up error typologies as part of the project workflow, allowing revisers (or vendors performing other roles) to highlight a particular error, assign a category, sub-category and severity, propose a change to the translation ('Suggested correction' in Figure 8.1), and enter a comment to rationalise the change ('Enter new comment'). Upon completion of the task, the project manager can then produce an LQA report that lists the various errors, types, severities, and comments, as well as a 'score' for the translation (if requested) using the formula presented above. Figure 8.1 shows the 'Enter LQA error' dialog in memoQ.

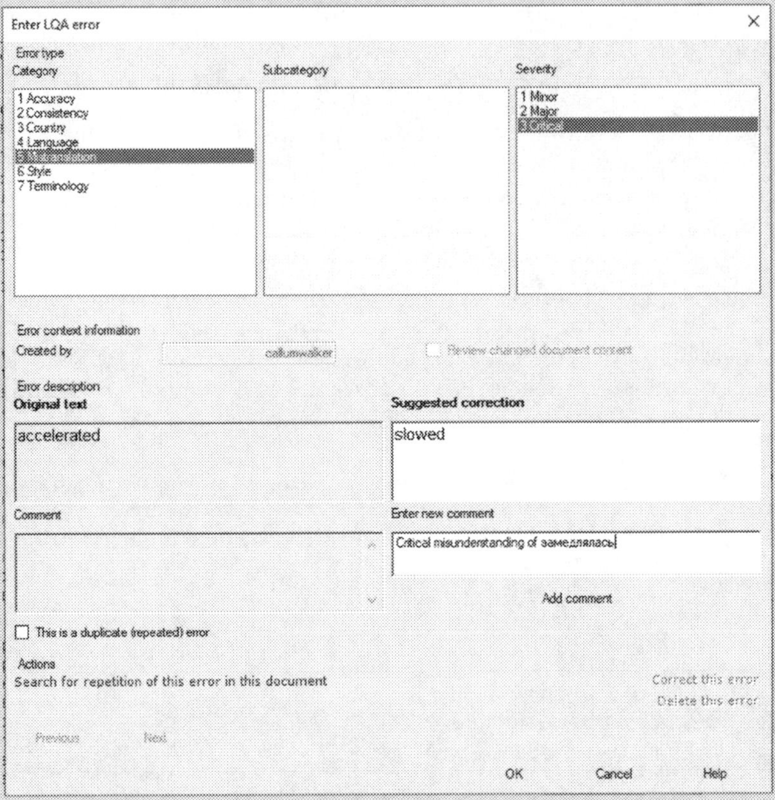

Figure 8.1 LQA error functionality of memoQ

of the error. In the main, error scores are implemented within specific CAT tools and allow an independent vendor (or a suitably trained PM) to examine a translation, propose corrections using Track Changes (if required), and annotate all observed errors by assigning them a category and severity rating. The categories available and severity grades differ from one LQA model to another, but they can also be designed in a bespoke way by an LSP according to its own needs and the nature of its work. The points assigned to each identified error offer a crude method to determine whether a translation has 'passed' or 'failed' depending on the stipulated 'pass threshold'. The normalised error score is calculated using the following formula:

$$Score = 1 - \frac{Total\,Points}{Total\,Words}$$

The default 'pass threshold' tends to be 0.90 (implying a translation score of 90% or higher). A 500-word translation in which 2 critical errors, 1 major error, and 3 minor errors were present (a total of 28 error points using the LISA error typology outlined in Box 8.2), for instance, would still score a 'passable' mark of 0.944 (= 94%), which raises questions about whether PMs, vendors, or clients would be happy with two potentially meaning-critical errors in such a short text(?). In practice, LQA models are rarely used to 'pass' or 'fail' a translation; they are used most frequently for on-going quality assessment measurement and, in some cases, as a form of enhanced quality assessment where recurrent issues have been identified with a particular vendor over a protracted period of time.

As many will immediately recognise, reading a translation in detail, highlighting errors, categorising them, and assigning them a severity is a time-consuming venture. For this reason, micro LQA scores are often sought only on a sample basis. Matis (2011, pp. 152–153) proposes four 'levels' of sampling that are used in quality assessment workflows:

- **End user**: the person carrying out the LQA work acts as the end user, reading it at a normal speed to check for readability and logic, checking only in more detail where hesitations occur;
- **Sample**: error scoring is carried out on a certain percentage of a full text, or chunks of text selected at regular intervals;
- **Full**: the entire text (or project) undergoes full error scoring and checks for terminology, style, grammar, spelling, etc.
- **Extended**: this is similar to a 'full text' approach, but the depth of reading is more superficial, or the checks focus on only specific aspects (e.g. transfer of meaning, spelling, etc.).

Although micro LQA scoring might seem like a panacea for quality assessment, it is not without its limitations. First, it is highly dependent on the sample chosen. Just because one 500-word sample is error-free (or free of serious errors) does not mean that the subsequent 500-word sample is equally error-free. Second, as noted above, even with appropriate sampling, it is extremely time consuming to analyse a translation on such a minute level and assign error categories and scores to identified errors (in addition to comments and corrections, in some cases). It also requires clear guidance and/or training so that vendors understand and apply the categories consistently. Third, it is very easy for vendors to lapse into critiques of subjective matters (especially stylistic preferences), and this in turn can easily descend into a cyclical 'blame game', which is in no way beneficial to the project as a whole. Fourth, based on studies focusing on reviews of post-edited translations, reviewers can differ in their opinions. While they may agree on what constitutes a 'good' or 'bad' translation in general terms, they will often disagree on the error typology (see Guerberof Arenas, 2017). Finally, LQA models are not used consistently or even particularly widely in the industry, making it very difficult for LSPs to compare vendors (in terms of quantitative feedback on job references, for instance) or for clients to compare LSP performance. Despite these shortcomings, LQA scoring is used in the industry to varying degrees and, once collected, still needs to undergo analysis in order to make sense of the broader trends, either for individual translators or for all vendors as a whole, which can in turn help to identify possible defects in the project management process or the guidelines supplied to vendors for various tasks.

The more client-focused form of measuring quality requires far less explanation here, as most readers will already be familiar with how the opinions of customers are regularly sought by companies. LSPs will often resort to both formal and informal methods of collecting feedback on projects. At the more formal end of the spectrum, many LSPs send out surveys to clients to request feedback. These surveys might be sent out after each project is completed, but, more often than not, they will take place less frequently (e.g. monthly, quarterly, or even yearly), as this will typically prompt better engagement and higher response rates from clients. At the less formal end of the spectrum, the feedback offered directly to project managers by email (or by other means: telephone, post-mortem meetings, etc.) can be logged in a central feedback register and/or forwarded to senior members of the LSP's management team, depending on the size and internal structures of the LSP. Both of these approaches can collect both numerical and non-numerical data from clients, which can help to measure, in broad terms, the overall quality of the products and services being supplied to clients and clients' satisfaction with these products and services.

Analyse

The analysis stage can be approached from a number of perspectives, typically drawing on some form of basic (or indeed more complex) statistics. As can be seen in Box 8.1, qualitative LQA scorecards can easily be quantified using 1-to-5 Likert scales, for example, from which descriptive statistics such as means, medians, minimums, maximums, and standard deviations can all be easily computed using commonly available software packages. Equally, the same approach can be applied to the scores generated from error typologies and classifications (as in Box 8.2).

One important factor to decide upon is the *level* of the analysis. Is the project manager (or other member of the company) interested in analysing trends on an **individual vendor level** or on a **higher level,** such as specific language pairs, specific domain, projects managed by a specific project manager, or even all of the LSP's projects. On the one hand, a highly granular vendor-specific analysis of data can help to identify underperforming vendors who might then undertake certain training, or it may prompt the creation of new guidelines, or – in the worst cases – it may result in the vendor being removed from the LSP's database. On the other hand, a higher cross-sectional analysis of trends can help to highlight specific problem areas in the delivery of translations or in the performance of specific workflow stages. For example, particularly poor scores in more 'technical' aspects of error scoring might suggest that vendors are either not reading and adhering to style guides properly or the style guides are not sufficiently clear and may need redrafting.

As with any form of statistical analysis, it is very easy to create what is sometimes referred to as a 'data explosion', meaning that so much data and so many statistics are available that it is difficult to identify broader trends, often resulting in fairly negligible issues being unduly foregrounded. Since the official Six Sigma methodology is better suited to manufacturing processes, it would not be appropriate in most cases to undertake a strict Six Sigma 'defect per million opportunities' analysis to identify the LSP's current sigma (defect) level. There are, of course, a multitude of analytical approaches that could be used, but one approach that is well adapted to the nature of translation services – and is also relatively easy to calculate – is the Pareto analysis (see Box 8.3 for more details).

Box 8.3 The Pareto principle and Pareto analyses

A Pareto analysis (and the corresponding chart) is based on the so-called Pareto principle. Developed by Joseph Juran and named after Italian economist Vilfredo Pareto, the Pareto principle holds that approximately 80% of certain effects are caused by 20% of causes. Pareto himself developed these ideas in economics, where he observed that, in Italy, roughly 80% of the land was owned by 20% of the population. This principle has been expanded to a wide range of fields since: in software engineering, it is said that 80% of bugs are found in 20% of program modules; in taxation, 80% of tax income in the US comes from the top 20% of earners; and so on.

Conducting a Pareto analysis is relatively simple. First, in the context of quality in translation projects, you would need to list all of the relevant error typologies (e.g. all of the sub-categories from the LISA error typology, for instance). Next, you would list the frequency with which each error was observed. These error typologies are then sorted in decreasing order of frequency from high to low and plotted on a bar chart, with frequency on the left-hand vertical axis and the error categories along the horizontal axis. Next, you would need to calculate the percentage of each error type out of all the error types combined (e.g. in Table 8.5: (B2 ÷ B18) × 100). Finally, you would add up each percentage in turn until you reach the last error category (reaching 100%). These cumulative percentages should then be plotted on the same chart using the right-hand vertical axis (see Figure 8.2).

Table 8.5 Example Pareto distribution table

	A	B	C	D
1	Error Type	Freq.	% of total	Cumulative %
2	Language: Spelling	77	23.69%	23.69%
3	Language: Punctuation	57	17.54%	41.23%
4	Terminology: Glossary adherence	33	10.15%	51.38%
5	Language: Grammar	32	9.85%	61.23%
6	Consistency	24	7.38%	68.61%
7	Style: General style	22	6.77%	75.38%
8	Language: Semantics	19	5.85%	81.23%
9	Country: Company standards	18	5.54%	86.77%
10	Mistranslation	12	3.69%	90.46%
11	Accuracy: Omission	10	3.08%	93.54%
12	Style: Register/tone	8	2.46%	96.00%
13	Terminology: Context	5	1.54%	97.54%
14	Country: Country standards	3	0.92%	98.46%
15	Accuracy: Addition	2	0.62%	99.07%
16	Style: Language variants/slang	2	0.62%	99.69%
17	Country: Local suitability	1	0.31%	100.00%
	Total:	325		

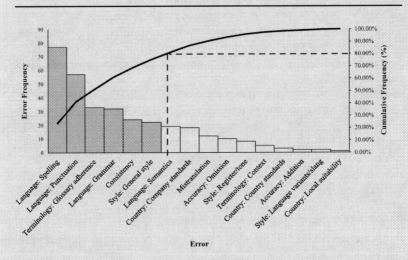

Figure 8.2 Example Pareto chart based on LISA error categories

> Once the chart has been drawn up (Figure 8.2), a line can be drawn horizontally across from 80%, and another line can be drawn vertically from where the 80% line meets the cumulative frequency line. All categories to the left of this vertical line are considered to be the 'vital few' that account for 80% of the errors; those to the right of this line are the 'trivial many' that account for only 20% of the errors. Hence, by focusing on reducing or eliminating errors among the vital few (shaded in dark grey), we can improve translation error rates.

Other methods of measurement can also be analysed in both quantitative (i.e. numerical) and qualitative (i.e. non-numerical) ways. Post-project client surveys, for instance, might have some numerical elements such as a Likert scale to gauge project satisfaction (e.g. 1 = Very dissatisfied, 5 = Very satisfied), but they will also likely offer opportunities for clients to provide so-called narrative feedback, where they describe how they feel about the service provided and certain elements that worked well or poorly. Such qualitative data is more difficult to analyse but is, in many respects, more valuable than purely numerical data alone, as it offers important *nuance* to the numbers derived from error scoring or other quantitative methods. It may take longer to process, as it cannot be neatly imported into Excel and processed via mathematical formulae, but the time spent reviewing feedback from surveys and the less formal feedback that filters through project managers is worth it.

The key takeaway here is that all of the analysis carried out by project managers and other members of an LSP's senior management needs to have an underlying purpose. Analysis of various types of quality metrics is time-consuming, and it is important that the analysis does more than simply generate a number of visually appealing charts and summary reports. In addition to having a purpose, it is also common that these sorts of in-depth analyses stem from a deeper problem. It may be that persistent complaints have been received about a specific vendor, or about a number of projects managed by a specific project manager, or about projects delivered to a specific client, all of which should serve as a preliminary warning sign that something may be amiss in the linguistic or project management processes. Hence, most detailed analyses will have a very narrow focus; high-level analyses will likely only take place intermittently, given the amount of time that such exercises can take.

Improve

Inevitably, the main purpose of measuring and analysing quality in translation projects is to bring about improvement. There is no guaranteed

186 *Evaluating Translation Project Constraints*

method of success for translation, as in most industries, but there are certain measures that, once specific defects have been identified, can help to improve the quality of the output or at least the quality of the process. Improvements do not guarantee client satisfaction, of course, but improvements in the product's quality will go a considerable way towards eliminating client satisfaction issues.

The type of response adopted will ultimately depend on the nature of the quality issues identified, but some measures that can be used in certain instances include

- writing in-house **style guides** to explain clearly any spelling conventions (e.g. colour or color), punctuation conventions (e.g. semi-colon, comma, or no punctuation at the end of bullet points), and conventions relating to units and measurements (e.g. use of currency symbol or codes and their placement, thousand separators and decimal places, spaces before unit measurements, etc.);
- introducing and implementing a clear **query procedure** so that vendors can raise queries as they carry out their various tasks. This aims to avoid vendors sending over last-minute queries that cannot be resolved easily prior to delivery, which can in turn result in mistakes or outstanding queries being retained in project deliverables;
- requiring delivery of a **clean QA log** to show that the automatic QA alerts in the particular CAT tool used for the project have all been checked and corrected, if necessary. Many common CAT tools allow you to export a QA log upon completion of the automated QA checks to show that each alert has been either marked as 'Ignore' or corrected;
- **training for new vendors and PMs** on the requirements of a regular client with particularly demanding specifications for their translations. Training might cover corporate branding (e.g. words or phrases to avoid and alternatives to use in their place), the company's style guide more generally, and any unique workflow stages specific to the relevant client(s);
- changing **recruitment practices** to introduce translation tests, for example, or raising the minimum candidate specifications required to be added to the LSP's vendor database (e.g. a postgraduate qualification in translation, professional membership, etc.); and
- encouraging the use of simple proactive solutions such as spellcheckers, reinforcing basic instructions on ignoring locked segments or protected tags, requiring strict adherence to project glossaries, etc.

As can be seen from the list above, nearly all of these issues can be resolved by making adjustments to the translation project *process* or, rather, the tools and procedures used to support this process, as opposed to targeting very specific linguistic or other failings on the part of vendors. Many of these problems also have very simple solutions too. Quality assessment offers suitable methods to measure quality, but it does not, in and of itself, mitigate deficiencies in the original processes. Rather, it helps to identify the deficiencies themselves and single out focal points in the workflow or body of human resources where deficiencies have occurred most frequently. Sometimes the processes that are adopted for specific projects are not suitable for the content, for instance. As such, QA processes are no substitute for poor quality project management in the first place. Quality comes from a whole host of factors associated with good project management practices: the need to establish clear guidelines (a translation brief), to manage terminology, to maintain style guides, to provide suitable context and reference materials to vendors, and to adopt appropriate query resolution processes during the project lifecycle.

Control

The final stage of the DMAIC methodology is *controlling* quality. The control stage is an on-going process of revisiting earlier stages in the DMAIC cycle: a problem is identified, an improvement is implemented, and the improvement is then measured, analysed, and improved again, if necessary. The focus is therefore on sustaining the improvement in the long term, ensuring that the identified improvement actually yields results, and – equally as important – monitoring implementation over time to ensure that standards do not slip again in the future.

In order to effectively control quality standards, those responsible for monitoring quality need to establish a baseline standard (i.e. measurements prior to improvements being implemented) that can serve as the basis for all comparisons. If, for instance, a project manager has identified regular complaints from clients about inconsistent punctuation and spelling conventions, the suggested improvement may be to produce a video or run a training session on a new style guide for all vendors. The baseline measurement of quality will be prior to the introduction of these new measures. After the new style guide is introduced and the training has been offered to all relevant vendors, new measurements and analyses can be carried out periodically (e.g. monthly or quarterly, as appropriate) and compared with the baseline measurement. Using simple charts and statistics, it is relatively straightforward to quantify the improvement (or indeed further decline) and determine whether additional improvement measures are needed.

As such, quality control is an on-going process of periodically verifying that quality is at the required level for each project and each client (taking into account the level of quality specified in the briefs, of course) and deciding whether existing improvements need to be further adapted or additional measures are needed to bring quality to a higher level still.

The Bigger Picture: Cost of Quality

Like any other service, translation is a client-driven industry: if a client is unhappy with the service provided by an LSP, that client will look elsewhere in future. Client satisfaction is therefore incredibly important in terms of retaining clients, in addition to attracting new clients through word of mouth. However, 100% client satisfaction is a chimera: no client-facing company will satisfy all clients all the time. And more importantly, an LSP cannot strive for 100% satisfaction *at any cost*. Each additional workflow stage to check and (hopefully) improve the quality of a deliverable adds to the cost that the LSP has to pay its vendors, which may or may not be passed on to the client (who may or may not be willing to shoulder such cost). There are of course occasions where, in order to satisfy a particular client, an LSP has to take a financial hit, so to speak, and cover the cost of extra remedial work to improve the quality of a deliverable. This may result in a loss on a particular project, but it could ensure that the client is happy and willing to pay an invoice in full after possible issues earlier on in a complex project. Needless to say, adopting a 'kitchen sink' attitude to all projects (see Chapter 7) is not sustainable business practice in the long term. If we return to the Kano diagram (Figure 7.1), it is simply not advisable or financially viable to over-engineer every project in order to achieve the illusive 'maximum quality'. Not only is this costly, as already noted, but it is also too time-consuming for many projects. Project managers are therefore forced into a careful balancing act in order to achieve the 'right amount' of quality to satisfy the client. On the one hand, there is a need to not scrimp on quality to save money (and increase profits), which could cause more problems further down the line. On the other hand, project managers should not over-spend and lumber the LSP with needless expenses, further reducing the profit earned on a particular project. This balancing act has both short-term and long-term dimensions, which will be discussed briefly below. It is important to stress, however, that the discussions below are all based on cases where a good (but not necessarily outstanding) level of quality is required and expected by the client (i.e. the translation is not simply for 'gist' or 'information' purposes, where quality standards can be lower).

In the **short term** (see Figure 8.3), a project with a low standard of quality (Q_1) will not cost the LSP very much (C_1). The reason for this should be clear: an inexperienced and/or poorly qualified translator who charges very little for his or her services will not cost the LSP a lot of money, especially if the translation is not followed up with revision or other quality-focused workflow stages. At the opposite end of the spectrum, a highly experienced and qualified translator, who is then followed by equally qualified revisers, reviewers, and proofreaders (high quality overall: Q_2), will cost the LSP a lot of money for the same project (C_2). The diagram in Figure 8.3 is, however, an over-simplification of a far more complex situation. In the case of a low-quality (low-cost) translation, there is a chance that the LSP could 'get away with' such cost-cutting measures: the translation may be delivered to the client and the client might not remark on the quality at all, thereby yielding a tidy profit for the LSP. There are, of course, many ethical issues related to such practices.

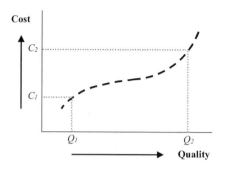
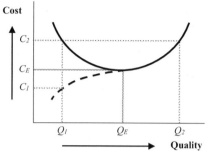

Figure 8.3 Short-term cost of quality   Figure 8.4 Long-term cost of quality

If, however, the LSP gets 'caught out' doing this, then the client will not only be dissatisfied but will also likely demand that the LSP rectify the situation. In some cases, the client may ask for a discount, in which case the LSP will need to decide whether to reduce the vendor's payment in turn. If not, this adds yet more cost to the project. In other cases, the client might ask the LSP to improve the project's quality, which would require revision, at the very least, or possibly re-translation, in addition to various other post-translation workflow stages. In the **long term**, therefore (see Figure 8.4), the cost of a low-quality translation (Q_1) could be very high indeed (C_2), and even as much as paying for a very high-quality translation in the first place (Q_2). Hence, as part of this balancing act, project managers will usually try to achieve an **equilibrium** in terms of quality and cost (Q_E, C_E), such that the project is delivered with the 'right amount' of quality, but without spending more money than necessary to do so.

In project management literature, this concept is closely linked to another quality-related methodology called **cost of quality** (**CoQ**). CoQ is made up of two primary elements: prevention and appraisal costs, and failure costs.

Prevention costs include any work to prevent quality issues from arising and are incurred before the work begins on a particular project. In the context of a translation project, this stage will normally involve the creation of project specifications and documentation (e.g. style guides, glossaries, etc.) and/or the set-up of CAT tools with relevant resources and appropriate project settings. Prevention costs may also include training costs in certain contexts. **Appraisal costs** are incurred in connection with any measurement and monitoring of quality-related issues (see sections above as part of the DMAIC methodology, for instance) and will often involve payments to additional vendors involved in the quality assessment process (e.g. revisers, reviewers, and proofreaders, as well as anybody else involved in analysing the quality data) on a one-time or more regular basis. Both prevention and appraisal costs are known as **costs of good quality** (**CoGQ**), as they both

190 Evaluating Translation Project Constraints

contribute to a positive impact on the quality of deliverables. As can be seen in Figure 8.5, and consistent with the paragraphs above, prevention and appraisal costs are inevitably at their lowest for low-quality projects and at their highest for high-quality projects.

Failure costs might be internal or external and constitute **costs of poor quality** (CoPQ). **Internal failure costs** are costs that have been incurred before project deliverables are handed over to the client and are typically picked up during post-translation steps in the workflow. In some cases, additional cost can come about through unnecessary work (e.g. extra pages being translated that did not need to be), work that is of such a poor quality that it needs to be re-translated from scratch, or the more obvious corrective actions required to amend translations and rectify errors or problems spotted during internal quality checks. The cost of carrying out any quality assessment and control processes may also be categorised under internal failure costs if such processes have been implemented for a specific project in response to identified shortcomings. **External failure costs** are costs incurred to rectify quality issues after delivery to the client when the product does not meet the client's specifications or expectations. Often, such problems are identified upon delivery (e.g. missing files) or shortly after delivery (e.g. obvious 'visual' errors such as missing pages or paragraphs), but many quality problems can occur some time after delivery, once the translation starts to be used. Such external failure costs are, in many ways, not unlike warranty costs for manufacturing companies, when failed parts need to be replaced or repaired.

The difficulty for project managers is finding the **sweet spot** in Figure 8.5, where the cost (both in terms of money and time) invested in prevention and appraisal is not excessive but equally does not allow quality to fall to a standard where failure costs grow. At both ends of the scale – Poor Quality and Exceptional Quality – the costs of quality are very high, but the centre of the graph, where prevention and appraisal costs are balanced against

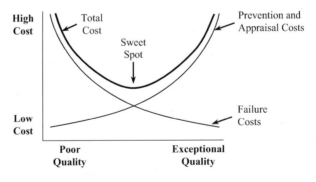

Figure 8.5 Cost of quality

failure costs (allowing a certain controlled amount of risk), is where the best balance of cost, time, and quality is achieved, keeping project costs low enough to guarantee decent profits while not tolerating a high risk of quality problems creeping into projects.

* * *

Translation is highly dependent on quality; it lies at the very heart of what we do as translators and at the very heart of what project managers do in setting up and monitoring the execution of their translation projects. As this chapter has shown, quality is a slippery concept that shifts and morphs according to the perspective, the brief, and the relative criteria against which it is judged. While it is, of course, impossible to *guarantee* high quality – or indeed the necessary level of quality – suitable tools and processes have been widely documented in project management literature to undertake the best possible endeavours to maintain high standards of work, such as the Six Sigma and related DMAIC methodology. Various forms of macro- and micro-level LQA can be carried out in translation projects, alongside industry-wide error typologies, to offer a veneer of objectivity to these processes. Though they may never be fully objective (or indeed widely accepted or reliable), they can, in certain contexts, serve a useful purpose to maintain the required standards. As the final part of this chapter has shown through its discussion of the cost of quality, focusing on low-cost solutions is a risky venture and can often come back to haunt the project manager and LSP at a later date. Hence, over time, with experience and the necessary data, project managers can hope to find the equilibrium or sweet spot in terms of the relationship between cost and quality.

* * *

Topics for Discussion and Assignments

1. Using any assessed translations that you might have (e.g. from your university studies), try to categorise your errors based on your tutors feedback. Do this across a number of translations and assess their severity using the LISA model in Box 8.2. When complete, compile a Pareto distribution table (Table 8.5) and chart (Figure 8.2) to see in which areas you might improve your own practice.
2. Using user guides or video guides, find out how one or more of the CAT tools you use implements LQA error typologies. Try using the CAT tool to error-score one of your peers' translations. Write a brief report – drawing on the numerical score and breakdown of errors – on your peer's performance and areas for improvement.
3. Discuss the following quotation with reference to industry publications, academic literature, and your own experience (including experience of

using CAT tools in your work): 'The technology-driven modus operandi and technology-based infrastructure on which translation increasingly rests adds to quality concerns' (O'Hagan, 2019, p. 2).

Further Reading

Mitchell-Schuitevoerder (2020) provides further insights into how error scoring and vendor feedback operate on a practical level in Section 3.7.3 (p. 63–64), as well as the wider quality assurance dimensions of CAT tools and how project managers and vendors use the tools (Chapter 5, p. 92–112).

The edited volume by Koponen et al. (2021) offers a number of useful chapters relating to various forms of quality assurance and the project workflow, including 'Preferential Changes in Revision and Post-editing' (Nitzke & Gros, 2021), 'Differentiating Editing, Post-editing and Revision' (do Carmo & Moorkens, 2021), 'Post-editing Human Translations and Revising Machine Translations' (Daems & Macken, 2021), 'Revision and Quality Standards' (Schnierer, 2021), and 'From Language Check to Creative Editing: Exploring Variation in the Revision Stage of the LSP Workflow' (Korhonen, 2021).

Drugan's (2013) book *Quality in Professional Translation: Assessment and Improvement* is also an excellent point of reference for quality assurance processes from the perspective of translation companies and international organisations but also individual translators.

References

Basu, R. (2009). *Implementing Six Sigma and Lean: A practical guide to tools and techniques* (1st ed.). Elsevier Butterworth-Heinemann.

Bowker, L. (2019). Fit-for-purpose translation. In M. O'Hagan (Ed.), *The Routledge handbook of translation and technology* (pp. 453–468). Routledge.

Cronin, M. (2013). *Translation in the digital age*. Routledge.

Daems, J., & Macken, L. (2021). Post-editing human translations and revising machine translations: Impact on efficiency and quality. In M. Koponen, B. Mossop, I. S. Robert, & G. Scocchera (Eds.), *Translation revision and post-editing: Industry practices and cognitive processes* (pp. 50–70). Routledge.

do Carmo, F., & Moorkens, J. (2021). Differentiating editing, post-editing and revision. In M. Koponen, B. Mossop, I. S. Robert, & G. Scocchera (Eds.), *Translation revision and post-editing: Industry practices and cognitive processes* (pp. 35–49). Routledge.

Drugan, J. (2013). *Quality in professional translation: Assessment and improvement*. Bloomsbury.

Guerberof Arenas, A. (2017). Quality is in the eyes of the reviewer: A report on post-editing quality evaluation. In A. L. Jakobsen & B. Mesa-Lao (Eds.), *Translation in transition: Between cognition, computing and technology* (pp. 187–205). John Benjamins.

International Organization for Standardization. (2015). *Quality management systems: Fundamentals and vocabulary (ISO 9000:2015)*. International Organization for Standardization.

Koponen, M., Mossop, B., Robert, I. S., & Scocchera, G. (Eds.). (2021). *Translation revision and post-editing: Industry practices and cognitive processes*. Routledge.

Korhonen, A. (2021). From language check to creative editing: Exploring variation in the revision stage of the lsp workflow. In M. Koponen, B. Mossop, I. S. Robert, & G. Scocchera (Eds.), *Translation revision and post-editing: Industry practices and cognitive processes* (pp. 131–147). Routledge.

Matis, N. (2011). Quality assurance in the translation workflow – A professional's testimony. In I. Depraetere (Ed.), *Perspectives on translation quality* (pp. 147–160). De Gruyter.

Mitchell-Schuitevoerder, R. (2020). *A project-based approach to translation technology*. Routledge.

Mossop, B. (2014). *Revising and editing for translators* (3rd ed.). Routledge.

Nitzke, J., & Gros, A.-K. (2021). Preferential changes in revision and post-editing. In M. Koponen, B. Mossop, I. S. Robert, & G. Scocchera (Eds.), *Translation revision and post-editing: Industry practices and cognitive processes* (pp. 21–34). Routledge.

O'Hagan, M. (2019). Introduction. In M. O'Hagan (Ed.), *The Routledge handbook of translation and technology* (pp. 1–18). Routledge.

Pym, A. (2019). Quality. In M. O'Hagan (Ed.), *The Routledge handbook of translation and technology* (pp. 437–452). Routledge.

Schnierer, M. (2021). Revision and quality standards: Do translation service providers follow recommendations in practice? In M. Koponen, B. Mossop, I. S. Robert, & G. Scocchera (Eds.), *Translation revision and post-editing: Industry practices and cognitive processes* (pp. 109–130). Routledge.

Smith, B. (1993). Six-sigma design (quality control). *IEEE Spectrum*, 30(9), 43–47. https://doi.org/10.1109/6.275174

9 Benefits

> **Learning outcomes:**
> - Understand the meaning of benefits as a project constraint
> - Develop an awareness of the lesser-acknowledged benefits of translation projects
> - Understand the role of a business case in identifying and pursuing benefits
> - Consider the reasons for the existence of the translation industry and the value of translation beyond mere monetary terms
> - Show sensitivity to the ways in which benefits differ for the various stakeholders involved in a translation project

Benefits is perhaps one of the least intuitive and self-explanatory constraints of the PRINCE2 project constraints model, largely because the most obvious – or at least self-evident – benefit of business is the prospect of generating profit and increasing wealth, which is the very underpinning of a capitalist economy. This view, however, is a rather simplistic impression of the benefits of business and, more specifically, of projects. That is not to say that profit is not one of the benefits of running an LSP and providing translation services, but rather that profit is one benefit among potentially numerous benefits, some more obvious than others. By the end of this chapter, readers should have a clearer understanding of some of the lesser-acknowledged benefits of translation projects, beyond the most obvious prospect of accruing profit.

When we speak of benefits in the context of project constraints, project managers and business owners will need to engage in some ways with a more macro-level, top-down view of individual projects and groups of projects within the wider context of a business's operations. As you might recall from the very start of Part 2 of this textbook, PRINCE2's definition of the benefits constraint was as follows:

DOI: 10.4324/9781003132813-11

Why are we doing this? ... The project manager has to have a clear understanding of the purpose of the project ... and make sure that what the project delivers is consistent with achieving the desired return.
[Office of Government Commerce, 2018, p. 10]

This definition marries well with broader business-level definitions of a **business benefit,** which is a measurable outcome of an action that will help a stakeholder to meet its business objectives. Evidently, in this textbook, we are focusing more on the project level, but the above definition is perfectly adequate, especially if we substitute the word 'business' with 'project'. Indeed, the PMBOK offers its own definition of a **project benefit:** 'the outcome of actions, behaviors, products, services, or results that provide value to the sponsoring organization as well as to the project's intended beneficiaries' (Project Management Institute, 2017, p. 33). In essence, to understand the value of benefits and how benefits operate as a constraint in project management, we need to boil this concept down to a series of easily understandable questions. These questions could be formulated as follows:

- Why are we doing this?
- How and when will the project benefits be delivered?
- How are benefits to be measured?
- Who are the beneficiaries (i.e. the people or entities that benefit)?

On a general level, projects serve a number of purposes and will be initiated due to any possible number of reasons. The PMBOK, for instance, suggests that projects might be initiated as a result of market demand, a strategic opportunity or business need, a social need, environmental considerations, a customer request, technological advances, a legal or regulatory requirement, and/or an existing or anticipated problem (Project Management Institute, 2017, p. 546). Using the PMBOK quotation above as a question prompt, and before reading any further in this chapter, how would you answer the following:

? Is there a market demand for translation services?
? Are there any strategic opportunities or business needs, or even social needs, that are met by translation projects?
? Are translation services driven by customer requests?
? Are there any legal or regulatory requirements that influence translation projects?
? Do translation projects respond to an existing or anticipated problem?

By breaking it down in this way, you should hopefully already have some ideas of the benefits offered by or secured as a result of carrying out translation projects.

Justification for Translation Services

The PRINCE2 project management framework focuses on the delivery of outputs in the form of products, which is, in many respects, a good fit for the translation industry, where most outputs are tangible products or at least semi-tangible services (although this is open to debate, as discussed earlier in this textbook). Even interpreting, where there is no physical product produced, could arguably be described as a product in the sense that it is observable and recordable and results in the delivery of an ephemeral, spoken product. The use of these products (or delivery of these services, depending on your perspective) brings about change in the business environment: they improve the *status quo* in some capacity – by making an incomprehensible foreign-language text comprehensible, by facilitating the signing of an international business contract, or by making your video-on-demand viewing more enjoyable by enabling you to watch a film produced in a language you do not understand. All of these **outputs** – the tangible translation products or services – are responsible for these changes. These changes are referred to as **outcomes**, and an outcome, in simple terms, refers to the process or phenomenon that has been (hopefully) improved as a result of the output. The **benefits** are the measurable impact of the outcome. Outputs, outcomes, and benefits are all closely linked to the notion of **business case** (see Box 9.1). While the business case may overlap for the LSP and the client, each party will often have different (and sometimes competing) elements within their respective business cases.

To offer one very simple example, the successful completion of a contract translation from Polish into German (the output) meant that the LSP's client was extremely happy with the translation service (the outcome for the LSP). In turn, the Polish client was able to secure a major international contract with a German business (the outcome for the client). For the LSP, the result of this change in situation was that the Polish client pledged to return to the LSP for any future translation requirements, which, in the future, will account for 5% of the LSP's total profits each financial year (the benefit for the LSP). For the client, the signed contract with the German business will result in 10% higher profits in the future (the benefit for the client). In this straightforward example, the benefits are measured primarily in monetary terms (future profits both for the LSP and for the client in their respective industries), but there are also intangible forms of benefit, such as client satisfaction, quality of service delivery, and business image, for both the LSP and the client.

Hence, projects enable change; they bring about progress and advance a business's situation from A (the current state) to B (a future state). They do this through measurable improvements, or benefits. The first stage of our benefits analysis is to consider the question of 'why': why do we provide translation (and related) services?

Box 9.1 Business case

When thinking about the benefits brought about by a particular project, businesses will often turn to a **business case**. The business case helps businesses to think about the measurable improvements they want to make to their business. These improvements can be on a higher business-level scale (e.g. investment in equipment to speed up certain processes) or they can be on a lower-level scale (e.g. taking on a specific project because it will generate income for the business and improve business goodwill with the client).

According to the PRINCE2 framework (Office of Government Commerce, 2018, p. 47), projects should always have a business justification, which helps to understand whether a particular decision (project-level or business-level) is

- **desirable**: what is the balance between the costs, benefits, and risks of the project?
- **viable**: is the LSP, in this case, able to deliver the promised services and products?
- **achievable**: is the subsequent use of the products by the client likely to result in the intended outcomes and the resulting benefits?

A good business case is not a static entity; it will change throughout the course of a project. That is not to say that the business case for each project needs to be fully documented and recorded (although the PRINCE2 framework would argue otherwise, and this may be true for costly business-level changes), but these considerations are worth bearing in mind. Ultimately, if the business case is no longer applicable (e.g. the LSP can no longer deliver what it has promised), the project manager needs to rethink the project. Can it continue? Does the project need to be adjusted? How can the project be put back on course in order to achieve the intended benefits?

In a formal context, a business case will set out the 'costs, benefits, expected disbenefits, risks and timescales against which the viability is justified and continuing viability is tested' (Office of Government Commerce, 2018, p. 48). In the context of translation services, these considerations will encompass some of the points discussed later in this chapter.

At this point:

? What occurrences might make you think, as a project manager, that a project is no longer viable?
? What might you consider to be a disbenefit (i.e. the opposite of a benefit) in the context of a translation project?
? How might the project manager continually monitor the viability of a project? And against which constraints might this monitoring be particularly prominent?

? Why do translation services exist?
? What benefit do translation services offer to different stakeholders (e.g. LSP, clients, vendors)?

The two sub-sections below present two possible answers to these questions, but many more answers exist beyond these responses.

Facilitating Intercultural Communication

In response to the question prompts above, many readers will have already likely come up with the notion that translation helps to facilitate intercultural communication. Looking at the simple definition of a project (or indeed business-level) benefit as an action that drives a business's situation forward from A to B, translation (broadly defined) can provide the very technical infrastructure by which this can take place. Many clients who have never procured translation services in the past overlook this simple fact. Indeed, DePalma argues that 'most people don't recognize the value of translation until they can't read the language in which something they need or want is available' (2020, p. 363). There has almost certainly been no shortage of businesses that have tried to globalise their operations without translation, most likely to their detriment.

Translation plays a 'key mediating role … in global connectivity and the movement of people and information around the world' (Bielsa, 2020, p. 2). Indeed, because globalisation has resulted in such a rapid rise in mobility and growth of the so-called 'information superhighway', the role of translation has been rendered increasingly invisible as technological developments have started to eliminate many of the most evident problems caused by the language barrier (see Bielsa, 2005). Many of these complexities are being perpetually minimised in the eyes of end users when services such as Google Translate make it so easy to 'convert' a text in Language A into a text in Language B. But one of the inherent tensions in translation in a globalised world is between the 'global and the local': products and services are being sold to the global masses, but knowledge and understanding of the local element still plays such a fundamental role, not only in how the product is marketed and the instruction manuals are presented, for example, but also in the very way in which the product or service is designed.

We should also remember that translation – and communication more generally – goes beyond mere writing on a page or spoken language. The growing attention now being paid to multimodality in translation studies (see, for instance, Boria et al., 2020) highlights the fact that we communicate not only in written and spoken form but also visually, pictorially, through gestures and body language, through actions, and through the very discourse embedded in product and service designs. To offer a well-known example, consider the eminent success of home furnishing retailer IKEA's approach to globalisation. Instead of focusing on the translation of written instructions,

IKEA's products use their now iconic step-by-step images to guide users in assembling their products, and the company also purposely uses words of Scandinavian origin as product names. This approach has been eminently successful, such that many commentators have referred to a process known as 'IKEAzation' (see, for instance, Beninatto & Johnson, 2017, p. 65). The solution does have its critiques, of course, and many readers may have experienced their own frustration in assembling such products at various points, but this brief example shows that 'translation' can take many forms.

? How has IKEA harnessed translation to realise its commercial benefits?

To offer another example, never has the fundamental importance of translation services been more apparent than in humanitarian and other forms of crises. As Federici reports (2020, p. 182), 'the awareness of multilingual communication and its significance is often confined to last-minute requests for language services from anybody who could offer them'. Lack of access to information not only in a language but in a *form* that is understandable to the end user is widely recognised to be a type of discrimination. Enabling such access is a benefit in the rawest of forms: it allows the end users to fulfil a (basic) communicative need. The business case of humanitarian organisations will typically involve varied commitments relating to providing support for affected communities, and the language (and translation) element is a core component of the overarching crisis response strategy. As an addendum to this example, it is always important to remember that benefits, business cases and the like need not be in a strictly commercial environment. From private clients right up to huge multinational companies, and with non-governmental organisations on the side, benefits are sought by everybody, but they will often look different for different types of stakeholders (more on this below).

? How could humanitarian organisations better incorporate translation into their workflows and processes to realise their intended benefits? It may be helpful to consult the chapter by Federici (2020), as well as other publications in the field of 'crisis translation', if this is an area that interests you.
? How would you, as a project manager, potentially advise humanitarian organisations as to the value of translation (broadly defined)?

Translation project management plays an important role in all of these examples, and this wider discussion around intercultural communication also reminds us that project management takes place in situations far removed from the traditional client–LSP–vendor model. But the project manager as an individual can also add value to these transactions, in all contexts. Understanding the client and their needs (and ideally their strategic goals, too) can then feed into the project manager's understanding of the way in which the intercultural communication can be best facilitated, depending on the medium and the context, as well as the more pragmatic matters of cost, time, and quality, among other constraints, all of which are aimed at helping the client to derive maximum benefit from their venture. This brings us to the next sub-section: fulfilling a need.

Fulfilling a Need

The market for language services was valued at $49.6 billion in 2019 (CSA Research, 2019), of which translation accounted for the largest share among translation, interpreting, localisation, and engineering. This demand is met by LSPs and freelance suppliers in the main, and the number of translators and interpreters has grown rapidly since the turn of the millennium, with numbers in the US increasing from 15,000 to 53,000 between 2000 and 2017 (Moorkens, 2020, p. 325), for example. The translation industry is huge and worth a great deal of money to investors, as shown by the large number of mergers and acquisitions that have taken place in recent years (Slator, 2019).

This huge market demand comes from numerous sources: the corporate world, the governmental and supra-governmental sector, non-profit organisations, and private clients, among others. But the source of the demand comes, on a lower level, from the vast data explosion witnessed in the global economy (DePalma, 2016; in DePalma, 2020). Even if only a small fraction of this content needs to be translated, it still creates considerable demand for translation services. In many cases, clients will need to make use of the translation themselves (internally), but sometimes, as we know, translations are geared towards external end users, such as user manuals to accompany a product or websites to draw in new customers.

The problem, for the translation industry, is that many businesses fail to understand the need for translation or to appreciate the potential that it could bring to their operations. Indeed, as DePalma notes, 'it's often the result of business analysis showing limited revenue potential that causes companies not to translate their websites' (2020, p. 363). But yet, as he goes on to observe, 'not supporting the right languages excludes many prospects from starting the customer journey because they have a huge but not surprising preference for consuming information in their native language' (DePalma, 2020, p. 364). Many businesses therefore fail to recognise or to capitalise on the benefits that translation can bring. The wider globalised world can hold considerable potential demand for a company's products and services, but without appropriate translation (or indeed localisation) support, it is not possible to tap into these markets and exploit their full potential.

Most businesses tend to bring in language support only when they successfully identify rising market demand, or an economic analysis points to opportunities in a specific area (DePalma, 2020, p. 364). Questions also arise over the government procurement of language services, especially in multilingual nations or in nations where accessibility and equal opportunities laws feature more or less prominently or demand is more or less substantial.

Translation therefore tends to be a relatively *reactive* industry. A need arises for a particular entity, the entity seeks out a service provider, and the service provider satisfies the need. Satisfaction of the need can bring about benefits for the original entity (and for the service provider), but, as observed in most other economic sectors, this reactive approach – fulfilling needs only as and when they arise – is not necessarily the most productive way to capitalise on potential benefits.

Measuring Success

Success is said to be in the eye of the beholder, and this aphorism could not be more true of benefits in translation project management. Before reading any further, consider the following questions:

? What does success look like in a translation project?
? How do we measure project success?
? What factors impact success?
? How will success differ for different stakeholders?

This section aims to engage with these questions from different perspectives. We have already mentioned above that profit is one of the most obvious forms of benefit to be derived from a translation project, but there are more complex questions to consider here. Who is profiting? In what way? And is there more to business than profit alone? The three sub-sections below consider briefly the profit angle (as well as the *non*-profit angle), client satisfaction, and functionality as three dominant ways to approach the matter of success in translation projects.

More Than Just Profits?

Profit is an obvious benefit. Moreover, profit is a benefit that is appreciated by all stakeholders across the project lifecycle (and beyond). A vendor will always have an eye on their own income (i.e. freelance profit), LSPs are businesses and aim to generate profit as one of their aims, clients will procure translation services usually with a view to enhancing their business in some way (and therefore generating more profit), and end users will in some cases (but not all) make use of translations to enhance their own operations in some way. These principles are not difficult to understand, and the merits of profit generation are clear for all to see.

For LSPs, there are two financial considerations to bear in mind here. Firstly, there is the 'project profit', so to speak, which is often referred to as the 'margin'. As discussed in Chapter 6, this is essentially the money paid by the client for a project minus the money paid out to vendors to carry out the work. Achieving a positive balance at this stage is crucial, of course, because these are not the only expenses involved in running an LSP. The 'true' profit, in essence, would be calculated on the basis of other costs such as utilities (electricity, gas, water, communications, etc.), staff costs (salaries), rent or mortgage payments, insurance, and the numerous other on-going overheads that businesses commit to. Clearly it is difficult to calculate these on a 'per project' basis, as it is virtually impossible to appreciate how much electricity is used, or how many hours of a project manager's time is allocated, for example, for one specific project. Profit is therefore calculated on a higher level and reflects a business-level benefit as opposed to a project-level benefit directly. This level of benefit is usually beyond the remit of most project managers, but they will still need to bear these considerations in mind: the ways in which they cost their projects and manage them in order to satisfy their clients will have a direct bearing on the overall profitability of the LSP.

For clients, the profitability of an investment in translation can be a minor point of tension when procuring translations. Time (and patience) permitting, clients might shop around for quotations because they want the best price and this, in turn, feeds into potentially higher returns on investment. Higher returns on investment are just one of many indicators that can serve as a reflection of benefits. However, project managers still play an important role here, not only in trying to offer the best possible price to the client (thereby maximising their benefits, in their eyes) but also – and arguably more importantly – in highlighting the value that they, as a project manager and as an LSP more widely, add to the project to justify the potentially higher cost that might be incurred if the translation is procured through that specific LSP as opposed to another. A benefit for one stakeholder can therefore be a benefit for another stakeholder if it is approached in the right spirit of cooperation and collaboration; a successful project brings benefits (monetary and otherwise) to both of these key stakeholders if done well.

But what about non-profit work? A small emphasis is placed on non-profit projects in the translation industry. Evidently, these are not a staple of an LSP's project diet but constitute a very important supplement to the wider business landscape. Profits are not the 'be-all and end-all' of business; non-profit work can be just as rewarding in terms of business goodwill and reputation. Many non-profit organisations are set up precisely for this very purpose, such as Translators Without Borders (see Box 9.2), and many LSPs 'volunteer' their services directly to such organisations, either on an on-going basis (e.g. a certain amount of content each month) or in response to one-off shocks and events such as the earthquake and tsunami in Japan in 2011, or the Russian invasion of Ukraine in 2022.

> **Box 9.2 Translators Without Borders**
>
> According to its website, Translators Without Borders (TWB) is a 'global community of over 80,000 translators and language specialists offering language services to humanitarian and development organizations worldwide'. Founded in 1993, it was set up to connect translators with non-profit organisations focusing on health, nutrition, and education, and to this day continues to work to 'close the language gaps that hinder critical humanitarian and international development efforts worldwide'.
>
> TWB reports that it translates more than ten million words per year by working with thousands of volunteer translators around the world, and its work focuses on 'crisis response, development, capacity building, and advocacy'. Many LSPs also partner with TWB as sponsors, providing not only financial support for its work but also project support in the form of free or reduced-price translation services. Volunteers can also apply to work as translators alongside project managers and graphic and web page designers, and TWB runs a Community Recognition Program to reward volunteers. TWB also offers numerous language resources and glossaries.
>
> Explore the TWB website (https://translatorswithoutborders.org) and consider the following questions:
>
> ? Why does TWB exist and what benefits does it derive from its work?
> ? What benefits do the end users derive from the work of TWB?
> ? What about the volunteers? Do they see any benefits from their contributions?
> ? How does TWB incentivise the involvement of volunteers (both freelancers and LSPs)?

? Can you find specific case studies on LSPs' websites where they have provided translation services *pro bono* (free of charge)?
? Under what circumstances did they provide the services?
? Why do you feel that the LSP made this decision?

Client Satisfaction

Client satisfaction is another potential benefit for all stakeholders involved in the project lifecycle. Again, vendors will be keen to impress the LSP, the LSP will be keen to impress the client, and the client, in turn, will be keen to impress the ultimate end users of the translation (if the translation is not being used internally). The problem, as noted in the *SDL Translation Technology Insights 2020* survey, is that 'clients ... assume [a good baseline of quality is] a given, and then proceed to put pressure on translation professionals to produce it more quickly, cost-effectively, or both' (SDL, 2020, p. 5). This causes immense pressure on LSPs across various project management constraints.

This is where the client–LSP agreement (see Chapter 2) is particularly important in terms of ensuring that project benefits are properly realised. A clear delineation of goals, responsibilities, and expectations in the client–LSP agreement will ensure that all parties are 100% clear on what will be delivered, what services will be undertaken in pursuit of those deliverables, and any specifications with regard to quality standards or other requirements. As with the profit element above, the project manager plays a key role here (as discussed at great length in Chapter 2): the project manager needs to manage the client's expectations and not promise too much (which might prove unfeasible), but also not promise too little (which could be off-putting for the client). It is therefore a careful balance between satisfying the client's wants and needs in this client–LSP agreement and actually ending up with a contractual arrangement to deliver a 'fit-for-purpose' translation. This concept has come up at various points in this textbook, most notably in Chapters 7 and 8. Fit-for-purpose does not necessarily mean 'poor quality', but simply the necessary level of quality to satisfy the client's needs. Sometimes this will mean lower quality is satisfactory, but at other times very high quality might be necessary. This is precisely why clear targets need to be specified in the client–LSP agreement.

On the client side, ensuring that the translation fulfils its intended purpose is a key determinant of the client's own customer satisfaction. If the translated user manual is unintelligible, buyers of that particular product will be deeply dissatisfied with the client's product and leave negative reviews, and this will impact on the client's business reputation. Similarly, if the client's website is poorly localised, it will reflect badly on the client's services and other offerings, likely resulting in less incoming business and rendering the initial website localisation project a poor investment.

Satisfaction can of course be measured. We spoke in Chapter 4 about the importance of feedback, and this plays an important role in determining client satisfaction. Gauging client satisfaction at the end of a project is useful on a lower level, but semi-regular 'check-ins' (e.g. quarterly, annually) with regular clients will help project managers to touch base with them, understand their satisfaction with the LSP's services, and adapt if necessary. This is precisely how satisfaction is gauged in other industries, so why not translation too? Keeping clients happy and showing a willingness to change practices, act on (positive and negative) feedback, and accommodate their needs will always have a beneficial impact on a client's desire to bring business back to an LSP. Clients whose benefits have been realised through a successful translation project will in turn bring about likely benefits for an LSP through repeat orders. Benefits for the various stakeholders, although different in nature, are usually complementary: a benefit for one stakeholder will often have an accompanying benefit for another across the production process.

Functionality and Usability

Another benefit, albeit one that is much more client oriented, is the functionality of the translation. For all the focus that Translation Studies as a discipline has placed on the 'purpose' of the translation (see various literature on the functionalist paradigm, such as Nord, 2018, *inter alia*, for a good introductory text), target readers and end users' *real* (as opposed to assumed) needs and reception have been marginalised at times in the academic realm. In the corporate sphere – i.e. translation practice – the picture is better, but there are some LSPs that are guilty of a 'fire-and-forget' approach to project completion.

Project managers spend a lot of time trying to understand what the client (and, in turn, the end users) wants or expects from a translation, but how often in practice do we truly understand whether those wants, needs, and expectations were satisfied? In a market dominated by calls for tenders (often, sadly, awarded to the lowest bidder), innovation is key for project managers: finding new ways to add value, diversify their offerings, and deliver on client benefits while also protecting their own benefits. One of the key ways in which this can manifest itself is in ensuring that the translations are 'functional', in the sense that they fulfil their intended function.

Despite the prevalence of commentary on usability and functionality in Translation Studies, it is an area that has not been subject to a great deal of attention. However, one of the most extensive studies is Suojanen et al.'s (2015) book *User-Centered Translation*. While it goes beyond the scope of this textbook to review this content in any depth, there are two concepts from this work that are particularly worthy of note and may be areas that project managers would consider discussing with clients during the preparation of a project: **usability** and **user experience**. These concepts are defined as follows:

> Usability refers to the ease with which users can use a product to achieve their goals; they should be able to achieve their goals according to their expectations and without obstacles or hindrances.
> [Suojanen et al., 2015, p. 2]

> Usability is ultimately about the *user's* relative experience of the success of use. Usability is thus, in essence, user- and context-dependent. … It is indeed central to consider the context of use, which consists of several elements: user characteristics, the quality of the task, the

equipment and the environment. If usability is ultimately the user's subjective experience that the use has been successful, it is also relevant to gather information about user experience, not just about the problems that the user experiences when using the product.

[Suojanen et al., 2015, p. 14]

What is of particular interest in Suojanen et al.'s book is that user-centredness is a process, and an iterative, cyclical one at that, 'where users are analyzed and usability is evaluated via recursive usability research methods' (Suojanen et al., 2015, p. 4). Although the project manager is not likely to be responsible for testing usability in such a comprehensive (or indeed scientific) manner, the process delineated in the book is of considerable benefit to the project manager when thinking about the benefit for the client of a 'usable' translation.

Firstly, the authors outline that there must be a translation need (i.e. 'a communicative need for the translation' [Suojanen et al., 2015, p. 4]) and that part of this need will involve defining users to ensure that the translation meets their expectations (especially in interactive media such as websites). Next, a written specification is required to ensure 'mutual understanding of the goals of the translation between the stakeholders' (Suojanen et al., 2015, p.5). Importantly, they stress that this is not a 'wish list, but is to be drafted in dialogue and in mutual respect of the other party's expertise', including 'desired quality level' and 'agreed measurements to assess it' in terms of 'whether or not the translation's agreed *usability* goals have been reached' (Suojanen et al., 2015, p. 5). The process also involves mental models of the intended users and an on-going assessment of usability (including dedicated usability testing with target groups), followed by a project post-mortem and even subsequent reception research (Suojanen et al., 2015, p. 6).

Such extensive testing would go beyond the scope of the vast majority of translation projects that project managers are required to handle, but there will be some instances where nothing is off the table and user experience (or UX) data is paramount. Indeed, the PRINCE2 project management framework explicitly states:

Although one of PRINCE2's principles is a focus on products, it is important to remember that the benefits underpinning the business justification of the project are delivered through the use of the products produced by the project, not just their delivery. As the project's outcomes and benefits are often only realized after the project has closed, it is easy for project teams to become focused solely on creating products (the outputs). The link from the project's outputs to outcomes and benefits needs to be clearly identified and made visible to those involved in the project, otherwise there is a danger that the original purpose of the project can get lost and benefits will not be realized.

[Office of Government Commerce, 2018, p. 54]

Thus, the project manager will need to use his or her expertise to tie together the intended benefits for the client – in terms of the product's usability and the user experience of its end users – with the specifications for the project itself and what the project deliverables will look like. The benefits for the LSP also factor in here, of course: if the intended client benefits are suitably realised, then the LSP's own benefits – reputation, profit, success, etc. – will also likely be realised if the project is well managed from the perspective of other project constraints (cost in particular). Ultimately, the project manager and the vendors that carry out the work need to represent the end users: they are the stakeholders who are likely to have the most complete picture of the needs and expectations of the end users, given that their expertise offers the all-important bridge between the multiple cultural perspectives in the context-dependent situation of the project.

Who Benefits and in What Ways?

Benefits accrue to different stakeholders in different ways, depending on their role in the project lifecycle, their aims and objectives, and their direct (or indirect) contribution to the project's success. All parties in the project lifecycle will play a role in shaping their own fate with regard to the benefits that they derive from a project, but the project manager has a particularly important role here in terms of trying to secure the success of the project, which will in turn have a substantial impact on whether the benefits for the LSP itself are realised or not.

To discuss this further, let us use a tangible case study. The case study presented in Box 2.1 (Chapter 2; also revisited in Chapter 7) is a relatively straightforward project for this purpose, and one that is also incredibly commonplace in the translation industry nowadays. To recap briefly, the client was a website designer who wanted to rebrand and redesign its own website and have it translated into Arabic, French, German, and Spanish with a view to tapping into demand in new international markets. Before you read further:

? Who are the stakeholders involved in this project?
? What are the contributions (i.e. the individual projects or tasks) of each stakeholder (vendors, of which there may be many, LSPs, clients, and end users)?
? What are their outputs and outcomes (i.e. the tangible product or service that they are delivering either for themselves or for another stakeholder) and what do they facilitate or improve?
? What are their benefits (i.e. the measurable impacts of their outcomes)?

The possible stakeholders in a translation project are many, but, for the purposes of our discussion here, we will limit our scope to one vendor (a translator in this case), the LSP as a whole, the client, and the end user.

Beginning with the vendor, his or her 'project' or specific involvement in the wider project will in this case be limited to translation of the original English copy into one of the specified target languages. On a lower level, therefore, the role is one of 'transferring' the message of the content (linguistically, culturally, etc.) from one language and locale into another language and locale according to the specifications on the project brief, which may also specify the use of specific terminology, or require adherence to a specific style guide provided by the project manager. This stage will likely be prior to another vendor taking on the subsequent task of revising the initial translation, and it will also be performed concurrently with other vendors working on the translations into the other specified target languages. This particular vendor's project is therefore one part of a larger whole. Individually (and collectively), the vendor's outcome is the production of translated copy in the specified target language in accordance with the stipulated brief. The translation may – in this case – have also been carried out in a specific CAT tool and delivered in a specified file format (e.g. Trados return package, .sdlrpx). This file is a tangible (in a sense) outcome of the vendor's project that he or she can deliver to the project manager. The benefits that he or she derives from the completion of this project include LSP satisfaction, an improved relationship with the LSP, income from completion of the project (in proportion to the amount of work carried out), the potential of future work from the LSP, and an improved reputation in the eyes of the LSP and the wider translation community (when listed on the vendor's CV, for example). Of course, this is a very idealistic picture, as this assumes successful (near-flawless) completion of the project. Varying degrees of dissatisfaction can result in varying degrees of 'disbenefits' or at least reductions in benefits, including a very perceptible reduction in income for poor performance if appropriate, which would then have a substantial knock-on effect on reputation, the vendor–LSP relationship, and, of course, the potential for more work in the future.

For the LSP (represented by the project manager), the project, outcomes, and benefits change. The project or 'task' is, of course, one of project management: ensuring that the web design packages are suitably prepared, translated, and localised, and that project constraints are appropriately managed. During the course of the project, the LSP will produce various forms of documentation or files in order to manage these processes (quotations, client–LSP agreement, CAT tool project packages, etc.) and bring the project to a successful conclusion. The tangible outcomes of the project will be the localised web design packages in the various specified languages, satisfying the quality standards agreed with the client (having also gone through the required processes stipulated in the client–LSP agreement), as well as ancillary outcomes in the form of TMs, TBs, and other resources. The benefits of successful completion include heightened client satisfaction and a stronger client–LSP relationship, profit from the project, increased potential for repeat custom in the future, and repeat validation of project management processes (i.e. showing that the processes worked as intended). The ancillary outcomes (TMs, TBs, etc.) are also a form of benefit in that they can be recycled and re-used in future projects, subject to any specific arrangements with the client.

For the client, its own project is to procure translation services for its updated website so that it can market its services internationally in a number of new markets. On the one hand, this entails the successful recruitment of a suitable LSP, and, on the other hand, it entails successful (on-going) communication with the LSP to ensure that its needs and expectations are suitably communicated at the start of the project and throughout the project lifecycle. The outcome of the project, in this case, will not be produced by the client but will, in fact, be *received* by the client from the LSP (who in turn will have received various components of the project from different vendors). But, ultimately, the client will end up with a new website in English (created in-house by the client), as well as the Arabic, German, Spanish, and French versions supplied by the LSP. The benefits of this outcome could include new business deals with international clients in Arabic-, German-, Spanish-, and French-speaking countries, increased sales of web design services (the main offering of the client), increased profits, an enhanced reputation for web design services over time, and an overall expansion of the business.

Finally, we come to the end user. In this case, the end user is likely to be another company that is looking for web design services, most likely from one of the new locales targeted by the investment in the translated website. The end user's project, therefore, will be one of procuring web design

Stakeholder	Project	Outcomes	Benefits
Vendor (Translator)	Translation of website copy; initial 'transfer' from ST to TT prior to next stage in production phase (e.g. revision)	Translated copy as a CAT-tool project package	Enhanced LSP satisfaction; enhanced LSP relationship; income; potential for return custom; reputation
LSP	Project management; delivery of localised web design packages; successful management of project constraints	Localised web design packages; TM and TB resources	Enhanced client satisfaction; enhanced client relationship; profit; potential for return custom; successful project management processes
Client	Procure translation services for international business expansion (website localisation)	New website in EN, in addition to AR, DE, ES and FR	New business deals with international clients via localised website; increased sales and profits; increased reputation; expansion of business
End user	Procure web development services from international web developer	New company website for end user's company	Same benefits as client (see above), but in a different domain

Figure 9.1 Stakeholder benefits

210 *Evaluating Translation Project Constraints*

services from the client (the web designer). Its outcome will be a new company website to advertise the end user's products or services, and the benefits that it derives from this new website will likely be very similar to those of the client (new business, increased profits, enhanced reputation, etc.).

We should also bear in mind that there is a potential added benefit here for the LSP. Through the LSP's own enhanced relationship with the client following successful delivery of the translated website, if the end user is also interested in having its new website translated, there is an excellent opportunity for word-of-mouth referral (something that the project manager could mention and capitalise on at the time of the project's final sign-off). The opportunities for benefits on the back of the project outcomes are therefore numerous for all parties involved (see Figure 9.1 by way of summary).

* * *

Although some elements of benefits are beyond the control of the project manager, he or she still plays a key role through the way in which the project is managed. The project needs to be managed in such a way that it enables vendors to do what they do best (provide their expert linguistic, cultural, and translation know-how and expertise) and allow them to focus solely and exclusively on this task. This can, of course, be achieved by setting up a forum (e.g. a carefully configured project in a CAT tool) in which they can produce the best possible outcomes and maximise their own benefits, which will in turn allow the LSP to produce its own outcomes by drawing on various vendors and maximise its own benefits. If the LSP is able to do this successfully, this will in turn allow the client to derive the intended outcome from the project and realise the intended benefits, which in turn enables the end user to do likewise. The project manager can also help the client to understand which elements of a proposed translation project will enable the realisation of specific benefits, and even propose new or alternative ways to achieve those benefits that the client might not have even considered. The whole process – the entire 'benefit chain', if you will – is intrinsically interconnected: acting in the best interests of the project as a whole (as opposed to the best interests of one stakeholder) will enable all stakeholders to benefit from the project, provided that the specifications have been clearly defined and expectations carefully managed by the project manager.

* * *

Topics for Discussion and Assignments

1. Using one of the case studies on the TS Portal, and perhaps drawing on a previous quotation that you have drawn up, work out the total profit that your LSP will generate from the project. (Ignore the cost of overheads, wages, etc., which are difficult to factor into these calculations.) What is

the profit as a percentage? Do you feel satisfied with the profit? How do you feel personally about the level of profit generated?
2. Reflect on the role of translation in the globalised economy. What role does translation play? What is its value to the global economy? In what ways does it facilitate or impede cross-cultural communication? How do these questions and answers feed into the day-to-day work of a project manager? Your response could form the basis for an in-class discussion, a written assignment, or a presentation.
3. Using another of the case studies on the TS Portal, conduct an analysis of the benefits for each stakeholder, using Figure 9.1 as a template.

Further Reading

Beninatto and Johnson (2017) offer a discussion of the three core functions of LSPs (pp. 134–194), looking at how different stakeholders contribute to the value chain and the value added at each stage. While not addressing benefits directly, it deals with many of the same points covered in this chapter but from a different perspective, as well as looks at how vendor management can contribute to the overall realisation of business benefits.

Bielsa (2005) and Bielsa (2020) are good points of reference to look at the wider role of translation in the context of globalisation.

References

Beninatto, R., & Johnson, T. (2017). *The general theory of the translation company*. Nimdzi.
Bielsa, E. (2005). Globalisation and translation: A theoretical approach. *Language and Intercultural Communication*, 5(2), 131–144. https://doi.org/10.1080/14708470508668889
Bielsa, E. (2020). Introduction: The intersection between translation and globalization. In E. Bielsa & D. Kapsaskis (Eds.), *The Routledge handbook of translation and globalization* (pp. 1–10). Routledge.
Boria, M., Carreres, Á., Noriega-Sánchez, M., & Tomalin, M. (Eds.). (2020). *Translation and multimodality: Beyond words*. Routledge.
CSA Research. (2019). Global market for outsourced translation and interpreting services and technology to reach US$49.60 billion in 2019. Retrieved 23 July 2020 from https://csa-research.com/More/Media/Press-Releases/ArticleID/546/Global-Market-for-Outsourced-Translation-and-Interpreting-Services-and-Technology-to-Reach-US-49-60-Billion-in-2019
DePalma, D. A. (2016). *The calculus of global content*. Retrieved 9 May 2022 from https://insights.csa-research.com/reportaction/36512/Toc
DePalma, D. A. (2020). Language demand and supply. In E. Bielsa & D. Kapsaskis (Eds.), *The Routledge handbook of translation and globalization* (pp. 363–374). Routledge.
Federici, F. M. (2020). Translation in contexts of crisis. In E. Bielsa & D. Kapsaskis (Eds.), *The Routledge handbook of translation and globalization* (pp. 176–189). Routledge.

Moorkens, J. (2020). Translation in the neoliberal era. In E. Bielsa & D. Kapsaskis (Eds.), *The Routledge handbook of translation and globalization* (pp. 323–336). Routledge.

Nord, C. (2018). *Translating as a purposeful activity: Functionalist approaches explained* (2nd ed.). Routledge.

Office of Government Commerce. (2018). *Managing successful projects with PRINCE2 2017 edition* (6th ed.). The Stationery Office Ltd.

Project Management Institute. (2017). *A guide to the Project Management Body of Knowledge (PMBOK® guide)* (6th ed.). Project Management Institute, Inc.

SDL. (2020). *SDL translation technology insights 2020. Coping with the rise in pressure: Why humanizing technology is key to translation success.* Retrieved from https://www.rws.com/localization/products/resources/translation-technology-insights-2020/

Slator. (2019). *Slator 2018 Language Industry M&A and Funding Report.* Retrieved 9 May 2022 from https://slator.com/data-research/slator-2018-language-industry-ma-and-funding-report/

Suojanen, T., Koskinen, K., & Tuominen, T. (2015). *User-centered translation.* Routledge.

10 Risk

> **Learning outcomes:**
> - Understand and use key terminology on risk management
> - Employ the 'Identify, Assess, Plan, Implement' method to manage risk
> - Develop an awareness of who has responsibility for risk management and in what ways
> - Analyse – both qualitatively and quantitatively – the impact of risks
> - Prepare possible responses to tangible risks that might arise in a translation project

Risk is one of the most difficult aspects of translation project management, as, by its very nature, risk is unpredictable and difficult to control directly. It can, however, be managed and manipulated, sometimes for gain, but often simply to reduce some of the negative effects of risk if left unchecked. All projects are risky, as they combine varying degrees of complexity and an on-going drive to deliver benefits, all the while being influenced by other project constraints (timescales, costs, quality, etc.), assumptions, and stakeholder expectations (which can be conflicting and/or changing). An LSP's approach to risk management should be controlled so as to generate value, but still balance risk and reward. Project risk management is therefore inextricably linked with project success. The PMBOK's explanation is particularly useful here:

> Individual project risk is an uncertain event or condition that, if it occurs, has a positive or negative effect on one or more project objectives. ... Project Risk Management aims to exploit or enhance positive risks (opportunities) while avoiding or mitigating negative risks (threats). Unmanaged threats may result in issues or problems such as delay, cost overruns, performance shortfall, or loss of reputation. Opportunities

DOI: 10.4324/9781003132813-12

that are captured can lead to benefits such as reduced time and cost, improved performance, or reputation.

[Project Management Institute, 2017, p. 397]

What is particularly noteworthy – and often overlooked – is that risk need not be something negative. Indeed, risk can be positive and beneficial. As noted in the above quotation, a synonym for a positive risk is an **opportunity**. Many tend only to think of risk as negative (a **threat**). In basic terms, project risk management is about increasing the likelihood and impact of positive risks and reducing the likelihood and impact of negative risks. In project management terms, risk is therefore defined as the relationship between the **probability** of a threat or opportunity occurring and the scale of its **impact** on the project's objectives (Office of Government Commerce, 2018, p. 120).

Lammers provides a succinct example of a negative project risk in his chapter 'Risk Management in Localization' (2011, pp. 212–213, paraphrased). A number of files are sent to a translator, but the word count is double the original estimate. As a result of this unexpected increase in volume (the **condition**), the vendor cannot complete the work on time (the **event**), which in turn causes delays later in the project workflow (the **impact**). This simple example seems to have a relatively straightforward cause: either the client underestimated the volume of the project, or the project manager failed to calculate the correct volume. Both of these eventualities are likely avoidable, illustrating the importance of carrying out pre-production tasks carefully. Although it might not seem like it, the feasibility study (see Chapter 2) is an excellent example of pro-active risk management: by carefully examining the source files, finding out the availability of suitable vendors, devising a workable schedule, and calculating an accurate quotation, the project manager is anticipating possible negative risks and implementing clear strategies to avoid them. Reacting to a negative risk after it has occurred will never be as successful as a pro-active approach to risk management. A pro-active approach to risk management implies that appropriate project management processes are in place at the LSP and have been followed. Hence, if such processes are followed, negative risks should automatically reduce in probability and impact, and positive risks should increase in probability and impact. How these elements can be analysed and managed in practice will be the focus of the second half of this chapter, beginning with an assessment of project and organisational risks for LSPs and closing with risk responses.

Risk Assessment

Risk management plays an important role in project management as well as business management more generally, as the level of risk and uncertainty varies throughout the project lifecycle. As a preliminary point for consideration, it is helpful to analyse how risk changes throughout the project lifecycle compared with how the cost of changes to a project might change, as this gives an important insight into the specific relevance of risk management to translation projects. Figure 10.1 plots project risk and the cost of changes to the project over time, from project start to project end. Risk and uncertainty are highest at the start of the project, as no work has been carried out and, in some cases, this might be the first project working for a particular client or outsourcing a translation to a new translator. Over time, however, these factors decrease as the project progresses and certain deliverables are accepted or milestones reached. As noted at various points in this book, pre-production is the period when the project manager has the greatest control over a project, and it is at this time that the project manager's influence over the end product is highest, in terms of the preparation put into preparing the project and associated resources and instructions. However, while risk decreases over the course of a project (risk never disappears entirely), the cost of making changes increases constantly from the moment that a project begins until it is delivered to the client.

Consider a translation of a tourist brochure, for example. In pre-production (see T_1 in Figure 10.1), when the project manager is preparing resources and the work breakdown structure for the various vendors involved, the cost of any change to the scope or required quality of the product will be negligible (C_1); it will simply require more time for the project manager to adjust the materials. In production, once the vendors are midway through the translation (T_2), the risk of uncertain events occurring has dropped (R_2), but the cost of making changes – if the client suddenly decides that a portion of the ST needs to be changed, for example – will have risen (C_2). Once the project has been released to the client (T_3), if the client suddenly realises that there is a problem with the deliverables, the cost of making any changes will have risen significantly (C_3), but the risk of such extensive, unexpected changes

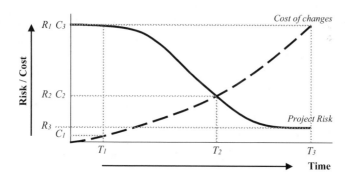

Figure 10.1 Project risk and cost of changes over time
Adapted from Project Management Institute (2013, p. 40)

occurring are very low (but not non-existent) (R_3). This is, of course, a fairly crude generalisation of project risk and the cost of changes, but, for many projects, these basic principles hold true.

It goes without saying that not all projects require the same level of risk assessment as others. Indeed, since projects are a constant in the life of an LSP, it would in fact be impractical to carry out detailed risk assessments for each and every project. What will likely happen, for most LSPs, is that risk assessment takes place on a macro level – i.e. by directors and senior executives of the company – for all types of risk that might be encountered across the business as a whole, including projects, while smaller-scale, micro-level risk assessments might take place only for projects that are particularly complex, or involve a large budget or a complicated schedule, thereby requiring an assessment of risks specific to that project. The PMBOK refers to the 'tailoring' of risk assessments, depending on the project's size, complexity, importance, and development approach (Project Management Institute, 2017, p. 400). If, for instance, the project is sufficiently small in scale, or simple in scope, or not especially important to the business's overall strategy, a simplified risk assessment might be more than adequate, and this will likely be the case for the vast majority of translation projects.

Hence, in this chapter, we will be taking an LSP-level perspective on risk management, drawing on the sorts of risk assessments that directors and senior managers might appraise when setting up a new LSP, or when holding regular reviews of risks over the last quarter or year, for example. Risk management is an iterative process; it does not end once an initial risk management meeting has taken place. Risks need to be identified, assessed, and planned for, and plans need to be implemented continuously, alongside comprehensive and thorough risk communication throughout the organisational hierarchy (see Figure 10.2), as more and more risk data becomes available from the LSP's operations.

Risk Management Plan

Risk management planning involves determining what the approach to risk management will be. This will cover how risks are identified and assessed, how risk responses are determined and implemented, and how risk management is communicated throughout a project and after it is complete (see Office of Government Commerce, 2018, p. 121). One of the first aspects to consider is who the risk owner is. Consider the following questions:

? Who is responsible for risk in a translation project?
? Which stakeholders play a role (in any capacity) in risk management?

There is a variety of different stakeholders involved in translation projects and the management of LSPs more generally – senior executives, project managers (senior and junior), support staff (e.g. ICT specialists),

Risk 217

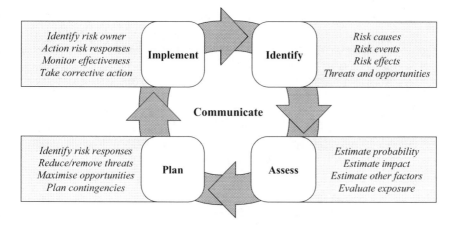

Figure 10.2 Risk management procedure
Adapted from Office of Government Commerce (2018, p. 123)

Box 10.1 Describing attitudes to risk

Businesses will likely want to give some thought to how much risk they are willing to allow in their operations. There are four related terms that concern a business's views on risk:

Risk exposure: 'the extent of risk borne by the organization at the time' (Office of Government Commerce, 2018, p. 121)
Risk appetite: 'the degree of uncertainty an organization or individual is willing to accept in anticipation of a reward' (Project Management Institute, 2017, p. 720)
Risk tolerance: 'the threshold levels of risk exposure that, with appropriate approvals, can be exceeded, but which when exceeded will trigger some form of response (e.g. reporting the situation to senior management for action)' (Office of Government Commerce, 2018, p. 131)
Risk threshold: 'the measure of acceptable variation around an objective that reflects the risk appetite of the organization and stakeholders' (Project Management Institute, 2017, p. 721)

These concepts are difficult to quantify and are often loosely defined in fairly qualitative terms. However, it is possible to consider tolerances and thresholds in quantitative form when talking about constraints

> such as timescales and costs. For very specific types of risk (e.g. missed deadlines, budget overspends, etc.) it is relatively straightforward to set thresholds of acceptable risk exposure. For instance, with regard to a specific project budget, the risk threshold for the project's costs might be based around the minimum *required* margin (i.e. profit on the project) for the LSP to cover that project's contribution to the LSP's running costs and overheads. Up to that threshold, additional costs can be tolerated if it means that the project is delivered in line with its specifications (the anticipated reward of making a profit), but, beyond that threshold, the potential costs become so great that some form of response is required.
>
> ? In your opinion, is the risk appetite of an average LSP likely to be low, medium, or high? Why?
> ? How might an LSP's risk appetite differ depending on the type of translation offered or the domain focus?
> ? How might an LSP's risk appetite (and associated tolerance and thresholds) correlate with other industries – for example, investment banking, insurance, legal services, accounting, logistics, etc.?

vendors, clients, etc. – all of which play their own individual role in risk management. Who is responsible for each element of risk management ultimately depends on the nature of the risk identified and the planned response.

In order to analyse the risks inherent in translation projects and an LSP's operations more generally, project managers and senior executives will need to consider the descriptions and scope of specific translation projects (for project-level risk management) and any risks identified at a business level. There is no single list of possible risks for different industries and different types of projects: all risk management processes tend to be developed as bespoke solutions for a specific business or a specific project. This is where expert judgement comes into play. As a newcomer to the translation industry, this might offer little solace, but inexperience does not preclude the identification of possible risks. Indeed, most forms of risk identification take place in meetings involving multiple members of staff at different levels of the business hierarchy.

These meetings offer opportunities for identifying possible risks that could occur in different areas of a business or different types of translation projects. Many risk management approaches will start with a high-level overview of different forms of risk, typically referred to as a **risk breakdown structure** (**RBS**) (see Box 10.2). Typically, members will then **brainstorm**

Box 10.2 Risk breakdown structure (RBS)

Project management frameworks such as the PMBOK Guide and PRINCE2 offer examples of a generic RBS, and, ultimately, the specific contents of an RBS will be tailored to the industry in question. An example of an RBS is provided in Figure 10.3, drawing on versions of the PMBOK and Lammers (2011). An RBS breaks down possible sources into a hierarchy of increasing levels of detail and serves as a prompt for risk management meetings to consider the sorts of risks that might be inherent in a project or across the business as a whole. Sometimes the higher-level categories are based on a PESTLE analysis (political, economic, social, technological, legal, and environmental risks), but, in a translation context, the higher-level categories could equally be different phases of the translation lifecycle, different stakeholders, and, more generally, any higher-level categories that work.

Figure 10.3 Example risk breakdown structure (RBS)

Adapted from Project Management Institute (2008, p. 280), Project Management Institute (2017, p. 405), and Lammers (2011, p. 213)

Ultimately, an RBS is solely a prompt; it only needs to function for the purposes of a risk management meeting to aid in identifying possible project or business-level risks. Using the RBS in Figure 10.3, one source of 'External Risk' is the 'Market'. Within this category, risks could include exchange rate fluctuations (see Box 6.2 in Chapter 6) or the appearance of a new direct competitor offering near-identical translation services in the same locality and same specialisms. In the same general category of 'External Risk', 'Environment' might include man-made or natural disasters such as power cuts, flooding,

220 *Evaluating Translation Project Constraints*

> hurricanes, and tornadoes, etc., all of which would interfere with a vendor's ability to carry out their tasks properly.
>
> ? What additional sub-categories for project risk and/or organisational risk can you think of under 'Technical', 'Project Management', 'Commercial and Organisational', and 'External' risks?
> ? Using the categories in the RBS in Figure 10.3, try to identify at least one specific example of a risk for each sub-category under 'Technical', 'Project Management', 'Commercial and Organisational', and 'External' risks.

possible risks, drawing on the diverse expertise of staff from different roles and different departments of the LSP (project management, sales, marketing, accounting, legal, etc.). Other sources of inspiration for identifying possible risks include a **risk register** (more on this below) and general lists or records of previous risks specific to the LSP or the industry more generally. Meetings can also be held with key clients to seek their views on possible sources of risk.

The risk management plan is therefore about laying down broad directives regarding the LSP's attitudes towards risk, identifying general categories of risk that might occur either within projects or during the LSP's operations more widely, and giving some thought to who has responsibilities for risk management within the organisation.

Risk Identification

LSPs will need to give some consideration to specific forms of risk that they might encounter during the course of their operations and during specific projects. Sometimes possible risks can be easily identified from project documentation, such as specifications on the project's scope and required quality (i.e. what specific tasks, processes, and deliverables are required), the project schedule (i.e. what are the key project milestones, deliverable dates, scheduling assumptions, etc.), and project cost (i.e. any uncertainties or estimates used in the costing). Others can also be found by looking at the client–LSP agreement and moving beyond the specifics of the project itself. For instance, clauses on confidentiality, payment terms, or non-compete clauses could all be seen as potential threats or opportunities, depending on the types of risks identified. Equally, industry standards, benchmarks, and even legislation or regulations can be possible sources of risk for a project or for an LSP.

As noted in the preceding section, different forms of structural breakdowns can serve as a prompt at risk management meetings, where the various meeting participants can each provide their own perspective on possible risks. We have already looked at **risk breakdown structures (RBS)** (see Box 10.2) in the context of higher-level risk categorisation and possible sources of risk. A similar category-based approach is a **SWOT analysis** (Strengths, Weaknesses, Opportunities, and Threats), which is typically used more in business strategy plans. Both RBS and SWOT approaches can be used together to identify risks and their **effects** for specific projects and across the LSP as a whole (or indeed the industry more widely). Once specific risks and their effects have been identified, a **root cause analysis** can be considered to identify the underlying **cause** of a specific risk or a specific **event** that might give rise to a risk. For example, if 'poor quality' is identified as a possible risk, the root cause may be inadequate checks of vendor qualifications, not requesting references from previous customers, or poor (or non-existent) testing of vendors before outsourcing work to them. An example of a risk event might be a sudden drop in exchange rates, leading to a decrease in a project's profit margin.

? Having now read about the RBS approach and briefly about SWOT analyses, try to draw up a list of possible risks that could occur for a translation project.
? Draw up a similar list of risks for an LSP on a business level.

It can also be helpful to think of specific risks in terms of the various project constraints – timescales, costs, scope, quality, and benefits – and to use these broad categories to identify specific examples of possible negative risks (threats) and positive risks (opportunities). As some readers may have noted over the preceding chapters, project constraints tend to be associated with a certain number of assumptions. For instance, in Chapter 5 we mentioned the 'industry-standard' assumption that translators can translate 3,000 words per day. However, making such assumptions without checking these with the vendors in question is inherently risky. These sorts of assessments are referred to as an **assumption and constraint analysis**. Threats can arise if assumptions are inaccurate, changing, inconsistent, or incomplete, but opportunities are also possible if restrictive assumptions (such as the aforementioned words-per-day throughput) can be relaxed (e.g. if a translator can in fact translate 4,000 words per day).

We will briefly explore four examples of possible risks that might be encountered in translation project management, on both a project and business level, to serve as a prompt for readers to consider different types of risks in the translation industry.

> **Example 1** The first example is the non-payment of fees for translation services (a negative risk). Unfortunately, this is one of the more common risks in the translation industry and often reflects poor business practices on the part of the client (poor organisation and payment processes) as opposed to anything that the LSP has done

wrong specifically. Using the RBS provided in Figure 10.3, this risk could fall under several categories: Commercial and Organisational Risk > Contractual Terms and Conditions, Client-Business Relations, or Funding. Using these categories as a springboard for reflection, we could consider the possible root causes of this risk. Perhaps the client has gone bankrupt, begging the question of whether this eventuality could have been avoided (see below in 'Risk Response'); perhaps a technological fault has meant that the client's bank is unable to make transfers; or perhaps the client is having payment issues with its own clients in turn. These possibilities highlight that one seemingly straightforward risk can in fact have multiple root causes, which, in turn, constitute separate risks in different areas.

Example 2 The second example is the loss of a client (a negative risk). If it transpires, at a later date, that a client no longer wants to use the LSP's services (RBS: Commercial and Organisational Risk > Client-Business Relations), this could have multiple root causes. Perhaps they were dissatisfied with the quality of the final deliverables; perhaps they were dissatisfied with how the project managers handled the quality complaints; perhaps the client's feedback was not sought by the project manager, which failed to reveal their dissatisfaction with the deliverables; or perhaps the client simply found cheaper services through another LSP.

Example 3 The third example is early delivery of a translation (a positive risk). For a particular project, the early delivery of a translation by several days is clearly an opportunity (RBS: External > Vendors, among others) and would bring with it a certain number of intangible benefits, not least the increased satisfaction of the client (hopefully). If such practices became widespread, could this be considered a 'Strength' of the business in a SWOT analysis, looking across the LSP's database of vendors more generally, or would this be a rare case? Indeed, one particular vendor who delivers early could potentially offset the threat of the late delivery of other vendors, which is a clear advantage of this specific strength. What about its root causes? There are potential positive and negative causes. On the positive side, the early-delivering vendor may have been able to leverage more TM matches than anticipated. On the negative side, just because the translation is delivered early does not necessarily mean that the quality is at the required standard.

Example 4 The final example is poor communication between project managers and vendors, resulting in some quality issues upon delivery (RBS: Project Management > Communication). The root causes of this risk are harder to pin down but could include inadequate instructions when the project was assigned, poor responses to queries raised by vendors, or failure by the project manager to check on project progress with the vendors at key milestones.

? Conduct a root cause analysis of some of the risks that you identified in response to the task above. Consider both positive and negative risks, and consider both project-level and business-level risks.

Identifying risks, their effects and possible root causes (which, in turn, can identify further risks) should also aid in identifying who owns each specific risk, as in most cases it will be quite clear who is responsible for a given risk (e.g. on-time delivery will be shared between the vendor and project manager). In other cases, such as non-payment, while the project manager will play a role, other LSP departments such as accounting or senior management might play a more extensive role in chasing late payers.

Risk Analysis

The mere identification of risks, effects, and causes, however, is only part of the risk management process, as, in order to determine appropriate risk responses, we need an assessment of the likely probability and impact of each risk so that the responses can be prioritised towards those that will be most likely to occur and/or have the most significant effect. The problem with risk probability is that the likelihood of a specific cause or event occurring is inherently unpredictable; it can only be quantified in terms of probabilities, and, in order to create such probabilities, previous risk data are needed. Hence, previous experience and a risk register play an important role in analysing risks.

A **risk register** is essentially a log of identified project risks. Initially, when an LSP is first set up, this will be made up of the risks identified in initial risk management meetings and will be based entirely on hypothetical situations (i.e. risks that *might* arise). Over time, however, data can be added to the register to record precisely how often certain risks occur and what their impact was in terms of a project's timescale or cost, for example. These valuable additions to a risk register during the course of an LSP's operations are a rich source of data for risk analysis and response planning, as they provide a log of *actual* occurrences, *actual* effects (as well as causes), and feedback on what worked and what did not in terms of the risk response (see Project Management Institute, 2017, p. 417).

Before we turn to how probability data might be used in risk analysis, we can make slightly more use of the RBS drawn up in the previous sections. Once a list of risks has been identified, each risk can be categorised under specific RBS sub-categories, allowing management teams to see the concentration of risk exposure in specific areas. If most risks tend to be focused under 'Project Management Risk', this would suggest that the risk response efforts in turn need to focus on this area. This approach is relatively simple and would work well for smaller LSPs, but larger LSPs with more complex operations and higher project turnover will want a more comprehensive approach to analysing risks.

224 *Evaluating Translation Project Constraints*

This is where **probability/impact matrices** can play a useful role (see Box 10.3). Identified risks can be categorised depending on their probability (i.e. how likely it is that they will occur or, possibly, how often such risks have occurred in the past) and on their impact (i.e. what is the likely

---

Box 10.3 Probability/impact matrices

A probability/impact matrix (or grid) is used to rank the probability of a risk occurring against its anticipated impact on a project or the business as a whole, depending on the level of analysis (see Figure 10.4). In most cases, such matrices are approached from a qualitative angle. Using the four risk examples discussed above, these can be plotted from 'very low' to 'very high' probability and impact: (1) – non-payment – might be classified as 'low' probability, but if it occurs (assuming the project to be relatively large), it could have a 'high' impact on the LSP's ability to pay its vendors; (2) – loss of a client – is not expected to be very probable, but if that client is one of the largest accounts for the LSP, the impact will be 'very high'; (3) – early delivery of a translation – may be considered 'medium' probability (it is not especially rare), but the impact may only be 'low' if the project was not especially urgent anyway; (4) – failures in communication, causing lack of clarity and confusion – might be classified as 'medium' probability and 'medium' impact (changing depending on the specifics of the project and associated corrective costs, of course). By categorising these risks in this way, it is easy to see that those risks that are closer to the top right of the chart (where it is shaded the darkest) require the greatest prioritisation, while those towards the bottom left might even be able to be ignored.

Very High					
High					
Medium		(3)	(4)		
Low				(1)	
Very Low					(2)
	Very Low	Low	Medium	High	Very High

Probability (vertical axis) / **Impact** (horizontal axis)

Figure 10.4 Example probability/risk matrix

This qualitative approach is not particularly systematic and is based solely on intuition. Probability/risk matrices can be quantified based on actual data, where available. Using data in a hypothetical risk register, let's assume that risk (1) – non-payment – has occurred in an average of 33 of the 112 projects completed by the LSP in the past year, yielding a 'probability' (or rather 'actual rate of occurrence') of 0.29. Let us now assume that the overall impact, in monetary terms, was −£31,500 (several cases where payment has still not been made, plus late payment charges and interest applied by vendors). Risk (2) – loss of client – occurred only once in the same 112 projects last year (probability of 0.01), but the lost client brought in an average profit each year of £85,000, which has now disappeared (−£85,000). Risk (3) – early delivery, defined as one day or more ahead of schedule – occurred 28 times across the 112 projects (0.25), but this had no financial impact whatsoever as no client paid any premium or bonus for early delivery and no cost savings occurred elsewhere in the lifecycle as a result (£0). (That being said, this could be quantified in the form of an intangible asset – business goodwill – but we will keep it simple here.) Finally, risk (4) – communication problems between project managers and vendors – occurred to some degree in 50 of the 112 projects last year (0.45, suggestive of particularly poor project management practices!), and the average cost of corrective action per project was £200 (a total of −£10,000 for 50 projects). We can now convert the four impacts into a standardised score between 0 and 1 using the following formula for each value: $x_{new} = \dfrac{x - x_{min}}{x_{max} - x_{min}}$, where x is the value that you want to standardise, x_{min} is the lowest of the values in the group, and x_{max} is the highest of the values in the group.

This formula yields values of 0.59, 1.00, 0.00, and 0.12 for each of the four risks. These can now be plotted on a chart, as in Figure 10.5 (left). This shows that, while the impact of the loss of a client was considerable, the overall probability (based on the risk register data) is incredibly low. By using real data, this changes the positioning and assessment of risks from a merely qualitative judgement by one or more members of a team.

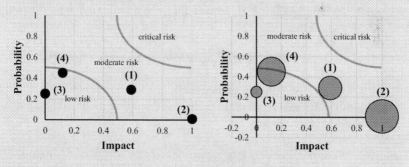

Figure 10.5 Example quantified probability/risk matrices

(Left) Probability plotted against Impact; (Right) Probability plotted against Impact, with Manageability represented by the size of the bubble

> Probability/risk matrices can also add another dimension by using bubble charts to incorporate a third element to the assessment. The right-hand chart in Figure 10.5, for example, adds 'Manageability' (judged intuitively on a scale from 0 to 1) to the previous matrix by encoding it in the size of the bubble.
>
> **?** Using some of the risks that you previously identified in Boxes 10.2 and 10.3, try to position them on a probability/risk matrix. You could draw a matrix on an A4 sheet of paper and use post-it notes to move the risks around the matrix as you add them.

effect of the risk on cost, time, etc. or what was the effect in past instances of this risk occurring). Risks that are appraised as being high probability and high impact should be prioritised for risk responses; low probability and low impact risks may not need a planned response at all. However, there are other dimensions to risk beyond their likelihood of occurrence and what their impact might be. The PMBOK helpfully delineates a wide range of different factors that can be considered depending on the nature of the risks and the nature of the industry itself (Project Management Institute, 2017, p. 424):

Urgency: how quickly would a risk response need to be implemented in order to be effective?
Proximity: how much time would there be before a risk could impact on one or more project objectives?
Dormancy: how much time might pass between a risk occurring and it being detected?
Manageability: how easy would it be for the risk owner to manage the occurrence or impact of the risk?
Controllability: how much control does the risk owner have over the risk's outcome?
Detectability: how easy is it to detect the risk occurring?
Connectivity: to what extent is the risk linked to other project risks?
Strategic impact: what is the potential impact of the risk on the organisation's strategic objectives?
Propinquity: to what extent is the risk perceived to be important by different stakeholders?

Answering some or all of these questions for some of the most potentially damaging (or potentially beneficial) risks can offer a much more robust sense of which risks need to be prioritised than assessments of probability and impact alone.

? How likely are high probability/high impact risks in the translation industry? Can you think of any possible examples?
? At the opposite end of the spectrum, can you think of any low probability/low impact risks?
? Which additional risk factors (as defined above) might be most relevant in a translation context?

One further method of risk analysis that could be used is a Pareto diagram (see Chapter 8, Box 8.3). Following the logic of the Pareto principle ('the vital few and the trivial many'), it might be sensible to assume that 80% of risk events come from only 20% of risk causes/types. By plotting causes of risk in decreasing order of frequency on the *x*-axis ('Risk Type') against a count of the number of risk cases in a given time period on the *y*-axis ('Risk Frequency'), then plotting a cumulative percentage frequency line, it is easy to identify the risk causes that need to be addressed as a priority by identifying, approximately, which 20% of causes account for 80% of risk events (see example in Figure 10.6). The diagram could also be adapted to show risk impact (in monetary terms, for instance) instead of risk frequency.

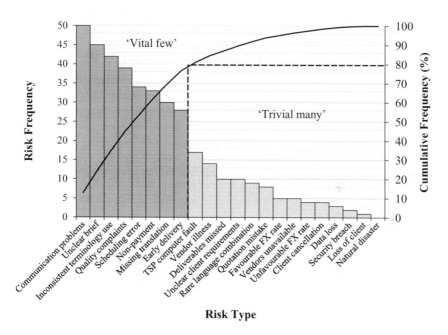

Figure 10.6 Example Pareto analysis in risk management

Various combinations of qualitative and quantitative risk analyses can therefore be combined on a business level and/or project level and take place at pre-defined points in time (e.g. quarterly, annually) and/or in the planning stages of particularly complex projects. It is important to stress, however, that all of these approaches only help to determine *which* risks to prioritise; it is impossible (and in many cases unnecessary) to fight fires on all fronts all of the time.

On a business level, a risk analysis reveals a wide range of possible risks that could be encountered throughout the life of an LSP, often with a longer-term perspective and a broader scope that will be addressed by senior members of the management team. On a project level, the analysed risks are far more specific and tailored to the unique features of the project at hand, yielding more clearly defined issues for the project manager to tackle in the risk response stage.

Risk Response

As with the entire enterprise of risk management, experience (in the form of an individual member of the team or a risk register) is of considerable assistance when it comes to determining the best possible response to a risk, referred to as **treatment** in ISO 31000:2018 (International Organization for Standardization, 2018). But even without prior personal or documented experience, planning risk responses is an important step on both a business and project level. This sub-section is split into risk responses for threats and for opportunities.

Threats

The PMBOK identifies five strategies that are considered appropriate for dealing with threats (Project Management Institute, 2017, p. 442–443).

Escalate. Escalation is an appropriate response when the threat is considered to be outside the scope of the project or the response would go beyond the remit of the project manager. To be more specific, the risk might not affect the objectives of the project in hand itself, but it might affect the LSP on a wider organisational level.

> • <u>Example</u>: *Discussions with various vendors on a series of interrelated projects reveal widespread dissatisfaction with rates of pay and the organisational processes put in place for the project. While certain aspects of these complaints (e.g. translation workflow processes) fall within the remit of the project manager, authorisation to increase pay for vendors (and to increase charges to clients and/or project margins) may need to be escalated to the LSP's senior management.*

Avoid. Avoidance is a response undertaken by the project manager to eliminate a threat or isolate the project from the threat. This response is particularly appropriate for high-probability, high-impact negative risks and will likely involve adjusting the project management plan or project objectives with a view to reducing the probability of occurrence as much as possible. Avoidance also involves isolating the project from the impact of a risk if it does occur.

> • *Example*: In a previous project for a particular client, negative feedback was received regarding poor translations of specialised terminology. Since this is a high-probability risk and the impact could be high (the client may take their business elsewhere if the same problem occurs again), the project manager could decide to work together with the client to produce a glossary of approved terminology and potentially involve one or more vendors to assist in the process. This glossary preparation stage would need to take place before the project starts, hence the project schedule would need to be adapted accordingly.

Transfer. Transferring a risk means transferring ownership of the risk to a third party and making the third party responsible for managing the risk and sustaining any impact of the risk if it should occur. Such transfer will often involve some form of payment for taking on the risk. Insurance is a very basic example of risk transfer, as an insurance company agrees to cover the cost of certain risks if they occur.

> • *Example*: A project is already underway at an LSP, but the client suddenly announces that they would like to add a new language pair to the translation. Unfortunately, the LSP does not have the necessary expertise to provide the requested language pair, so the project manager decides to outsource ('sub-contract') this particular language pair to another LSP that specialises in the language pair.

Mitigate. Mitigation means taking steps to reduce the likelihood of a risk occurring and/or the impact of that risk. It should be noted that this is a pre-emptive step to be taken in advance of the risk occurring, instead of a corrective step after the threat has already occurred. Mitigation steps might involve simplifying complex processes and integrating greater redundancy and leeway into schedules and resource allocation, for example.

> • *Example*: An LSP needs to recruit a new team of vendors to respond to a client enquiry for a new language pair and area of expertise beyond those normally handled by the LSP. In order to mitigate the potential impact of a poor translation being delivered to this new client (which could be quite lucrative for the LSP in the future), the LSP decides to undertake enhanced checks on the new vendors to screen them for qualifications and experience and will also ask them to carry out test translations that will be verified by one or more trusted independent vendors.

Accept. Acceptance may seem to be a counter-productive form of risk response, but in some cases it is entirely reasonable. Acceptance merely recognises that the threat exists, but the potential impact of the threat (or the likelihood of the threat) is so low that no response is needed. Acceptance can be 'active' or 'passive': active acceptance is arguably an example of a contingency-based risk response (see 'Contingency' below), while passive acceptance simply involves periodic monitoring of the threat to ensure that its potential probability and/or impact does not significantly change. The aforementioned terms 'risk appetite', 'risk tolerance', and 'risk threshold' are particularly relevant to the 'acceptance' response (see Box 10.1).

> • *Example*: *Approximately one hour before the delivery deadline for a translation, the translator contacts the project manager to request a one-hour extension due to encountering a minor technical problem. The project manager decides that there is sufficient leeway in the schedule to allow this extension and does not need to inform the client of the slight delay.*

Contingency. Adopting a contingency plan is mentioned in the PMBOK under 'acceptance' (the guide refers to a 'contingency reserve, including amounts of time, money, or resources to handle the threat if it occurs', Project Management Institute, 2017, p. 443), but it is listed as a type of risk response in the PRINCE2 framework (Office of Government Commerce, 2018, p. 132). In layman's terms, a contingency response is a form of 'Plan B': a backup plan or workaround if the risk materialises. Hence, no action is taken unless the risk occurs. A contingency response might also be a subsequent step if one of the risk responses above does not work as intended (typically the 'acceptance' response).

> • *Example*: *A project that is currently in progress at an LSP has a very tight deadline and very large volumes. As a contingency plan, the project manager decided to keep a small number of additional vendors on standby in case any unexpected problems occur for the contracted vendors. If such problems occur, the additional vendors can be easily mobilised to fill in or supplement the work of the other vendors.*

All of the above responses are aimed at removing or reducing threats. If the threat is only reduced (instead of removed), the remaining risk is referred to as 'residual risk' (Office of Government Commerce, 2018, p. 132); if the residual risk is deemed too high with reference to the project specifications or the LSP's risk tolerance, several risk responses can be combined to reduce the risk probability and/or impact to the lowest possible level. It is also important to be aware that a response to one risk can in turn change certain elements of a project. This is called a 'secondary risk' (Office of Government

Commerce, 2018, p. 133), and these risks need to be identified, assessed, and controlled in precisely the same way as the 'primary' risks.

Opportunities

After all of the preceding discussion on risk identification, analysis, and threat responses in particular, it is easy to lose sight of the fact that risks need not be negative; remember that risk can be positive too (typically referred to as an opportunity). As will become apparent from the examples given below, many opportunities operate on a business level or have more business-level impacts beyond the level of individual projects. This does not mean, however, that project-level opportunities do not exist.

Escalate. Escalating an opportunity is used in precisely the same way and in the same contexts as escalating a threat. Namely, the risk falls outside the remit of the project manager and may need to be assessed and 'owned' by a member of the senior management. The only difference with opportunities is that the escalated risk will potentially have a positive impact on the project or business.

- *Example*: A client mentions to the project manager that they will soon be calling for tenders on a major long-term, high-value translation services contract. Because of the far-reaching scope of the tender, this exceeds the remit of the project manager and the tender will need to be analysed, prepared, and submitted by the senior management team.

Exploit. Exploitation of an opportunity is closely related to 'enhance' below, but unlike 'enhance' (where the aim is simply to improve the probability/impact of an opportunity), exploitation looks to increase the probability of an opportunity occurring to 100% and to secure the maximum possible benefit from a project. This response is therefore reserved for high-priority opportunities.

- *Example*: The LSP decides to respond to a large call for tenders issued by a major international organisation for translation services. Because of the highly lucrative contract on offer, the LSP includes in the tender documentation its most trusted, most experienced, and most reliable vendors and supplies their CVs and samples of their work as part of the tender application. While not guaranteeing success (as is the case in any competitive tender), it does maximise the chances of the LSP being awarded the contract.

Share. Sharing an opportunity is similar to transferring a threat, as it involves assigning ownership of an opportunity to a third party so that the third party can share some of the benefit if the opportunity is realised. As with transferring a threat, there may be some form of payment involved between the parties to secure the sharing arrangement.

> • <u>Example</u>: *Two small LSPs working in a similar niche domain in the translation market in the same region approach one another to discuss the possibility of a merger or joint venture between the businesses, with a view to capturing a larger share of the market in that region and domain, and therefore increasing the benefits (i.e. profits) generated by the business.*

Enhance. Enhancing an opportunity is the opposite of mitigating a threat. Instead of reducing the probability/impact of a threat, enhancing an opportunity means making the opportunity more likely to occur and increasing its impact if it does occur. In short, it involves trying to improve the potential benefit generated by a project or business operations more generally.

> • <u>Example</u>: *A new client approaches an LSP with a small project but promises a larger, longer-term collaboration if they are satisfied with the LSP's project management. The LSP may therefore decide to dedicate more resources (human, technical, and technological) to the project to deliver it ahead of schedule, with a view to impressing the client and securing the prospect of longer-term collaboration.*

Accept. Acceptance of an opportunity is identical to acceptance of a threat in that no proactive action is taken to enhance, share, exploit, or otherwise handle the risk. Typically, this would only be used for low-priority opportunities where the additional expenditure or resources are too costly (in monetary or temporal terms) for the potential benefits that the opportunity would bring.

> • <u>Example</u>: *Vendor recruitment at an LSP does not normally take place proactively. Typically, the LSP receives lots of applications through its website from freelance vendors and the vast majority are relatively inexperienced and/or poorly qualified. Most of these applications are ignored or rejected. Occasionally, however, the LSP receives small numbers of applications from very well-qualified, experienced vendors, which it will keep on record for its projects. Because the LSP does not need a new influx of vendors at the present time, there is no need to dedicate time and resources to approaching possible vendors through reputable translator associations.*

It is important to remember that, despite opportunities having a clearly beneficial impact on a project or business, not all opportunities need to be pursued (actively or passively). Indeed, there are times – as alluded to above – when opportunities can or should be rejected. Notably, the time or cost that would be required to escalate, exploit, share, enhance, or even accept an opportunity may be disproportionately high compared to the benefits that the opportunity might bring. It is at this stage (for both opportunities and threats) that the chosen response(s) may need to be analysed.

Response Analysis

The identified risk response(s) should always be proportionate to the probability and/or impact of the risk, whether positive or negative. In particular, project managers should consider the realistic (tangible) impact of risks on project constraints (time, cost, scope, and quality, in particular) and on LSP–client relations. As noted above (under 'Escalate'), some responses go beyond the remit of a project manager and may have a higher, business-level impact, in which case the LSP's senior management may need to decide on the broader impact on the LSP's business operations, image, and relationships with clients and stakeholders. There are also some instances (e.g. in relation to fraud, confidentiality issues, etc.) when risks can bring with them a reporting obligation under certain laws or regulations.

While we will not delve into this in any detail in this textbook, it is at this point that a **cost-benefit analysis** can prove useful. For threats, the project manager may need to decide whether the risk response is more costly (in monetary or temporal terms) than the potential impact. For instance, if the risk (threat) is as simple as a slight delay in delivery, and the only available vendor to assist with the translation is very expensive, it may be that the potential displeasure on the part of the client (if any) or potential discount that the project manager has to offer the client to apologise for the situation is still smaller than the additional cost of enlisting the support of the expensive vendor. Equally, if an opportunity presents itself to pursue a high-value translation contract tender with only minimal chances of success, but the LSP cannot spare the time of multiple members of staff without compromising their day-to-day operations, the cost will inevitably be greater than the potential benefit. Hence, the cost of the risk response itself should be compared with the expected monetary value (or time) of the risk both with and without the risk response. If the cost of the risk response is less than the reduction in monetary value, the risk response is arguably worth undertaking (see Office of Government Commerce, 2018, p. 133).

Hence, not all risk responses should be pursued outright with no consideration for the wider impact of the responses on the project or business operations more generally. The same approach as noted earlier in this chapter – that of 'tailoring' risk assessments, depending on the project's size, complexity, importance, and development approach – should also be applied to the matter of risk response.

Implementation

Inevitably, after this process of identifying, analysing, and determining responses to risks, the final stage is to implement the risk response, monitor its effectiveness, and adjust its implementation if the response does not match the expectations. With this in mind, it is essential, in the risk response planning stage, that the **risk owner** and **risk actionee** are identified, and in some cases, these might be one and the same person.

> **Risk owner:** 'a named individual who is responsible for the management, monitoring and control of all aspects of a particular risk assigned to them, including the implementation of the selected responses to address the threats or to maximize the opportunities'; and
>
> **Risk actionee:** 'an individual assigned to carry out a risk response action or actions to respond to a particular risk or set of risks. They support and take direction from the risk owner'.
>
> [Office of Government Commerce, 2018, p. 134]

In many cases, the risk owner will be the project manager, who will be responsible for managing and monitoring the risk response, and the risk actionee may be a vendor, who will carry out certain tasks associated with their linguistic role to either minimise threats or pursue opportunities. Equally, project managers will often act as the risk actionee too – for instance, by assigning additional resources (human, technical, or technological) to a project to keep it on time, within budget, and in line with the specifications.

The PRINCE2 project management framework identifies one further stage to risk management: communication. As stressed at various points throughout this book, communication should always be a fundamental element of a project manager's role, and this is especially the case when handling risk. However, communication also extends to documentation responsibilities. So documenting the risk, risk response, and an evaluation of this risk response in a risk register or similar will help to improve risk management practices in the future through indirect communication with future project managers and other stakeholders.

Crucially, a project's or a business's exposure to risk is always changing. Hence, effective communication between all stakeholders is essential to identify new risks or changing risks on a continuous basis and for these stakeholders to work together to analyse such risks and decide upon appropriate risk responses.

* * *

As this chapter has shown, risk management is a theme that runs throughout all aspects of project management more generally. Experience does of course help in being able to anticipate potential risks and in being able to plan appropriate responses, but that is not to say that those new to project management will struggle to undertake effective risk management. What is most important, arguably, is that risk management is *proactive* instead of *reactive*. It is always better to play ahead for possible risks in order to response to

Risk 235

them quickly and effectively with a view to mitigating the negative effects of a threat or maximising the positive effects of an opportunity.

* * *

Topics for Discussion and Assignments

1. Prepare a full risk assessment for one of the case studies on the TS Portal. It can be presented in any form (written document, in-class presentation, etc.). In your assessment, you should look to identify risks, analyse them using qualitative and/or quantitative methods, devise appropriate risk responses, and consider how you will monitor implementation of these responses.
2. How do the risk assessments that you have carried out change in the context of an audiovisual translation project (e.g. subtitling)? Or software or website localisation? Or an interpreting assignment? How do these different modes and media bring about new threats or opportunities that the project manager will need to address?
3. According to ISO 31000:2018 (Risk Management – Guidelines), 'the purpose of risk management is the creation and protection of value. It improves performance, encourages innovation and supports the achievement of objectives'. To what extent do you agree with this assertion in the context of the translation services industry?

Further Reading

Chapter 10 of the PRINCE2 framework (Office of Government Commerce, 2018, p. 119–136) and Chapter 11 of the PMBOK (Project Management Institute, 2017, p. 395–458) provide considerably more detail on the intricacies of managing project risks. In the same publication series as the PRINCE2 framework, there is also a book specifically on risk management: *Management of Risk: Guidance for Practitioners* (Office of Government Commerce, 2010).

An essential point of reference on risk management in a translation context is Lammers (2011), which covers many of the same points addressed in this chapter but with a specific focus on software localisation.

References

International Organization for Standardization. (2018). *Risk management – Guidelines (ISO 31000:2018)*. International Organization for Standardization.
Lammers, M. (2011). Risk management in localization. In K. J. Dunne & E. S. Dunne (Eds.), *Translation and localization project management: The art of the possible* (pp. 211–232). John Benjamins.
Office of Government Commerce. (2010). *Management of risk: Guidance for practitioners* (3rd ed.). The Stationery Office Ltd.

Office of Government Commerce. (2018). *Managing successful projects with PRINCE2 2017 edition* (6th ed.). The Stationery Office Ltd.

Project Management Institute. (2008). *A guide to the Project Management Body of Knowledge (PMBOK® guide)* (4th ed.). Project Management Institute, Inc.

Project Management Institute. (2013). *A guide to the Project Management Body of Knowledge (PMBOK® guide)* (5th ed.). Project Management Institute, Inc.

Project Management Institute. (2017). *A guide to the Project Management Body of Knowledge (PMBOK® guide)* (6th ed.). Project Management Institute, Inc.

11 Post-mortem

> **Learning outcomes:**
> - Understand the wider industry context in which translation project management takes place, including the influence of client expectations, working conditions, and the technologisation of translation procurement and translation practice
> - Consider the importance of maintaining strong client–PM–vendor relationships as a project manager
> - Appreciate the dual role of a project manager as both a professional providing a service and a principal 'buying' a follow-on service from vendors
> - Analyse the impact of information asymmetry, goal incompatibility, adverse selection, and performance ambiguity on translation project management and the translation industry more generally
> - Identify possible areas for future research and projects in this field

As will hopefully become apparent as you read this chapter, this 'post-mortem' is not intended in the same sense introduced in Chapter 4 (i.e. a post-project debrief). Rather, the title is intended figuratively, in the sense that this chapter is intended to wrap up and tie together a number of overarching and, in some cases, more or less apparent themes that run throughout the entire book. Being a conclusion (of sorts), it offers a summary of the wider context in which translation project management takes place and the ways in which it operates.

Indeed, it may raise more questions in the minds of readers than it offers answers. But this is also one of the pleasing consequences of how this chapter is designed. Because translation project management has been subject to so little attention in scholarly literature, so many of these questions and wider issues are ripe for further exploration, either as part of undergraduate and masters dissertations, doctoral studies, or even post-doctoral projects. However, in light of the nature of this chapter, it does break the

DOI: 10.4324/9781003132813-13

238 Post-mortem

conventional wisdom of not introducing anything substantially new in the final concluding chapter, but the context and developing research avenues provided here offer a useful framework to bring the textbook to a fitting conclusion and pave the way for future studies in one fell swoop.

The Wider Context

Let us first reflect on the wider context in which translation project management operates. For this, we need to take a step back to look at the main parties involved in providing translation services: not just the LSPs and the project managers that work for them, but also the vendors themselves. For brevity, we will refer to them as 'translation professionals', although this term is not quite as straightforward as it initially appears.

The Status Quo

Figure 11.1 provides a simplified breakdown of the key challenges, pressures, and changes that the translation industry has been facing in recent years and is now facing with increasing vigour as we move into the future. Many of these factors can be described as 'disruptors', such is their impact on the way in which translation now takes place, while others have been persistent problems that are now changing in nature or intensifying in force.

Beginning with **client expectations**, we have noted at various junctures that some clients are increasingly coming to expect low-cost, high-quality translations delivered in record time. Based on data in the *SDL Translation Technology Insights* report for 2020, LSPs reported between 27% and 40% increases in the number of project files, project scope (number of words), number of customers, amount of outsourcing required to complete a project, variety/types of source content, number of target languages requested, and variety of file types (SDL, 2020, p. 4). The 2016 report revealed that 70% of respondents were faced with faster turnaround times than five years before alongside increased 'chunking' requirements or 'micro-translations[:] splitting of content into sections that are translated in isolation' (SDL, 2016, p. 13). In 2016, quality was more important than speed and cost, but, in 2020, the *pressure* lay firmly in cost, followed by speed, with quality ranking last among these three project constraints (SDL, 2020, p. 5). As we have seen in Chapters 5, 6, and 8 in particular (as well as Chapter 7 to a degree), these three main constraints are strongly inter-related, so when clients misunderstand what is realistic in a translation project in one or all of these dimensions, it can prove very difficult for project managers. The knock-on effect of any such difficulty, of course, is that cost, time, and quality pressures for project managers will inevitably have to be passed on to vendors, too, in some form.

Moving over to **working conditions**, there are so many issues to unpack within the three summary boxes provided in Figure 11.1, but, for the sake

Post-mortem 239

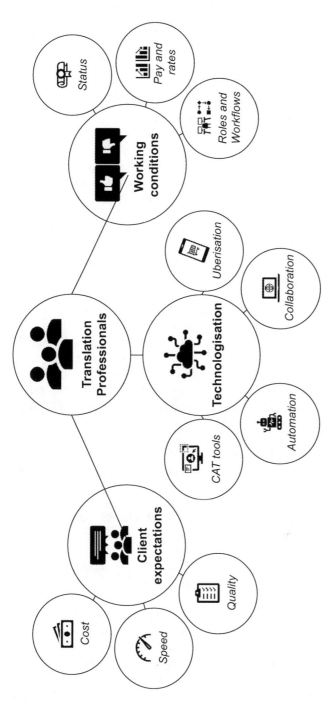

Figure 11.1 Summary of contemporary translation industry challenges, pressures, and changes

of discussion, it's important to address them, even if only briefly. The status of the translation profession is a fairly long-standing observation both in scholarly literature and among practitioners (Monzó-Nebot, 2019). Indeed, the topic has been addressed to such an extent that three special issues have been written on the topic (Dam & Zethsen, 2009; Sela-Sheffy & Shlesinger, 2009, 2010), in addition to it being covered in diverse works ranging from Pym et al.'s report on the status of the translation profession in the European Union (Pym et al., 2012) to the profession versus occupation debate (Tyulenev, 2015). Because the profession is largely unregulated in most jurisdictions, there are no barriers to entry for 'unqualified' translators (hence the prevarication over the use of the term 'translation professionals' above). This has led to pressure (often downwards) on pay and rates for translation services, especially in some of these 'less professionalized sectors of the market' (Nunes Vieira, 2020). As Pym et al. (2012) point out, for vendors, who are often employed on a freelance basis and sometimes work only part time, translation is a largely precarious venture, and it is often characterised by strong 'feast and famine' income patterns. Couple these problems with the dramatic growth in post-editing practices in the translation industry on the back of wholesale improvements in the quality of machine-translated output (see do Carmo, 2020) and it is clear that these pressures and disruptors are having a significant impact on the working conditions of translation professionals (see Lambert & Walker, 2022). These trends probably affect vendors more than LSPs and project managers, but the overall picture in terms of how translations are carried out (i.e. not just 'human translation' anymore) and the implications that this has for prices are changing the very face of the translation industry and the way in which translations are procured and managed. In turn, this raises a whole host of ethical concerns about responsible procurement, healthy working practices, and the sustainability of the profession in its present form, especially when vendors have seen their incomes stagnate or fall and many so-called 'super-LSPs' have seen their revenue soar in recent years.

This brings us neatly to the **technologisation** of the translation industry, which is arguably one of the underlying facilitators behind the heightened client expectations and change in working conditions. CAT tools are an obvious addition to Figure 11.1, as shown by the European Language Industry Association survey carried out in 2019, in which 34% of LSPs reported a desire to invest further in translation memory software (European Commission, 2020, p. 50). Automation – which not only refers to machine translation but also workflow automation – features very prominently in most industry surveys. In the same survey, 66% of LSPs intended to invest in machine translation in 2020 and 59% in automated workflow technologies. Of course, clients too have some insight here into automation, as nearly everybody has heard of Google Translate and will have used it in some capacity. These perceptions can feed into what clients believe to be reasonable in translation procurement in terms of cost, time, and quality, especially when freely available (and often free-of-charge) MT output is seemingly achieving levels of quality comparable to the products supplied via more expensive, more time-consuming human-driven methods. The ways in which translation professionals collaborate with one another has also changed drastically even over the last decade. While translation professionals are no strangers to working from home and working independently – and the conditions imposed in most countries as a result of the COVID-2019 pandemic were no different to the usual *modus operandi* for the vast majority – forms of collaboration have still evolved considerably. Since 79% of LSPs and vendors reported working with remote teams in some capacity in 2016 (SDL, 2016, p. 12), it is no surprise that CAT tools have evolved over the last one to two decades from predominantly desktop and package-based project management (handled via email and FTP servers), to real-time server-based projects, and most recently to cloud-based project management allowing for seamless live collaboration involving a wide range of shared resources. Such smooth operations have, however, facilitated what can be described as Uberisation in the translation industry (Fırat, 2021). Although many of these workflows and phenomena have been prevalent for years in various forms, with the growth in the platform economy, translation too has started to become more commoditised under the guise of streamlining translation procurement. Although this may seem a noble venture, if not done appropriately it can bring about a whole host of problems relating to bargaining power among vendors, status (again), income (again), and privacy concerns. That is not to say that such platforms are without benefits, but it is not unfair to argue that many of the benefits accrue to the companies that manage the platforms (which are, in a sense, fulfilling the same role as LSPs), as opposed to the vendors who carry out the bulk of the work in these disintermediated relationships.

There are so very many issues to unpack in the brief summaries above, and, in truth, the overviews barely scratch the surface of this area. The aim, in the sub-section below, is to draw on some of these trends and phenomena to put a more realistic spin on the translation industry and how project management works within it. Translation procurement is often presented in a rather idyllic manner: a client approaches an LSP, the PMs at the LSP decide how to manage it, the project is sent out to vendors, and the translation is magically produced and delivered to the client. In practice, procuring a translation – both for clients and, more importantly here, for *project managers* – is anything but idyllic. This is not to say that it is impossible (far from it!), but there is a complex array of relationship dynamics and competing factors that complicate procurement across the supply chain, for all stakeholders involved.

Client–PM–Vendor Relations

Liaising with both clients and vendors is one of the main roles of a project manager before, during, and after a project. Clients and vendors come in all shapes and sizes and in varying degrees of agreeability. Some are very easy to work with and some, to be completely honest, are not very easy to work with at all. However, strange as it might seem, 'niceness' is not the main determinant of how easy it is to manage these relationships. There are in fact numerous other socio-economic dynamics at play that, in most cases, covertly complicate the negotiation processes taking place on either side of the project manager.

To explore this further, we will refer to a concept in economic theory called the **principal–agent problem** or **agency theory**. To prevent this sub-section devolving into a theory-heavy discussion, we will try to avoid excessive use of jargon and abstraction in order to keep the focus firmly on translation. However, there are various secondary sources cited throughout this section for those who would like to read more about this area.

The principal–agent problem arises when 'one party (the principal) delegates work to another (the agent), who performs that work' (Eisenhardt, 1989, p. 58). The reason why such arrangements occur is precisely the reason why outsourcing exists in the context of translation: namely, 'recipients of expert services are not themselves adequately knowledgeable to solve the problem or to assess the service required' (Freidson, 1983, p. 41). In translation, for example, the client (the principal) will often not have the necessary linguistic, cultural, or wider translation skillsets to produce the translations in-house, so he or she will need to call upon outside experts to provide this service. In return, the service provider (the agent) – who may be an LSP or a freelance professional liaising directly with the client, of course – delivers translation services to fulfil the task that the client was unable to perform in-house.

So far, this is relatively straightforward. But economic relationships are very complex, and many are motivated by self-interest. This is the very essence of the principal–agent problem. The term 'self-interest' has something of an image problem, as it is immediately associated with acting selfishly or without due regard for others, but in this economic context the meaning is more nuanced. From the stance of personal ethics, any notions of selfishness – prioritising your own well-being over that of others, for instance – are frequently seen as abhorrent, but, in business ethics, prioritising your own corporate interests has a very different image, broadly in-keeping with the classic business mantra that 'the social responsibility of business is to increase its profits' (Friedman, 2007). Prioritising corporate interests, therefore (i.e. the self-interests of the client, or of the LSP, or even of the vendor, to an extent), is deemed more acceptable, and this plays a significant role in the ways in which different stakeholders interact in business relationships.

Hence, the principal–agent problem broadly revolves around this starting premise: **the desires and goals of the principal and the agent may be in conflict**. However, there is a secondary element to bear in mind: **it is ultimately difficult for the principal to verify what the agent is doing**, precisely because the principal lacks the necessary skills and/or knowledge to undertake the

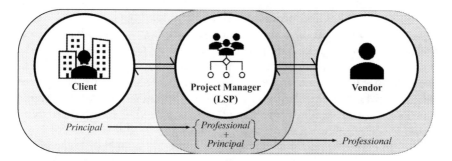

Figure 11.2 Principal–professional relationships in client–LSP–vendor interactions

task directly. This is one of the reasons that contracts exist: to obviate these difficulties by laying down clear expectations and specifications as to the standard of service provided and deliverables supplied.

Agency theory tends to be applied most frequently in strongly hierarchical relationships, such as shareholders (principals) and company executives (agents), as these environments tend to be where self-interest is more explicitly prioritised. Translation, however, is arguably a different case. Not to say that self-interest plays no role, of course, but the principal–agent problem is not strictly the most accurate form of this framework to apply. Sharma (1997) proposed an alternative model called the **principal–*professional* problem**. He argues that professionals undertake specialised technical tasks involving not only division of labour abut also division of *knowledge*. Abbott suggests that 'professions are exclusive occupational groups applying somewhat abstract knowledge to particular cases' (1988, p. 8). Professions are also characterised by selection processes (training, credentials, licences, etc.), self-regulation (peer monitoring, professional associations, disciplinary bodies, etc.), and trust (reputation, social networks, etc.) (Shapiro, 2005, p. 276). But Sharma also refers to a tension, whereby professionals have a much greater sense of calling to serve that needs to be balanced against the imperatives of doing business (1997, p. 766).

The parallels with the translation industry should hopefully be starting to come into contrast at this point. Not only the vendors but also the project managers are professionals who embody specialist expertise and impart this knowledge on clients to deliver a particular service and solve a posited problem. How this problem is solved is essentially negotiated and co-produced between the various stakeholders (client, project manager, vendor) in a complex double principal–professional chain. As shown in Figure 11.2, the project manager therefore occupies an interesting status: one of both professional (vis-à-vis the client) and principal (vis-à-vis the vendor(s)).

The four sub-sections below draw on four key constructs of agency theory, which we will examine briefly from the perspectives of the different stakeholders involved in the relationship: the client (principal), the project manager (agent and professional), and the vendor (agent). These four constructs – **information asymmetry, goal incompatibility, adverse selection,** and **performance ambiguity** – are hypothesised to be antecedents to the broader principal–agent/professional problem (Bhattacharya & Singh, 2018) and therefore provide a useful framework to explore how such relationships are managed in the translation industry. To offer a relatable contrast to the translation example – and picking up on the growing Uberisation trend across the services sector – we will use takeaway food deliveries for comparison in each of these areas to highlight some of the problems specific to translation. It may seem like a trivial choice, but since we are seeing similar Uberising trends in translation (as noted above), and since the vast majority of translation services are procured electronically online, the contrast is useful to illustrate these abstract concepts. It is not, however, intended to assimilate takeaway food delivery services to translation services; the two sectors and the supply chains involved are entirely different.

Information Asymmetry

Information asymmetry describes a situation where one party – typically the buyer (or principal) – has less information than another party – typically the seller (or agent/professional) – in a particular transaction. Such a situation results in an imbalance of power. Consider the relationship between a client looking to procure a translation and the project manager, for instance. If the client has never purchased any translation services in the past, he or she will likely have very little information on what to ask for, how long it will take, how much it will cost, and, more generally, what to expect from the service:

> The hiring party [the principal] has very limited knowledge about the specific tasks required and is, therefore, highly dependent on the professional not only to deliver but also to recommend the type and extent of service needed. This creates an asymmetry in which the professional agent is in a more powerful position than the less knowledgeable principal.
>
> [Sharma, 1997, p. 788]

The project manager, conversely, is in a strong position, as he or she will know broadly what is involved, how much it costs, how long it will take, etc. But not all project managers are alike here. Some translation project managers do not have training or experience as translators and some (rarely) may not even have any foreign-language skills. This in turn can create information asymmetries between the project manager and the vendor. Across the entire supply chain, therefore, the vendor is arguably in one of the strongest positions in terms of *know-how* and *know-what* (more on these terms in a minute) – even more so than the project manager. However, where the project manager has an advantage is in understanding better the costs and timescales involved, as the project manager will be dealing directly with the client to weigh up the client's expectations of costs/timescales against what is actually realistic. The dynamics between the three stakeholders are therefore by no means straightforward.

Information asymmetry operates on various levels, though. On a lower level, it can pertain to quite pragmatic elements such as how much translations actually cost: a client may have no idea about cost, the project manager has a good idea of what is achievable, and the vendor may have strong views on what he or she would *like* to charge, but not what is actually practicable. But on a higher level, information asymmetry plays out on a wider sociological scale. For instance, how does a client know what a good translation looks like, or what a good LSP looks like, if the client has no prior experience? Both of these questions are closely linked to the notions of adverse selection and performance ambiguity below, as we will see shortly.

In principal–professional exchanges, information asymmetry is particularly strong precisely because professionals have expert technical knowledge that the principals cannot assess. But this is only part of the equation. Sharma notes, for instance, that the principal will likely not understand *how* the professional carries out the work (*know-how*) or *what* it is that the professional does, strictly speaking (*know-what*). As noted earlier in this chapter, this tension surrounding translator status permeates so much of what takes place in the translation industry: if clients fail to understand some of the complexity inherent in translation activities, what is the likely effect of this on expectations around rates, timescales, quality, etc.? The answer is hopefully relatively obvious: the value of the service decreases. What is more, lack of knowledge increases the perceived risk of a venture, which can also decrease the price that a client is willing to pay for a particular service.

Information asymmetry works in all directions though, and project managers can all too easily have an improper understanding of many client-side factors. Despite enquiring about the purpose of a translation, or despite being told information about the client's budget or timescale for a particular project, it is often the case that project managers will not receive the full picture and may even be prevented from accessing the full picture, especially where the client's (actual) budget is concerned.

If we now bring in our takeaway food example, we can see that information asymmetry is perceptibly more problematic in translation. Admittedly, for cuisines different to those with which the buyer is most familiar there is still an element of the unknown. But it is at least very easy nowadays to find pictures online and descriptions of recipes and ingredients explaining what goes into a particular dish. Of course, the chef at the restaurant preparing the meal will still have much stronger know-how and know-what than the buyer, but the balance is much fairer in this sector because the physical product being delivered is less of an unknown when you are ordering a takeaway dinner. The buyer knows very clearly how much the food will cost because prices are readily provided on the ordering screen; the buyer will know roughly how long it will take because delivery times are provided, and buyers will normally have prior experience and know what sort of time is reasonable before they ring the restaurant to complain; and the buyer will have reasonable expectations about quality based on the price and customer reviews (more on this below under 'adverse selection').

Turning back to translation:

? For whom is the information asymmetry more acute: the client, the project manager, or the vendor?
? Is the information asymmetry uniform across all elements of the project, or are there some areas where different stakeholders have more knowledge than others, and vice versa?
? What role does the project manager play in trying to redress this information asymmetry?

Goal Incompatibility

Closely related to information asymmetry is the concept referred to as goal incompatibility. Put simply, different organisations and entities will have different motivations and interests at stake when business transactions take place. With the project manager in the middle, on one side is the client, who is requesting a low-cost, high-quality translation as quickly as possible, and on the other side is the vendor, who is requesting a highly-paid, 'fit-for-purpose' translation with a generous deadline.

In our takeaway food example, the buyer will want to have food that is as high quality as possible, delivered quickly, and not too expensive. This is of course in contrast to the restaurant, which – in an ideal world – will want to deliver food that satisfies the customer, generates a lot of income, and can be delivered when it is ready (without rushing). There is still some incompatibility here between the customer and the restaurant. But because the information asymmetry is less acute, the customers have a more realistic understanding of what raw ingredients cost, what wages might be paid to the kitchen and delivery staff, and how long it takes to cook one or more elements of a meal. These understandings will never be perfect (unless the customer is a chef or a restaurant proprietor of course, and even then, businesses operate differently), but they will still allow sufficient insight into what is at stake to rein in some of the disparity between the customer's and the restaurant's goals.

As noted above, in 'traditional' agency theory interpretations, self-interest tends to reign supreme for the party with the greatest power. In the tripartite LSP-mediated translation context, the power dynamics are difficult to trace with any certainty, but it is logical to surmise at least that the project manager is in the strongest position (a view also supported by Abdallah & Koskinen, 2007, p. 679). While rather mercenary in tone, the project manager effectively acts as a gatekeeper between the vendor and the client. The project manager is able to make his or her case to the client and negotiate for a particular costing, timescale, or otherwise, but the vendor will be more restricted in many cases, as he or she will be forced to work within the confines of the agreement already reached between the project manager and the client. Among super-LSPs in particular, this disparity in power relations between project managers and vendors is all the more apparent: if a vendor is unwilling to take on a project at a particular price point and/or with a particular deadline, provided that it is a suitably resourced language, the project manager can in many cases simply offer the work to another vendor.

There are, of course, ethical considerations here in relation to fair payment and terms of work, but it is all too easy to lay the blame at the project manager's feet when, in reality, other factors are working against his or her ability to command higher fees, longer deadlines, etc. The reason: information asymmetry. As noted above, if the client misunderstands what is realistic or not, this can have a significant impact on the client's willingness to agree to particular conditions. It is here that the project manager plays a vital role in *educating* the client and negotiating carefully in such a way that the project is not lost to a competitor, but also that the budget and timescale, in particular, allow fair working conditions to be passed on to vendors while still protecting the LSP's margin requirements. Each of the three parties has their own self-interests at stake here, but it's important to ensure that the vendors are not left short-changed by their weakened position in this transaction.

? If you were a client, what would be your main priority? Budget, deadline, quality, or something else?
? Are there any elements that you would be willing to sacrifice if the project manager reported that it was impossible to satisfy one of your demands?
? As a project manager, where do you have the greatest flexibility to adapt your offering to client demands?

Adverse Selection

Adverse selection describes situations where different parties are unable or find it difficult to select an appropriate agent (or professional, in this case) to carry out a particular task. The reason for this problem is that suppliers all look very similar to novice buyers (Bhattacharya & Singh, 2018, p. 4197), since all of them will claim to be superior to the competition (Aubert et al., 2003). The actual suppliers themselves (whether LSPs or vendors selling directly to end clients) will know best whether they are good at what they do or not, but because they hold all of the cards it is easy for unscrupulous suppliers to 'distort' the way in which they present themselves and even to lie outright.

'Good' suppliers will typically issue so-called signals in order to try and distinguish themselves from 'bad' suppliers, a process referred to as 'signalling'. The problem, however, as Pym et al. (2012, p. 152) note, is that signals are very easy to fake, and this then shifts the client's task away from one of assessing which supplier is 'good' or 'bad' towards one of assessing which *signal* is 'true' or 'false'. As such, clients will often resort to 'screening' as a means to explore and include/exclude other characteristics pointing to the quality of the product or service on offer. But because of information asymmetry, how easy is it, in reality, for a client to decide *which* traits are appealing or even which traits are relevant?

In the takeaway food sector, platforms such as Just Eat, Uber Eats and Deliveroo have rating systems that provide direct appraisals from customers of the quality of service provided. It is easy to see the average 'star ratings' given to a particular restaurant, as well as – in many cases – direct testimonials from customers attesting to the quality of the food delivered, and even restaurant responses to criticisms. This allows the buyers to see whether the quality was as expected, if the food was cold on delivery, etc., and what the restaurant had to say in response. In many countries, there are also regulatory rating systems. The United Kingdom, for instance, has an organisation called the Food Standards Agency that regularly assesses all establishments serving food and awards Food Hygiene Ratings on a scale of 0 ('urgent improvement is required') to 5 ('hygiene standards are very good') on the basis of how food is handled, stored, and prepared, and the cleanliness of the facilities. Moving out of the takeaway sector for a moment, there are also rating systems such as AA Rosettes and Michelin Stars for high-end, fine-dining restaurants. All of these systems help to create a clear picture in the minds of customers about the quality of service that they will likely receive, in addition to any promotional materials (e.g. photos, descriptions) on the restaurant's website or ordering page. Recommendations are likely to play a significant role in the local takeaway market too.

Rating systems do exist for translation companies, especially via websites such as Trustpilot and even Google's own rating and commenting system, but a cursory survey of a number of UK-based LSPs on both of these forums reveals not only a very low number of entries on each page but also largely negative feedback, presumably because clients are more likely to leave feedback if they are dissatisfied with the service than if they are satisfied. (Many of them even have feedback entries from vendors, incidentally.)

For clients, the first port of call (before even looking at independent rating sites) will usually be the LSP's website. LSP websites usually offer a number of carefully curated testimonials. This is common practice in business, of course, but it is often of little value to the client unless there is a named brand or company that is particularly close to the client's own business or particularly well-known to them. The websites will also usually feature a number of stock images of people working in an office environment and pointing suggestively at a screen showing complex charts, data, and text.

It's also likely that any website copy will prominently feature words such as 'quality', 'turnaround', and 'budget', as well as various words with strongly positive associations such as 'international', 'facilitate', 'accurate', and many more besides. The website description above is, naturally, a caricature, but there is a lot of truth in these points. And we should not criticise LSPs (or any other businesses, for that matter) for presenting themselves in this way. They are simply 'playing the game'. They know that these signals will appeal to clients and so juxtapose carefully curated images, text, and particular associations with what clients might understand about translation ('accuracy' is likely to be a key feature that clients expect, for example) in order to draw clients in.

LSPs (and vendors) can of course be accredited by, and/or members of, translator associations. Vendors in the United Kingdom can undergo accreditation processes and become 'Members of the Institute of Translation and Interpreting' or 'Chartered Linguists' in the United Kingdom, for instance, both of which should help to raise the status of their profile and offer a veneer of professionalism to their CV, especially when such statuses require checks on qualifications and/or professional experience. LSPs can also undergo ISO certification for ISO 17100:2015 or other standards. The trouble is that most clients will not understand what 'MITI' or 'CL' after a vendor's name means, or what 'ISO 17100:2015-certified' means in relation to an LSP. Indeed, Chan (2009, p. 165) confirmed in his study that respondents were generally ignorant towards or misunderstood signals such as translation qualifications and certifications.

But let's put ourselves in the client's shoes for a moment. How does the client know which signals are meaningful? If LSP A and LSP B both vaunt the 'outstanding quality' of their translations and a 'meticulous and diligent' approach to project management on their websites, how does the client know which one to trust? In essence, what does the client do when all of the competition looks the same to the untrained eye? The short answer – sadly – is that price tends to be the determining factor, due to information asymmetry: 'many buyers still select the lowest cost supplier without exploring the match between the supplier's skill and outsourcing requirements, due primarily to lack of available information' (Bhattacharya & Singh, 2018, p. 4197).

The same problem faces the project manager when recruiting vendors, though. If we take a similar look at translator platforms such as ProZ.com, or even translator association listings, we see profiles replete with grandiose claims about 'superior quality', 'reliability', and 'accuracy', vague notions such as 'professionalism' and 'versatility', and no small number of clichés about *not* being lost in translation. 'Bilingual' seems to be readily conflated with being a good translator, pseudo-certifications such as the ProZ 'Certified Pro' status abound, and claims are made about certain qualifications that may or may not be relevant (and – being particularly cynical – may or may not even be true or may be exaggerated). But again, these vendors are merely playing the game: promoting features or characteristics that they believe will make them more attractive to potential project managers (and direct clients).

For such an economically valuable industry, the widespread lack of regulation around qualifications, certification, and general access to the profession all cause a wealth of problems even for project managers, who are, of course, far more knowledgeable than the average client in the industry, especially when crowdsourcing and amateur translation is starting to bleed into the more professionalised sector of the industry, and when the lines between the 'bulk' and 'premium' markets are starting to become increasingly blurred.

? As a client, how would you select an LSP for a translation project?
? What trends do you observe when you explore LSPs' websites in terms of how they market their services? Why do you feel that they market their services in this way?
? As a project manager, what characteristics would you look for in a vendor? How can you be sure that what they tell you about themselves is truthful?

Performance Ambiguity

Finally, we come to performance ambiguity. In short, this refers to the principal's difficulty in assessing the outcome of a particular contract. Because outsourcing exists to provide services that cannot be carried out in-house, the vast majority of clients find it very difficult to assess the quality of what is delivered (Eisenhardt, 1989). Poor performance – or 'shirking', as it is called – can, for example, be down to an agent acting opportunistically (doing the bare minimum required in the hopes of passing off substandard work and still being paid), or it can be down to other factors such as mere mistakes in the product or processes involved in managing the project. Moreover (still in a very cynical light), because of information asymmetry, some extremely unscrupulous suppliers can use the client's lack of knowledge as a way to get away with poor performance by blaming it on other factors (Aubert et al., 2003).

Returning again to our takeaway food example, most customers will find it very easy to judge poor performance of the takeaway delivery 'contract'. Cold food (unless the food is supposed to be cold, of course!), undercooked poultry, over-seasoned sauces, or simply the food 'not tasting nice' are all realistic assessments of the quality of service provided by a takeaway establishment. The overwhelming majority of customers may not be Michelin assessors or even expert chefs, but most buyers can make fairly decent judgements about the quality or otherwise of the food delivered and whether it was as expected. In some cases, it can be very simple if the wrong food is delivered! There can, of course, be some cynical practices taking place at takeaway establishments, but by and large most performance issues will be down to mistakes (sending out the wrong food, not quite cooking the chicken for long enough, burning something, accidentally adding a little too much salt, etc.). Some problems are also very easy to measure objectively: if delivery is supposed to be made within 45 minutes and the doorbell rings after 90 minutes, clearly there are significant performance issues.

Missing deadlines in translation projects is equally easy to monitor for non-expert clients, but this is largely where the parallel ends in a translation context. How does a client with no experience in translation – and perhaps no experience even speaking or reading a foreign language – judge the quality of a translation? (Even many experts in translation cannot agree!) In many cases, clients will look at the formatting and appearance of the deliverables. Or they might copy the translation into Google Translate and translate it back into their main spoken language to see if it resembles the original text. Or, more commonly, they will simply not check the translation at all because they lack the necessary skills to make an informed judgement. Even assuming the client manages to recruit a so-called 'good' LSP or the project manager succeeds in finding a 'good' vendor, does this really guarantee that the quality will be up to scratch? There is therefore a huge amount of trust placed by the client in the LSP and, in turn, by the project manager in the vendor(s). The *SDL Translation Technology Insights* report for 2016, for instance, found that 59% of those surveyed (including LSPs and those involved in 'translation-related' roles in the private, public, or non-profit sector) 'don't measure translation quality at all, or use ill-defined or purely qualitative assessment' (SDL, 2016, p. 8).

As Olohan and Davitti rightly point out, 'trusting plays a major role in the assigning or non-assigning of translation work by the PMs to freelancers' (2017, p. 398). There is substantial risk involved in entrusting work to a particular vendor (and for clients entrusting a project to a particular LSP), and much of the risk is mitigated by working with trusted vendors (or LSPs) that have previously provided good services. However, this is not always possible, which is what makes performance ambiguity such a problematic concept in translation, as being able to assess the quality of what is delivered can be impossible without needing to bring in additional 'information systems' (in agency theory terms) to monitor performance and overcome the inherent information asymmetry. In translation, this can take the form of revision, review, and proofreading, but these information systems entail additional cost. But such costs would obviously need to be weighed against the inherent risk. This applies to both the client and the project manager, of course. The client may be wary of hiring an LSP for the first time, and equally the project manager might be wary of working with a vendor for the first time. But such solutions are not perfect and will never guarantee diligent performance of the tasks at hand; they merely help to redress the balance of the information asymmetry to a certain degree (Sharma, 1997, p. 769).

252 Post-mortem

- ? As a client, how would you appraise the quality of a translation?
- ? As a project manager, how could you help a client to understand the quality (or conformity) of the deliverables in a project?
- ? As a project manager again, are there any aspects of performance that you would find difficult to appraise in a project?

Summary

In a complex triadic relationship between clients, LSPs (and the project managers that embody the LSPs), and vendors, it is clear that information asymmetry, goal incompatibility, adverse selection, and performance ambiguity introduce considerable complexity into the context in which translation procurement takes place. Bhattacharya and Singh (2018) interestingly conceptualise information asymmetry and goal incompatibility as being antecedent factors that feed into adverse selection: if you have radically competing goals and lack the necessary information to make informed choices, then the risk of selecting a poor LSP (or a project manager selecting a poor vendor) increases. But in turn, they also argue – and have mixed data to support the claim – that information asymmetry, goal incompatibility, and adverse selection, cumulatively, result in performance ambiguity: lack of information, competing goals, and poor selection of agents/professionals increase, firstly, the risk of poor performance and, secondly, the inability of the principal to assess the performance itself.

The self-interests of all three stakeholders (and others besides), combined with the complicated dual role of the LSP (both professional and principal), combined further with the various forms of 'information systems' inherent in the transaction (the LSP itself arguably acting as an information system, in addition to lower-level processes such as revision, review, and proofreading), all result in a situation where priorities compete amid the drastically varying levels of information. Agency theory offers a toolkit to explore these relationships further, but translation industry studies literature has engaged with only some of these concepts (Chan, 2009, 2013; Pym et al., 2012). There is still much work to be done in this area to disentangle how project managers handle these pressures.

The Role of the Project Manager

So again, we return to the project manager. What is his or her role in this complex landscape?

- ? From everything you have read in this textbook, how do you define the project manager's role?
- ? What are his or her responsibilities towards clients?
- ? What are his or her responsibilities towards vendors?

? What 'soft skills' does a project manager need to manage translation projects effectively?
? Where does the project manager add value in the translation industry?

Moving beyond the technicalities and very pragmatic nature of day-to-day project management outlined in Chapters 2 to 4, in particular, there are two key areas where the *human* element of project management is essential to the success of projects and adds considerable value: client relationships and vendor relationships. This truism is encapsulated perfectly by Olohan and Davitti in their article on trust in project management:

> Our workplace observations reveal how the PMs are pivotal in their companies' business as the sole point of contact for the client who requires a translation and the translator(s) delivering that translation. There is no direct contact between client and translator; it is through the PM's intermediation that a successful transaction takes place.
> [Olohan & Davitti, 2017, p. 397]

As Olohan and Davitti explore in their article, there are two sides to this role: the client side and the vendor side. They note (Olohan & Davitti, 2017, p. 411) that project managers need to be 'calm and polite' and introverted with a view to developing a relationship with the client. These traits are particularly important in contentious situations, 'where PMs are expected to respond constructively and nonconfrontationally to clients' attacks' (Olohan & Davitti, 2017, p. 411). Interestingly, despite the increasingly online nature of the service sector, their research found that clients still tended to harbour more trust for those LSPs that were local, with LSPs capitalising on this by offering in-person meetings where possible.

Trust plays a key role in modern project management. Not only in clients deciding which LSP to contract for a project but also on the vendor side, as observed by Abdallah and Koskinen (2007, p. 674): 'the network needs to be "glued together" by trust relations', as vendors can often be several 'links' removed from the actual client in this production network. Abdallah and Koskinen rightly point out that 'trust-building therefore entails that the perspectives and interests of each stakeholder are addressed, knowledge is shared, and information is clear, accountable and legitimate as far as all parties are concerned' (2007, p. 678). These networks are difficult to manage, partly on account of the importance of trust, but also because the relationship dynamics with the client and the vendor will be markedly different, and the project manager needs to carefully balance the interests of all parties to ensure that everybody is fully satisfied, including the internal demands of the LSP's senior management. In such production networks, therefore, 'the preferred option ... is often to create indebtedness and reliance over the long term. In other words ... creating long-lasting and stable partnerships' (Abdallah and Koskinen, 2007, p. 678). In the traditional 'direct client' model, where freelancers work directly with their clients, these long-term trusting relationships are easier to maintain (and indeed in the best interests of the freelancer to maintain); the network organisation of LSP-mediated translation complicates the picture, however, as there is a tendency to prioritise the clients over the vendors (Abdallah & Koskinen, 2007, p. 680).

But 'trust is based on familiarity', according to Abdallah and Koskinen (2007, p. 681), and this is made more difficult by the geographically diffuse manner in which the translation industry now operates (despite the aforementioned preference for local LSPs). It does, however, underline the fundamental importance of a project manager knowing his or her client, but also – just as importantly – knowing, communicating well with, and respecting the vendors. This personal touch – which can take precious time to develop but is worth its weight in gold – can be the secret to long-lasting relationships and successful project management, even in the face of great adversity. If the client or the vendor seems to be comfortable with this personal approach (a path that needs to be trodden carefully), a brief enquiry about their recent holiday, congratulations on a recent success, or even simple anecdotes about recent common sporting events or the weather can help to cement a stronger bond on both sides of the project manager and introduce an important sense of humanity into this difficult role.

Project managers bring considerable technical skill and know-how to the table when managing projects, but they also bring considerable *interpersonal* skills by knowing their clients and knowing their vendors. Being able to explore and discuss options in a project, and even educate clients on why a certain choice is not advisable, requires considerable tact as well as knowledge. Being able to negotiate with vendors asking for higher rates when the budget simply will not stretch that far is difficult (and can even be distressing at times). Being able to hand out reprimands to vendors when deadlines are missed or there are evident quality issues in a deliverable is far from easy, but it is still an essential part of the job. Being able to 'on-board' new vendors and make them feel welcome and valued in the LSP's database and deciding to take that first leap of faith by placing a task with the new vendor requires warmth, adaptability, and trust. And being able to listen to clients' complaints – whether founded or not – and handle them to the client's satisfaction demands the greatest possible skills in diplomacy, delicacy, and restraint.

Being a project manager is incredibly challenging. It requires diverse skills going beyond an understanding of translation alone, and it can range from being exhausting to exhilarating. Testing though it may be, the vast majority of translation project managers would agree that it is a highly rewarding role and not merely a stepping stone from translator training into the translation profession (as many believe it to be) but a long-term aspirational career path with huge potential for promotion and career progression.

? The big question: Is project management for you?

Epilogue: Future Directions

We can bring this book to a close with an outlook on areas deserving of more research. As noted at various junctures throughout this textbook, translation project management has seen sporadic attention in translation studies literature, but it is still vastly under-represented, which is strange considering the fundamental role that it plays in the facilitation of so many business ventures around the world and in the livelihoods of hundreds of thousands of project managers and translators globally. The areas listed below are far from exhaustive but will hopefully serve as inspiration for future projects at all levels, drawing on methods such as observation, surveys, interviews, and other combinations of techniques.

Workflows

- ? What are the standard processes that project managers undertake in pre-production, from the initial client enquiry through to hand-off to vendors?
- ? What are the standard quality assurance processes undertaken by a cross-section of LSPs after the translation stage is complete, but prior to verification and release?
- ? When project success is at risk, what is typically the first constraint to be sacrificed – cost, time, quality, or other?
- ? Where do project managers add value in the project lifecycle?
- ? What are the leading causes and effects of risk in translation projects?

Economics

- ? How much do vendors charge for their services in different regions, for different specialisms, for different services, etc.?
- ? How much are clients willing to pay for translations?
- ? What is the common markup applied by LSPs in different regions, for different services, etc.?
- ? How much supply and demand is there in the global, regional, or segmental marketplace for specific services, specialisms, etc.?

Sociology of Translation

- ? How do vendors feel about the rates offered to them by LSPs?
- ? How do vendors feel about the rising threats of automation and Uberisation?
- ? What is the future of crowdsourced and/or non-professional translation and where does it fit into the common 'bulk' versus 'premium' market debate going forward?
- ? What is the professional status and prestige not only of translators, interpreters, etc., but of the translation industry more widely, including project managers?

Vendor Management

? How do project managers (or vendor managers) recruit new vendors? What traits, characteristics, qualifications, and credentials do they look for?
? What is the workflow surrounding translation test assessment?
? How do project managers decide which vendor to assign a task to?
? What is the project manager's ethical responsibility in relation to the various agents with which they work?

Client Management

? How much do clients really know about translation?
? Among the three main project management constraints – cost, time, quality – which takes precedence for clients?
? How do clients select LSPs and what factors inform their decision-making?
? How do clients appraise deliverables on completion? What features or characteristics do they look for in a translation?

And one final, broad question: What does the future of translation project management look like as we move into this increasingly technologised and automated age?

? What other questions can you add to those above?
? What interests you in project management?
? What gaps have you identified in current scholarly literature?
? What gaps are there in current professional and/or higher education training and publications?
? Can you design a research proposal setting out a review of existing literature, a method based around primary or secondary data collection, and proposed outcomes?

Readers would also be well advised to explore theoretical frameworks beyond translation studies (as in the agency theory discussion above), but also drawing on existing applications to translation studies, ranging from Latour's actor-network theory (see Tyulenev, 2014, p. 164–169, for an overview and further reading) to much more recent applications such as Olohan's inspired practice theory approach to exploring how and in what contexts translation (broadly defined) takes place. Notably, Olohan specifically draws attention, in her own 'emerging research agenda', to studies 'of the situated accomplishment of practices, focusing on specific sites where those practices are performed and reproduced', 'genealogical' studies on 'the trajectory or life of a practice', 'configurational' studies on 'how practices are interconnected and trans-situated', and 'dialectal' studies on 'the tensions, contradictions and power imbalances that keep practices in flux' (Olohan, 2020, pp. 128–129).

As we can see from even the broad-stroke questions outlined above, this is a field ripe for further investigation so that we can better understand how translation projects are managed on a practical level and the manifold social, economic, and technological factors that influence modern translation project management and the language services industry as a whole.

References

Abbott, A. (1988). *The system of professions: An essay on the division of expert labor*. University of Chicago Press.

Abdallah, K., & Koskinen, K. (2007). Managing trust: Translating and the network economy. *Meta: Translator's Journal, 52*(4), 673–687. https://doi.org/10.7202/017692ar

Aubert, B. A., Patry, M., & Rivard, S. (2003). A tale of two outsourcing contracts – An agency-theoretical perspective. *Wirtschaftsinformatik, 45*(2), 181–190.

Bhattacharya, A., & Singh, P. J. (2018). Antecedents of agency problems in service outsourcing. *International Journal of Production Research, 57*(13), 4194–4210. https://doi.org/10.1080/00207543.2018.1506179

Chan, A. L. J. (2009). Effectiveness of translator certification as a signaling device: Views from the translator recruiters. *Translation and Interpreting Studies, 4*(2), 155–171.

Chan, A. L. J. (2013). Signal jamming in the translation market and the complementary roles of certification and diplomas in developing multilateral signaling mechanisms. *The International Journal for Translation and Interpreting Research, 5*(1), 211–221. https://doi.org/10.12807/ti.105201.2013.a11

Dam, H. V., & Zethsen, K. K. (Eds.). (2009). Translation studies: Focus on the translator [Special issue]. *Hermes: Journal of Language and Communication in Business*, 42.

do Carmo, F. (2020). 'Time is money' and the value of translation. *Translation Spaces, 9*(1), 35–57. https://doi.org/10.1075/ts.00020.car

Eisenhardt, K. M. (1989). Agency theory: An assessment and review. *Academy of Management Review, 14*(1), 57–74.

European Commission. (2020). *European Language Industry Survey 2020*. Retrieved 2 August 2021 from https://ec.europa.eu/info/sites/default/files/2020_language_industry_survey_report.pdf

Fırat, G. (2021). Uberization of translation: Impacts on working conditions. *The Journal of Internationalization and Localization, 8*(1), 48–75.

Freidson, E. (1983). The theory of professions. In R. Dingwall & P. Lewis (Eds.), *The sociology of professions* (pp. 19–37). St. Martin's Press.

Friedman, M. (2007). The social responsibility of business is to increase its profits. In W. C. Zimmerli, M. Holzinger, & K. Richter (Eds.), *Corporate ethics and corporate governance* (pp. 173–178). Springer.

Lambert, J., & Walker, C. (2022). Because we're worth it: Disentangling freelance translation, status, and rate-setting in the United Kingdom. *Translation Spaces*. https://doi.org/10.1075/ts.21030.lam

Monzó-Nebot, E. (2019). Interviewing legal interpreters and translators: Framing status perceptions and interactional and structural power. In Ł. Biel, J. Engberg, M. R. Martín Ruano, & V. Sosoni (Eds.), *Research methods in legal translation and interpreting: Crossing methodological boundaries* (pp. 187–211). Routledge.

Nunes Vieira, L. (2020). Automation anxiety and translators. *Translation Studies*, 13(1), 1–21. https://doi.org/10.1080/14781700.2018.1543613

Olohan, M. (2020). *Translation and practice theory*. Routledge.

Olohan, M., & Davitti, E. (2017). Dynamics of trusting in translation project management: Leaps of faith and balancing acts. *Journal of Contemporary Ethnography*, 46(4), 391–416. https://doi.org/10.1177/0891241615603449

Pym, A., Grin, F., Sfreddo, C., & Chan, A. L. J. (2012). *The status of the translation profession in the European Union*. Publications Office of the European Union.

SDL. (2016). *SDL translation technology insights: Executive summary*. Retrieved from https://www.slideshare.net/SDLTranslationProductivity/sdl-translation-technology-insights-executive-summary

SDL. (2020). *SDL translation technology insights 2020: Coping with the rise in pressure: Why humanizing technology is key to translation success*. Retrieved from https://www.rws.com/localization/products/resources/translation-technology-insights-2020/

Sela-Sheffy, R., & Shlesinger, M. (Eds.). (2009). Profession, identity and status: Translators and interpreters as an occupational group [Special issue]. *Translation and Interpreting Studies*, 4(2). https://doi.org/10.1075/tis.4.2

Sela-Sheffy, R., & Shlesinger, M. (Eds.). (2010). Profession, identity and status: Translators and interpreters as an occupational group: Part II: Questions of role and identity [Special issue]. *Translation and Interpreting Studies*, 5(1). https://doi.org/10.1075/tis.5.1

Shapiro, S. P. (2005). Agency theory. *Annual Review of Sociology*, 31(1), 263–284.

Sharma, A. (1997). Professional as agent: Knowledge asymmetry in agency exchange. *Academy of Management Review*, 22(3), 758–798.

Tyulenev, S. (2014). *Translation and Society*. Routledge.

Tyulenev, S. (2015). Towards theorising translation as an occupation. *Asia Pacific Translation and Intercultural Studies*, 2(1), 15–29. https://doi.org/10.1080/23306343.2015.1013206

Index

actor-network theory 256
administration 22, 43–44, 90–106, 115
agency theory 241–252; adverse selection 247–250; goal incompatibility 246–247; information asymmetry 244–246; performance ambiguity 250–252
aggregation of marginal gains 84–85, 87, 107
archiving *see* documentation
assumption and constraint analysis 221
automation 239–241, 255

benefits 13–15, 50–51, 114, 194–212; definition 194–195
brief 24–25, 28, 42, 55–57, 63, 78–79, 131, 149
Brooks's Law 125
bulk and premium markets 145, 250, 255
burnout 125–126
business case 41, 150, 153–154, 158, 161, 196–197; *see also* business justification
business justification 155–156, 197, 206
buyer's guide 146–148; *see also* client education

certification 51, 53, 68–69, 156, 160–161, 172, 248–250
ceteris paribus: definition 132
check: definition 57–59; process 58–60, 116, 118
client education 25, 51, 87, 108, 151–153, 202, 247, 256
client–LSP agreement 22, 41–43, 49, 77, 95, 105, 116, 204, 220
commission *see* brief

communication 3, 9, 79, 86, 108–109, 123, 125, 148, 151, 209, 216, 219, 222, 224–225, 234
competence 30, 32, 52–54, 253–254, 256
competition 138–139, 219, 247, 249
computer-assisted translation (CAT) software 27, 33, 36, 39, 45–47, 61, 105, 115, 121, 125–126, 172–173, 175–176, 180
confidentiality 26, 42–43, 105–106, 220, 223
constraints 1, 12–15, 50–51, 68, 163, 190–191, 208–209, 221, 238, 255
consultancy 45–46, 67–68, 146–148, 206–207, 253–254; *see also* client education
content: definition 10
controlled language 61–62
conventions: text-type 10–11, 74; linguistic 57–58
copy *see* content
corrective action 50, 70–71, 86–89, 217, 225; definition 86–87
cost 13–15, 35–36, 40–41, 88, 114, 129–143, 159–161, 203–204, 238; factors affecting 131–135; LSP 135–137, 162–163, 188; vendor 37, 130–135
cost of living 136
cost of quality (CoQ) 187–191; appraisal costs 189; cost of good quality (CoGQ) 189–190; cost of poor quality (CoPQ) 190; failure costs 190; prevention costs 189
crisis translation 199–200, 203
critical path 117–118, 121
currency xviii, 36, 41–42, 58, 97, 186; exchange rate 136–137, 219

Index

death march 125–126
deliverables 6, 77–78, 82–86, 91–93, 115, 149, 156, 190, 207, 222
dependency 116–117
desktop publishing (DTP) 27, 49, 74–76, 118, 134, 166
DMAIC 174–191; analyse 182–185; control 187; define 175–176; improve 185–187; measure 176–182; documentation 97–106; administrative 99–100; task 100–104
domain 10–11, 25–26, 32, 53, 74, 133–134

editing: bilingual *see* revision; monolingual *see* review
enquiry 23–25, 28–29, 32, 157
error scoring 176–182; example 179–181; sampling 181–182; typology 179
estimate 33, 35; *see also* quotation
ethics 4, 101, 153–154, 240, 247, 256; intellectual property 104; money 136, 162–163, 247; self-interest 242, 246–247, 252
European Masters in Translation (EMT) Competence Framework xv–xvi
exchange rate *see* currency
expectations: of client 8–9, 13–14, 51, 68, 78, 89, 119, 146, 149–150, 153, 167–169, 172, 174, 238
experience: of project manager 120–121, 151, 218; of vendor 159

feasibility study 21–40, 130, 214
feedback 71, 83–90, 100–101, 108; client–LSP 84–89, 204–205; LSP–vendor 90, 176–182
file sharing 47, 78, 241
fit-for-purpose translation 68, 89, 145, 154–155, 173, 204, 246; *see also* quality
float *see* leeway
four-eyes principle 69, 160; *see also* revision
freelance translation xvii, 2, 7, 35, 96, 201, 240, 242
functionality *see* usability; *see also* fit-for-purpose translation

Gantt chart 121
glossary *see* termbase (TB)
gold plating *see* scope creep

Goldilocks principle 119–120, 126, 136, 188

harmonisation 30–31, 37–38, 72, 158
Hofstadter's Law 119

IKEAzation 198–199
in-house translation 2, 6–7, 9, 53, 242
income *see* remuneration; *see also* rates
intercultural communication 154, 198–200
international standards xv, xvi, 49; on controlled language 61–62; on pre-editing 61–62; on post-editing 51–52, 60–61, 63–66; on quality 172; on risk 235; *see also* ISO 17100:2015
invoicing 91–97; timing 91–96; content 96–98
iron triangle *see* project management triangle
ISO 17100:2015 5–6, 42–43, 49–52, 69

kaizen 84
Kano model 155, 164–168, 188; concepts 165–167
kitchen sink syndrome *see* scope creep

language pair 28, 31, 34, 35–36, 39–40, 131–135, 140–141
language service provider (LSP) 7, 9; super-LSP 240, 247
language services industry *see* translation industry
law of diminishing returns 124–125
law of triple constraints *see* project management triangle
leeway 31, 118–121, 126, 136, 154, 161
lifecycle 5, 11–12
linguistic quality assessment (LQA) 90, 175–182; *see also* quality assurance (QA)
locale 11, 46, 208
localisation 2–3, 9, 11, 75, 134, 175, 200, 204, 209

machine translation (MT) 30, 60–67, 87, 159–160, 162–163, 240–241
margin 36, 135–137, 201–202, 247, 255
market forces 131–132
milestone 95, 116–117, 122, 215, 220

minimum charge 35
MoSCoW method 155–164; concepts 156–157

necessity good 141–142
negotiation xvi, 40–41, 242
non-disclosure agreement (NDA) 43
non-profit work 202–203

opportunities 220–221, 231–233; *see also* risk
optical character recognition (OCR) 27, 46
outcome 13, 195–196, 207–210
outsourcing 2, 7, 9, 52, 55–56, 130, 238, 242, 250
over-editing *see* over-revision
over-revision 71–72, 92
overheads 35–37, 135, 162–163, 202

Pareto Principle 144, 183–185, 227
Parkinson's Law 126
pay *see* remuneration
performance 84–85, 89
PESTLE analysis 219
planning fallacy 119
planning horizon 122
platform economy 148, 239, 241, 244, 255
PMBOK (Project Management Body of Knowledge) 4–5, 13–14, 83, 114
post-editing (PE) 51–52, 60–67, 87, 151–152, 159–160, 163; definition 60; light 63–65; full 65–67
post-mortem 15, 106–107, 114, 182, 206
post-production 5–6, 12, 82–109, 114, 215–216
practice theory 256
pre-editing 4, 61–63
pre-production 5–6, 12, 21–48, 114, 215
preparation 22, 40–47
price elasticity *see* supply and demand
price equilibrium 132–133
price grid 35–36, 39, 129
PRINCE2 (Projects IN Controlled Environments) 4–5, 14–15, 82–83
principal–agent problem *see* agency theory
principal–professional problem *see* agency theory
prioritisation 155–169; client priorities 157–160; LSP priorities 160–164

pro bono work *see* non-profit work
probability/impact matrix 224–226
production 5–6, 12, 49–81, 114, 215
profit 194–196, 201–202
project management triangle 12–15
project management: definition 8–9
project manager: competences 53–54; role 49–50, 71, 74, 76, 79–80, 121–122, 129, 146–148, 173, 205, 210, 252–254
project: definition 8, 113; analysis 25–29; preparation 40–47
proofreading: definition 74; process 74–76
public holidays 122–123
purchase order (PO) 22, 44, 56, 116
purchasing power *see* cost of living

QA log 186
qualifications 5, 32, 52–54; *see also* competence
quality 13–15, 114, 119, 151, 158–159, 171–193, 203–204, 238, 250–251; definition 68, 171–173
quality assessment *see* linguistic quality assessment (LQA)
quality assurance (QA) 28, 67–76, 175–176, 255; *see also* linguistic quality assessment (LQA)
queries 50, 57, 74, 88, 186, 222
quotation 33–40, 130–142

rates 41, 130–131, 141, 161, 228, 238–240, 255
record keeping *see* documentation
recruitment 32, 52–54, 186, 209, 232
register: language 10–11, 24, 42, 57
relationships 148, 168, 207–208, 241–254
remuneration 65–67, 238–240; *see also* rates
reputation 8, 25, 31, 202, 204, 207–210, 213–214, 219, 243
resources 13–15, 30–34; human 30, 32; technical and technological 32–33
retranslation 71
review: definition 72–73; process 73–74
revision: definition 68–69; process 69–72, 118
risk 13–15, 41, 94, 114, 162, 213–236, 255; analysis 223–228; concepts 217–218; assessment 214–228; definition 213–214; identification

220–223; management 1, 50, 126; responses 228–235
risk actionee 234
risk breakdown structure (RBS) 218–223
risk owner 216–217, 226, 234
risk register 100, 107, 220, 223, 225, 228, 234
rolling wave planning *see* planning horizon
root cause analysis 221–222

satisfaction 41, 88–89, 92, 150, 163–168, 188–189, 203–205, 208–209
satisficing 145
schedule 28–31, 118–126; factors affecting 122–126
scope 13–15, 114, 119, 144–170, 218; management 145–146; product 146–147; project 146–147
scope creep 65, 150–155, 160, 164, 188
sequencing 116–118
signalling 248–250
Six Sigma *see* DMAIC
skopos theory 23–24, 55
software 27–28, 32–33, 134; CAT *see* computer-assisted translation (CAT) software; project management 43–44, 99
specifications *see* brief
stakeholders 9, 207–210, 216, 218, 243
standards *see* international standards
status 39, 239–241, 245, 249, 255
student syndrome 126
style guide 43, 45–46, 58, 75, 186–187, 208
substitution 134–135, 138
success 22, 57, 83, 108, 130, 150, 201–207, 255
supply and demand 132–133; curves 132–133; elasticity of 138–142; for translation services 131–135, 195, 200–201, 255
surcharges 38, 96, 161, 164
SWOT analysis 221–222

technologisation 239–241
term bases (TB) 46–47, 61, 77, 90, 103–105; cleaning 103; preparation 46–47

terms and conditions 41–44, 104, 219, 222
threats 213, 217, 221, 228–231; *see also* risk
throughput 28–30, 96, 118–119, 221
time 13–15, 28–30, 113–128, 159–160, 203–204, 238
time zones 123–124
timeboxing 154
timescales *see* time
training 54, 141, 181, 183, 186–187, 189, 244
translation: definition 2, 6–7, 54–55, 115–116, 148–150; justification 196–201; process 54–57, 116, 118
translation industry 2, 4, 141–142, 200–201, 238–241, 243
translation memories (TM) 27, 36–39, 45–47, 77, 101–103, 105; cleaning 101–102
translation service provider (TSP) 9; *see also* language service provider (LSP)
translator associations 146–147, 249
Translators Without Borders (TWB) 202–203
trust 40, 120, 243, 249, 251, 253–254

Uberisation *see* platform economy
units 25, 27–28, 118, 130–131
upselling 146, 153–154
usability 172–173, 205–207
user experience (UX) *see* usability

vendor: definition 7; management 7, 32, 36, 44, 95, 135, 256
verification and release 51, 76–78, 83, 93

word count *see* units
work breakdown structure (WBS) 114–122, 148–150, 154
workflow 5–6, 9, 11–12, 60, 78–79, 207–208, 255–256; follow-the-sun 124; waterfall 12, 51–52, 67, 78–79
working conditions 4, 67, 238–240, 247

Printed in the United States
by Baker & Taylor Publisher Services